T0330250

Funding Civil Society

Funding Civil Society

Foreign Assistance and
NGO Development in Russia

LISA McINTOSH SUNDSTROM

Stanford University Press
Stanford, California 2006

Stanford University Press
Stanford, California

A portion of the material in Chapter Four was originally published
in "Foreign Assistance, International Norms, and Civil Society
Development: Lessons from the Russian Campaign," *International
Organization,* vol. 59, no. 2 (spring 2005): 419–49. Reprinted with
permission by Cambridge University Press.

Library of Congress Cataloging-in-Publication Data

Sundstrom, Lisa McIntosh, date –
   Funding civil society : foreign assistance and NGO development
in Russia / Lisa McIntosh Sundstrom.
      p. cm.
   Includes bibliographical references and index.
   ISBN 0-8047-5443-8 (cloth : alk. paper)
      1. Civil society—Russia (Federation) 2. Democracy—Russia
(Federation) 3. Economic assistance—Russia (Federation)
4. Non-governmental organizations—Russia (Federation)
5. Russia (Federation)—politics and government—1991–
I. Title.

JN6699.A15S86   2006
361.70947—dc22   2006017661

Typeset by BookMatters in 10.5/12 Bembo

For Greg and Nikolai,
with love and gratitude

Contents

Tables

Note on Transliteration

I have used a modified Library of Congress system for transliteration. Diacritical marks appear in the bibliography and list of interviews (Appendix 1), but have been removed from the text of the chapters for ease of reading. There are exceptions to the Library of Congress spelling when the names of well-known people and places are typically spelled differently in English-language publications. For example, El'tsin becomes Yeltsin and Iavlinskii becomes Yavlinsky.

June 1997, a summer resort on the Volga River near Toliatti, Russia. Gender studies scholars and leaders of activist women's organizations in Russia gather to participate in the Second Annual Russian Summer School on Women's and Gender Research—"Volga '97." The school is hosted by the Moscow Center for Gender Studies and Samara State University and funded by the U.S.-based Ford Foundation. The conference is mainly directed at exposing young Russian scholars to academic work in feminist theory and studies of women's status in Russian society. Toward the end of the summer school, however, conflict erupts briefly in discussions of the development of the Russian women's movement. Women from far-flung provinces of Russia suddenly express disapproval of the ways in which some Moscow and St. Petersburg women's organizations have begun to focus solely on obtaining funding from foreign foundations and governments. Some accuse these foreign-funded organizations of being populated by "feminist-entrepreneurs" rather than "real" feminists motivated by passion for their cause.

As a foreign participant in the room, I felt that a door had been opened through which I could peek very briefly at some of the tensions in the Russian women's movement, before the door swung shut again and the gathering reassembled its outward composure. This incident contrasted starkly with popular Western accounts of the Russian women's movement that characterized the movement as growing rapidly and becoming more united in pursuit of women's rights. I immediately became intrigued by the question of who was receiving funding from foreign donors, who was not, and what the impact of that funding was on the movement in reality.

As I looked more into these questions upon returning to the United States, I realized that they were relevant not only for women's organizations but also for all kinds of movements and organizations in civil society. Foreign donors, both governmental and private, had flooded into Russia beginning in 1991 with the collapse of the Soviet regime, with the goal of supporting democratic development in Russia. An ever-increasing component of this democracy promotion strategy has been assistance to civil society, since vibrant civil societies have come to be seen in recent years as a crucial element guaranteeing the durability of democratic regimes.

Because of the increasing size of the "democracy industry," policy analysts have begun to take interest in assessing the actual impact and consequences of democracy assistance. In the case of assistance to civil society development—an area of growing popularity in foreign aid—we in fact know very little about the actual effects of foreign donors' assistance.[1] During the 1990s, billions of dollars from the budgets of state foreign assistance agencies and Western nongovernmental organizations have been bet on the yet unproven assumption that assistance to nongovernmental organizations (NGOs) does in fact contribute significantly to the development of civil society and, in turn, to the institutionalization of liberal democratic regimes.[2]

Not only politicians and foreign aid practitioners are curious about the dynamics of foreign assistance, however. Scholars of international relations are also interested in studying its patterns, partly because this provides one avenue for understanding how states may modify the political regimes of other states—not by coercion, but by conflict-free promotion of changes in the behavior of citizens at the sub-state level. Scholars of civil society and regime transitions in comparative politics are concerned with whether or not transnational actors and norms are significantly shaping civil societies in democratizing countries, since existing theories have assumed that civil society development is largely a domestic process.[3]

When I landed in Russia in 1998 to begin my investigation of foreign donors' impact on civil society in Russia, my principal research questions were: "Are foreign donors having an impact, and if it exists, does their influence lead to positive developments for democratization in Russia?" I quickly discovered that, indeed, foreign assistance was having a huge impact on the size and shape of the Russian NGO community in terms of boosting the numbers of NGOs in existence and the priorities they pursued. Some of the developments appeared to foster democracy-promoting behavior, while others did not. Yet I was puzzled by the variation in outcomes that I observed among foreign-funded NGOs. Why was it that different NGOs with similar levels of funding from Western donor organizations varied so much in their levels of success in mobilizing? Why did the presence of foreign funding sometimes seem to facilitate NGO growth and even public policy successes and normative change in society, while other times it led to NGO stagnation that consisted of squabbling among activists and irrelevance to the public? This book provides an explanation for why we observe these divergent outcomes under conditions of similar transnational support.

I argue that foreign donors have the best chance of contributing to the successful development of Russian NGOs under two conditions. First, assistance programs are likely to make a difference when they promote NGO work on issues that can be framed in terms of norms, or "collective expectations about proper behavior for a given identity" (Jepperson, Wendt, and Katzenstein, 1996, p. 54), that are embraced universally around the world. There must be compatibility between the norms that foreign donors promote and the normative contexts encountered by the NGOs they support. In order to be successful in their local contexts, NGO activists must frame their campaigns in terms of the pursuit of norms that are accepted locally. This means that those norms must be either universal in nature or culturally specific to Russia. Since foreign donors are unlikely ever to promote norms that are particular to Russia, they will only succeed when they promote NGO campaigns based on universally embraced norms rather than specifically Western societal norms.

Second, foreign donors are likely to contribute to successful NGO development when they concentrate that development in regions where there is support from local political structures and elites. Where local elites are relatively supportive of the concept of an autonomous NGO sector (or at least do not actively harass NGOs), attitudinal and behavioral changes brought about by transnational assistance are substantial and thus likely to be long term. In contrast, in regions where transnational assistance has been concentrated intensively for several years, but where the local political environment is decidedly discouraging to NGOs, a typical outcome among NGOs is "decoupling"; activists make statements in private or to Western audiences that contradict the behaviors they exhibit in public life. Many of these activists, at a surface level, speak in terms familiar to Western activists but, at the level of behavior and deeper attitudes, harbor entirely different assumptions about their role in society and thus are not fully integrated into global understandings of civil society. It is possible for foreign donors to have a positive impact on civil society development in these contexts if they closely study the characteristics of NGOs that exist in those regions and choose carefully which ones to support, based on evidence of the NGOs' solid commitment to clearly identified goals. This careful approach to assistance is likely to become more necessary across Russia in the context of a more restrictive political opportunity structure for NGOs that has developed in the years of the Putin administration.

In developing the first proposition about the relationship between universal norms and successful NGO development outcomes, I compare the development patterns of two subsectors of NGOs—the women's movement and the soldiers' rights movement—that pursue different kinds of issues. In order to investigate the second proposition regarding different political contexts, I have chosen the method of comparing different regional political environments within the same state rather than adopting the classic comparative technique of comparing political environments across different states. The clear advantage that this method affords is the ability to hold constant many aspects of so-called "political culture" and socioeconomic variables that, in most cross-national studies, surface as problematic. I compare foreign assistance levels across seven Russian regions, combined with relatively positive or negative regional political environments (as concerns NGOs), to investigate how these different combinations of transnational and domestic political factors affect the local NGO community overall.

Scholars have rarely made systematic attempts to understand the role of transnational factors in civil society, while taking into account domestic factors as competing explanations affecting development. Research into transnational influences on civil society has seldom overlapped conceptually with work on the development of social movements within Russia. This book contributes to an area of empirical and theoretical knowledge about post-Soviet Russian civil society that is small, but quickly growing.[4] This study merely generates hypotheses from these cases about the relationship between foreign democracy assistance, societal norms, and local political conditions in explaining NGO development. I leave to future work the task of testing these hypotheses further.

Chapter Outline

Chapter One develops the theoretical arguments discussed here and considers alternative explanations for the patterns of NGO development that have occurred in Russia. It also outlines the details of the study design and explains my definition of the variables of foreign assistance, NGO development, and domestic political environment. Chapter Two introduces the domestic context of Russian civil society and presents the foreign donors that have interacted with Russian NGOs in the post-Soviet period. Chapters Three and Four present the detailed theoretical explanations and empirical evidence supporting the two components of my argument. And Chapter Five discusses the implications of the findings for theory on international relations and civil society in democratization, as well as for the practical design of democracy assistance programs, within the context of current developments in Russian politics.

Acknowledgments

I MUST FIRST THANK my husband, Greg, for hearing out all of my anxieties over the years and dutifully reading and providing the comments of a "real person" for each chapter. He kept my perspective down to earth with his rich knowledge of and experience in Russia. Late at night after work and during precious weekend hours, he ploughed through each chapter without even dozing off. I can only hope that I would be as patient and dedicated a partner if the roles were reversed. Thanks also to my son, Nikolai, now aged two, who had the grace to wait to enter the world until just after I submitted the manuscript for review, was a good napper through various parts of the process, and always reminds me that some things are much more important than my book manuscript. My parents, David and Pam McIntosh, by pushing me onto that first airplane to Russia, lending childcare support in desperate times, and assuring me that "of course" my book would be a success, helped me to see the project through.

This book began as a doctoral dissertation, so I naturally owe a tremendous debt to my dissertation advisers at Stanford University. David Holloway deserves the greatest praise, especially for his skills of subtle guidance—leading me to understand where the project was going without ever imposing a particular perspective. It takes considerable talent to grant students freedom and positive reinforcement, while still managing to make clear when they have stepped out of bounds or not met expectations. Michael McFaul has been a wonderful mentor, a gold mine of field contacts, and when needed, a young colleague to whom I could vent when I had lost all hope for political science. Gail Lapidus has been my solid and sustained tie to the Russian women's movement and academic thought on it from the very beginning of my graduate studies. She and Mike McFaul have challenged me the most concerning the empirical details of the book. I thank Gail particularly for her special way of singing the praises of her graduate students to others in the field. Finally, Steve Krasner has been my most formidable source of criticism on the logic and theory behind the project. I have discovered, though, that a friendly and supportive mentor lurks beneath the sometimes prickly exterior, and an honest, productive hunger for knowledge and debate is what drives his questions and doubts.

Many others have been generous with their comments on various versions of the material in this manuscript. In particular, Alfred Evans, Elisabeth Friedman, Sarah Henderson, Kathryn Hochstetler, Tomila Lankina, Masha Lipman, Kelly McMann, Richard Price, and James Richter offered constructive and thoughtful advice. I must especially thank Sarah Mendelson, who knows this topic at least as well as I do, for reviewing the manuscript and spending countless hours on the telephone with me giving detailed comments. Valerie Sperling also gave tremendously helpful feedback and suggestions as a reviewer, and it was an honor to obtain such constructive comments from this pathbreaking author on the contemporary Russian women's movement, who has inspired a great deal of work in those who have followed her.

I could not have seen this project through without the love and support of many friends. I can never adequately repay Jeanette Lee-Oderman in the Stanford Department of Political Science, who jumped at the numerous emergency requests I e-mailed to her from overseas during the field research for this book. Jane Edsell in David Holloway's office also helped me enormously with my long-distance filing of the final dissertation. Kathleen Collins and Laura Henry have always been willing to hear my ideas and read my work; they have been able to provide apt and objective criticism despite our close friendships. Inna Sayfer (with Grisha and Hannah) and Jennifer Daniell Belissent (along with Jacques and Nicolas) have been great friends, good listeners, and graciously opened their homes to me during my endless visits between trips to Russia.

My colleagues in the political science department at the University of British Columbia have been models of support, collegiality, and friendship. It is truly a rare blessing in this profession to work in a department of high scholarly calibre combined with generous warmth and humanity.

I must also thank the wonderful people who opened up their homes to me during my field research in Russia: Valia, Masha, Sasha, and Liubov Borisovna in Moscow; Liuba in St. Petersburg; Vadim in Ekaterinburg; and Liuba, Volodya, and Nastya in Izhevsk. Thank you all for being such welcoming hosts (even by Russian standards!), and for teaching me so much about your country.

My editors at Stanford University Press did a superb job of guiding the book through its final revisions. I am grateful to acquisitions editor Amanda

Moran and copy editor Mary Barbosa, who helped tremendously to limit my tendency toward verbosity.

Finally, I am grateful for several generous sources of financial support. They include the Social Sciences and Humanities Research Council of Canada; the Institute for the Study of World Politics in Washington, D.C.; the Center for Russian and East European Studies and the Institute for International Studies at Stanford University; and the International Research and Exchanges Board (IREX). These organizations made the research and writing of the book physically possible.

ABA-CEELI	American Bar Association's Central and East European Law Initiative
ARA	Antimilitarist Radical Association
CAF	Charities Aid Foundation (British NGO)
CEDAW	Convention on Elimination of All Forms of Discrimination Against Women
CIDA	Canadian International Development Agency
CPSU	Communist Party of the Soviet Union
CSM	Committee of Soldiers' Mothers (general)
CSMR	Committee of Soldiers' Mothers of Russia (name of united national-level umbrella organization, headed by Maria Kirbasova until 1996; see UCSMR and RCSM below)
EC	European Commission of the European Union
EIDHR	European Initiative for Democracy and Human Rights of the European Commission
EMAV	Ekaterinburg Movement Against Violence (*Ekaterinburgskoe dvizhenie protiv nasiliia*)
FALTA	Feminist Alternative (*Feministskaia alternativa*)
GFW	Global Fund for Women
ICIWF	Information Center of the Independent Women's Forum
INGO	International nongovernmental organization
IREX	International Research and Exchanges Board
IRI	International Republican Institute

ISAR	Initiative for Social Action and Renewal
LIEN	Linking Inter European NGOs, program of the European Union
MCGS	Moscow Center for Gender Studies
NDI	National Democratic Institute for International Affairs
NED	National Endowment for Democracy
NGOSS	NGO Sector Support
OSCE	Organization for Security and Cooperation in Europe
OSI	Open Society Institute, funded by the Soros Foundation
PCGI	Petersburg Center for Gender Issues
RCSM	Russian Committee of Soldiers' Mothers (the post-1996 organization headed by Maria Kirbasova, following the split with leaders from the current UCSMR)
RFE	Russian Far East
RI	Regional Initiative (new name of the former RII)
RII	Regional Investment Initiative (program of the U.S. government)
ROMIR	Russian Public Opinion and Market Research (*Rossiiskoe obshchestvennoe mnenie i issledovanie rynka*)
SMSP	Soldiers' Mothers of St. Petersburg
SWC	Soviet Women's Committee
UAW	Urals Association of Women
UCSMR	Union of Committees of Soldiers' Mothers of Russia (headed by Valentina Melnikova and formed several years after the 1996 split in the original CSMR)
USAID	United States Agency for International Development
USIA	United States Information Agency (recently dismantled and amalgamated into the U.S. Department of State)
UWR	Union of Women of Russia (*Soiuz zhenshchin Rossii*)
VTsIOM	All-Russia Center for the Study of Public Opinion (*Vserossiiskii tsentr izucheniia obshchestvennogo mneniia*)

Funding Civil Society

CHAPTER 1

Crossing Boundaries: Analyzing Civil Society and Transnational Influences

IN INTERNATIONAL RELATIONS theory, considerable debate surrounds the extent to which external actors can influence the domestic politics and regimes of sovereign states. This book investigates a particular slice of such influence, that of transnational actors on domestic civil society organizations. It is important not to evaluate the influence of transnational actors merely by their impact on the conduct and policies of governments: transnational actors also affect domestic politics by altering citizens' views and behaviors. If they succeed in changing the norms, preferences, and concerns of significant constituencies of citizens, transnational actors can potentially have a major impact on both government policies and broader societal behavior. In certain cases, transnational campaigns aimed directly at citizens have brought about important political and economic changes (Wapner, 1995, 2002; Mathews, 1997).

Questions of International Relations

Transnational actors who introduce targeted material support and training into domestic civil societies are commonly referred to as "foreign donors." Even if foreign donors do exert an influence on intra-state political processes, how significant is it compared to domestic political and normative factors? In recent years, scholars have begun to ask this question in relation to various domestic factors, such as the configuration of state institutions (Evangelista, 1995; Risse-Kappen, 1995), structure of civil society (Chilton, 1995; Risse-Kappen, 1995), and prevailing domestic norms and ideas (Keck and Sikkink, 1998). Some of the reasons for an increased intellectual interest in transnational networks are their growing numbers and their frequent impact on political outcomes.

Keck and Sikkink point out quite clearly, as does social movement theorist Sidney Tarrow (1998), that transnational advocacy networks (TANs) and, more generally, transnational challenges to domestic political regimes are nothing new. TANs consist of actors that are united in promoting political or social change on some issue—including international nongovernmental organizations (INGOs), social movements, foundations, media, governmental actors, and intergovernmental bodies such as United Nations agencies—and they have existed in different forms for centuries. What is new is their "number, size, and professionalism, and the speed, density, and complexity of international linkages among them" (Keck and Sikkink, 1998, p. 10). Organizations focused on issues of human rights, women's rights, peace, and the environment have proliferated spectacularly in recent decades, with especially rapid growth between 1983 and 1993.[1] Keck and Sikkink, as well as others, show that real and significant shifts are occurring in the frequency and effectiveness of transnational pressures on states, as well as in the extent to which nongovernmental networks of actors can effect domestic political changes (Keck and Sikkink, 1998; Clark, Friedman, and Hochstetler, 1998; Tarrow, 1998).

But what exactly is the nature of these actors? Although transnational NGO networks have grown in recent decades, I join several other authors in rejecting the term "global civil society" as an accurate conceptualization of existing transnational NGO networks (Clark, Friedman, and Hochstetler, 1998; Keck and Sikkink, 1998). Some authors, such as Ronnie Lipschutz, Mary Kaldor, and Paul Wapner, who have argued that civil society has become a truly global phenomenon, overstate the degree of transnational consensus and homogenization. They assume that transnational mobilization is growing more important than domestic civil society, and that national political opportunity structures are steadily declining in their relevance (Lipschutz, 1992; Wapner, 1995; Anheier, Glasius, and Kaldor, 2001). I, along with many others, find instead that domestic political opportunities and constraints, as well as domestic normative and cultural contexts, are key aspects in determining whether or not transnationally active NGOs succeed in their campaigns (Evangelista, 1995; Keck and Sikkink, 1998, p. 26; Tarrow, 1998; Risse-Kappen, 1994, 1995).

In the case of Russia, local political opportunity contexts vary tremendously from region to region. Many local governments, such as in the far eastern city of Khabarovsk, do not welcome NGOs as important to social and political life and do not seem to worry about the cross-regional and transnational contacts of NGO activists when deciding how to respond to critical activists. For example, one activist in Khabarovsk, Aleksandr Bekhtold of the For Human Rights network—which is part of the Moscow Helsinki Group network and linked into transnational human rights networks—claimed that his business was destroyed and that he faced repeated threats from the governor of Khabarovsk *krai* (region).[2] On the normative side, as discussed in Chapter Three, Western donors have invested enormous funds and training into the Russian women's movement, while most of the movement's activists and ideals are scorned by the majority of Russians—far more scorned than they are in the West. This book is concerned with how principles are transferred from the transnational to the domestic level in Russia by a particular group of actors: the liberal democratic states and Western NGOs and foundations that promote civil society development and democratization. It shows that, even in areas where foreign donors are present in force to promote certain values regarding proper NGO behavior, local political and normative conditions significantly affect the extent to which NGO activists adopt those values in their discourse and behavior. The transnational activities investigated here are focused primarily on strengthening Russian democratic institutions rather than directly changing particular state policies on issues such as the environment or human rights. The phenomenon under examination links the concerns of international relations theorists who are interested in foreign influences on domestic politics with the concerns of scholars of comparative politics in civil society and processes of democratic transition and consolidation.

Civil Society and Democratization in Comparative Politics

This section turns to defining civil society, its role in supporting democratic regimes, and the importance of NGOs as a component of civil society. But first, an explanation is in order regarding the importance of the Russian case for research into civil society development and the role of transnational actors in it.

RUSSIA AS A CASE

Russia is a particularly illuminating case for studying civil society development. First, it differs from many other third-wave democracies in that the Soviet regime actively repressed an already weak civil society—more actively than most authoritarian regimes from which democracies have emerged—by eliminating independent forms of social and political organization. Several authors, including Juan Linz and Alfred Stepan, have described the radical "flattening" of society that was carried out systematically in the Soviet Union, in which diversity of opinions and expression of interests were circumscribed more severely than in many other authoritarian regimes (Howard, 2002; Linz and Stepan, 1996, p. 247; Urban, 1997; Arendt, 1963). Thus, unlike civil societies in other regions, in which foreign donors have attempted to foster relationships with a civil society "resurrected" from the recent past—such as Southern Europe and Latin America, or even Eastern Europe—Russian civil society at the time of transition from Communism had been severely repressed for over seventy years.[3]

Groups of political dissidents, operating underground and opposed to the Soviet regime for various reasons, were a major component of the small realm of independent activity that did exist in Soviet society. However, most dissident organizations in the Soviet period were small and loosely organized, and the main opinion that united members was their opposition to the existing regime (Reddaway, 1972). The dissident community included individuals from a wide range of political orientations, such as Marxists, nationalists, social democrats, and liberal democrats, to name just a few. Once the regime collapsed, considerable dissensus emerged regarding the construction of a new regime, especially among more liberal democratic opposition organizations such as the Democratic Russia movement (Fish, 1995, p. 210).

Scholars of the "transitology" school, which advocates broad comparisons among all cases of transition from authoritarian regimes, have pointed out that this disintegration of consensus within opposition movements has been a common phenomenon in cases of transition (O'Donnell and Schmitter, 1986, pp. 55–56). However, in most other regions outside the Soviet Union—such as Latin America, Southern Europe, and even much of Eastern Europe—opposition interests were more differentiated into distinct groups that came together to form a united front against the authoritarian regime. These groups were then able to part ways in the process of regime transition but still remain relatively organized (Jaquette and Wolchik, 1998). While in most other authoritarian regimes, non-state organizations such as the Catholic church in Poland and much of Latin America provided at least some space for organizing individuals' interests outside the state, in Russia and the rest of the Soviet Union no such organizations were permitted until after 1985, with the installment of policies of glasnost and perestroika. Toleration of opposition groups was not formalized legally until 1990, first with removal of the Communist Party of the Soviet Union's (CPSU) guaranteed monopoly in public life from Article 6 of the Soviet Constitution, and then further with the Soviet Law on Public Associations of October 1990, which legalized political parties and independent trade unions.

The Russian case is distinctive not only because of the weakness of a pre-existing civil society. The especially severe and sustained efforts of the Soviet state to prevent independent contact between Soviet citizens and foreigners, and to regulate any contact that did take place, means that the direct influence of transnational actors on Russian civil society development is remarkably new. The perestroika period from the late 1980s on, including friendship exchanges with the West that were encouraged by Mikhail Gorbachev, brought about a considerable loosening of the restrictions on Soviet citizens' interactions with foreigners. Prior to this period, though, transnational contacts were severely restricted.[4] Although delegations from Soviet organizations attended international conferences on various occasions, the delegates sent were members of highly regulated state organizations and were observed constantly in their activities by representatives of the KGB.

The Soviet Women's Committee (SWC) provides one example: SWC delegates at international conferences were hand-picked by party loyalists within the Soviet regime and were monitored in their interactions with foreigners. It is important to note that, despite such restrictions, the ideas voiced by other countries' delegations at international conferences and the agendas presented at such forums did have identifiable effects on Soviet delegates. Several accounts by Russian women who were present in such delegations, and who are now members of other women's organizations, have attested to the dramatic ways in which attendance at international conferences opened their eyes to a different and broader understanding of issues shared by women around the world.[5] Yet the role of the SWC was much less to glean lessons from the experiences of women's movements from other countries than it was to present to the outside world a rosy and progressive image of the status of Soviet women (Sperling, 1999, p. 108). Zoia Khotkina, a scholar and activist with the Moscow Center for Gender Studies (MCGS), recalls the international role of the SWC that she and other scholars were required to fulfill at international conferences:

That organization had, like Janus, two faces: one for Soviet women and another for Western women . . . When foreign organizations came, I remember very well how we worked—Olga [Voronina, also of MCGS], Liudmila Zavadskaia, who has now become the deputy minister of Justice, and I. The three of us very often, in the presence of Western women, showed the great progressiveness of Soviet women and told them about the economic situation in our country, about the political situation . . . how we have such wonderful laws, how our laws are so full of equality for women.[6]

Given these two extreme characteristics of the Russian case—repressed civil society and a lack of access to transnational contacts—if effects of foreign democracy assistance are noticeable anywhere, they should certainly be visible in post-1991 developments in Russian civil society. According to one overview of Russian NGO sector development, only a few dozen NGOs were registered in 1990.[7] In such a context, foreign assistance programs can potentially play a major role in shaping the development of the Russian NGO sector. In the ensuing years, foreign governmental aid agencies and nongovernmental assistance foundations have focused significant amounts of energy and material resources on encouraging the activation and growth of civil society. Much of this funding has been distributed to other inter-mediary agencies and nongovernmental organizations for implementation. Russia is thus important as a case for studying influences of transnational actors on civil society development, since the levels of transnational in-volvement with civil society before and after the Soviet collapse are so different.

WHAT KIND OF CIVIL SOCIETY STRUCTURE PROMOTES DEMOCRACY?

Although scholars and foreign donors have generally assumed that civil society is crucial to democratization, the proper configuration and actual role of civil society in the process of creating and deepening democratic institu-tions have been topics of ongoing debate in academic literature on demo-cratic transitions. Most authors agree that civil society development is an important task for building stable and healthy democracies, since active civil societies are empirically closely linked with the persistence and depth of democratic regimes. It is argued that without the development of a strong and active civil society that demands citizen participation in governance, democratic rule cannot be thoroughly institutionalized (Diamond, 1996; Fish, 1996).

However, a number of important theoretical questions regarding civil society remain unanswered in the existing literature on democratization, such as how civil society should be organized and what the ideal balance is between state and society in order to support democratic institutions. Civil society is a notoriously difficult concept to define. Almost all authors concur that it is a sphere of public activities by citizens (that is, outside of their homes and kinship organizations) that lies outside of state institutions. However, scholars disagree regarding the extent to which the state should be involved and the kinds of non-state activities that should be included under the umbrella term "civil society." Most agree that commercial, profit-seeking organizations do not belong, since these represent self-oriented rather than publicly oriented activities.[8] Nearly all authors exclude political parties, since the prevailing aim of political parties is to take direct control of the state.[9]

I concur with these distinctions and advocate a definition of civil society that excludes state-run and state-organized groups as well as private busi-nesses and political parties. Civil society is viewed most appropriately as a realm of collective, publicly oriented activity by nongovernmental actors that is often formally organized (as NGOs, social movement coalitions, clubs, associations, and so on) but also includes many less formal networks of public discourse, such as nongovernmental mass media and informal networks among neighbors in a community. Yet this definition leaves wide latitude for controversy concerning the state's role in guiding and shaping civil society, and to what degree participants in a democratic civil society should act as adversaries or partners of the state. Debates among scholars on these questions relate directly to questions about the kind of civil society that is desirable or even possible in Russia, given a historical legacy that most would agree emphasizes communal ideas about public life as well as acceptance of heavy involvement by the state.

Scholars have generally agreed that Russia's political culture, in the wake of Communism, much more closely resembles a civic or corporatist understanding of state-society relations than a liberal one (Diligenskii, 2001; Kubicek, 2000; Phillips, 1999; Patomaki and Pursiainen, 1999; Malysheva et al., 1998). Of course, during the seventy-four-year history of Soviet rule, Russians did become accustomed to a corporatist, state-guided model of structuring citizens' participation in political life. Certainly the idea that the state should play a strong role in civic life continues to be widespread: for example, in a 1995 study of over 2,100 citizens in several regions around Russia, 62 percent of respondents answered that it was acceptable for NGOs to receive funding from the government, and 36 percent agreed with the statement that "in a normal democratic society, where the law defends citizens' rights, there is no need for NGOs" (Validata/Yankelovich, 1995). Almost a decade later, in a 2004 survey of over 2,000 citizens in forty Russian regions, carried out by the Russian organizations Tsirkon and the Agency for Social Information on behalf of the Donors' Forum (an organization of donors in Moscow), a majority of respondents (59 percent) agreed that the Russian state should be the primary charitable structure in Russia (Donors' Forum, 2005, p. 23). The next-ranking answer was Russian business organizations (43 percent). Russian charitable organizations, private individuals, and foreign organizations fell far lower on the list.

Sarah Oates and others have found through recent survey and focus group research that Russian citizens prefer state-run television news coverage to commercial television news. State media were viewed by many as "orderly" and "[w]hile state-run television was biased, many respondents felt that this was for the good of the country" (Oates, 2005, p. 68).

During the Soviet period, an authoritarian form of "state" corporatism dominated in structuring citizen participation. Paul Kubicek, in discussing developments in post-Soviet Ukraine, points out that "societal" or "democratic" corporatism as it developed in Western European states differs considerably from "state" corporatism of an authoritarian type (2000, p. 21). State corporatist systems focus mostly on mechanisms for the state to control and restrict public participation, and interest groups are meant to control citizens, rather than represent them (Schmitter, 1977). This, of course, is the kind of corporatism that existed in the Soviet regime. There is also much evidence that the current Putin regime in Russia is striving toward exactly this kind of corporatist model, by developing institutions such as the new Public Chamber (*obshchestvennaia palata*) created at the federal level, in which civil society representatives are chosen in a manner that makes them heavily loyal to the president (see Chapter Five). In contrast, corporatism may exist in democratic contexts, as it has done in several European countries (particularly Sweden); if power is not entirely centralized, various groups participate in shaping policy and remain largely independent, and competitive elections occur.

In attempting to change citizen and government attitudes toward political participation in Russia, foreign donors predominantly have promoted a liberal model of civil society in their assistance to NGOs, as we shall see in Chapter Two. Some critics have argued that such an approach is destined to fail, due to communal and statist traditions in Russia that stem from both the Soviet and pre-Soviet periods (Phillips, 1999; Patomaki and Pursiainen, 1999). In reality, though, there is a considerable amount of variety in Russian citizens' views of appropriate civil society models. NGO participants in particular often espouse fairly liberal notions of ideal relations between citizens and the state.

In my detailed interviews with sixty NGOs, in which I asked about their extent of interaction and cooperation with the state, ten of them expressed a preference for an adversarial or "watchdog" relationship with the state, which is one aspect of a liberal model of civil society. The organizations that advocated such a stance were mostly human rights (soldiers' rights) NGOs whose activists had backgrounds in the Soviet dissident community (see Sundstrom, 2001, Ch. 6). They included Elena Vilenskaia and Ella Poliakova of the Soldiers' Mothers of St. Petersburg (SMSP), who were active in the pro-democracy People's Front (*Narodnyi front*) in the late 1980s and up until the Soviet regime's collapse. Olga Lipovskaia of the Petersburg Center for Gender Studies was active in the dissident movement of the 1980s and published a *samizdat* (unofficially self-published) feminist journal. Two of the other adversarial NGO leaders were jailed as vocal dissidents in the Soviet era. Nikolai Khramov of the Moscow Antimilitarist Radical Association (ARA) was detained for several months in military prisons and psychiatric hospitals for refusing military service during the war in Afghanistan. In the late 1950s, Boris Pustintsev of St. Petersburg's "Citizen Watch" spent five years in a labor camp for protesting the Soviet invasion of Hungary. Thus, it is important to note that the leaders of nearly all of the NGOs I encountered who advocated an adversarial stance toward the state had developed their views long before the influx of foreign funding.

Moreover, these and other organizations also frequently described civil society as a realm for defending human rights, voicing public opinion, developing citizen activism, and making demands upon the state. These views indicated a more or less liberal approach to the role of civil society. The idea of "taxpayers'" right to control their government featured in some interviewees' statements. For example, Elena Vilenskaia, co-chair of the Soldiers' Mothers of St. Petersburg, expressed this idea when I asked her how she began thinking about concepts such as civil society: "The theme developed as the organization did; but, of course, in order to form such an organization, we were already thinking about this . . . that the citizens must control their army; we are the boss, we are the taxpayers . . . and we must control it."[10]

So, contrary to the arguments that certain scholars have made, the liberal character of the civil society model that foreign donors promote in Russia is not in itself a critical determinant of donors' success in their assistance to Russian NGOs.

A more fundamental problem with the particular liberal model that foreign donors promote in Russia is that it may not in fact strengthen democracy. Later chapters show that foreign donors have generally forwarded a very simplified model of civil society, as a sphere consisting of nongovernmental advocacy organizations, rather than as a more complicated realm including other kinds of networks of public discussion and participation. Several scholars of civil society have argued convincingly that much more sophisticated networks of civic relations are crucial to democratic civil society.

The powerful "social capital" thesis, as forwarded by Robert Putnam, argues against reducing definitions of civil society to include only politically relevant NGOs. He maintains, through comparative study of the diverging development patterns of northern and southern Italy, that the direct political relevance of associations and social networks is not important for creating a civil society that improves overall levels of trust and the quality of life in a society (Putnam, 1993, 1996). "Social capital" for Putnam "refers to features of social organization such as networks, norms, and social trust that facilitate coordination and cooperation for mutual benefit" (1996, p. 292). He argues that completely nonpolitical clubs and societies—as well as activities unrelated to organizational membership, such as newspaper readership—play just as large a role in creating social capital as political advocacy organizations that we typically call NGOs, and that "[t]o identify trends in the size of the nonprofit sector with trends in social connectedness would be [a] fundamental conceptual mistake" (Putnam, 1996, p. 296).[11] Even in the United States, Tocqueville's ideal of associational life, most citizens are not active members of formal NGOs, especially when mere check-writing activity is excluded. In addition, Putnam points out that as NGO membership is increasing in the United States, voter turnout and attention to political affairs are decreasing (1969, pp. 292–93).

Some other American scholars are concerned that the kinds of problems Putnam points to in civil society have been exacerbated by NGO funding patterns in the United States. They are concerned about how NGO funding structures shape civil society and democratic development in ways that are similar to my own concerns about foreign funding among Russian NGOs. For example, in a recent volume, Theda Skocpol analyzes the shift in American civic engagement patterns from large, broad-based, multipurpose, membership-based associations prior to 1960, to smaller, single-issue, largely elite professional associations in the present period. She points out, paralleling my findings in the Russian case, that patterns of funding to NGOs play a significant part in explaining the shift in the United States away from large membership organizations to professionally staffed ones. American associations prior to the 1960s largely depended on nationwide memberships and members' investments of time and finances for support (Skocpol, 1999). Yet in the contemporary world of American NGOs, organizations are often "sparked by well-connected leaders, [and] they frequently have—or soon obtain—outside funding from tax-exempt private foundations" (Skocpol, 1999, p. 501). John Judis similarly argues that NGOs today "have a far more tenuous connection to those whom they claim to represent directly" (Judis, 1992, p. 16). They are overwhelmingly organizations dominated by unelected professional staffs, funded by wealthy private donors, with little grassroots input. As Skocpol points out, there is nothing inherently wrong with this development; she merely cautions that "we should not imagine that these arrangements are democratic" (Skocpol, 1999, p. 501).

In the Russian context of foreign foundations supporting domestic NGOs to promote democratic development, this piece of American history prompts an important question. Can a strategy of supporting advocacy NGOs with professional staffs gleaned from among the elite intelligentsia promote a civil society that is characterized by broad citizen involvement in governance? Foreign donors in Russia, with few exceptions, have not experienced much success in increasing citizen involvement in public life or making civil society more influential in Russian politics. This outcome is in part a result of the narrowness of the range of principles and organizations that foreign donors are willing to support in the NGO community, which has exacerbated a pre-existing tendency for Russia's intelligentsia to dismiss the majority opinions of the masses.[12] When NGOs are encouraged to work in an insular way through the staging of NGO conferences, publication of analytical literature, and creation of specialized networks rather than working to build constituencies of interested citizens, they are not promoting civic participation or enlightening citizens about their efficacy in a democracy.

Donors' focus on civic advocacy organizations—often with the uncomfortable condition that they should be both politically relevant and nonpartisan—is much too narrow to encourage significant change in citizen behavior at large to bring the benefits expected from a civil society (Carothers, 1999; Van Rooy, 1998a; Ottaway, 2000). Important roles of civil society in a democracy are to foster a broad and participatory realm of discussion with relevance for all kinds of topics that concern citizens, and to create horizontal links that build a sense of inclusive and diverse community. This is done not solely by NGOs but also by more informal networks of civic interaction. The NGO-bound definition of civil society is thus inadequate for creating a civil society that plays a strong role in upholding democracy.

Nonetheless, this book focuses on NGOs for a number of reasons. Such organizations do comprise a large segment of civil society, and in institutionalized democracies they play important roles in encouraging citizen participation in public issues and defending the interests of various citizens. They also act as vehicles for dialogue with governments and state institutions. Moreover, as emphasized above, NGOs are the major form of civil society to which foreign donors direct their funding and technical assistance programs; thus, in order to evaluate the role of foreign donors in civil society as a component of democratization, investigation of their influence on the NGO sector is crucial.

For these reasons, the primary research presented in the book concerns Russian NGOs and their interactions with foreign donors, the state, and Russian society. The definition of NGOs employed is not as restrictive as that used by most foreign donors, however. It includes organizations that may receive funding and significant assistance from the state, but are nevertheless nongovernmental in constitution. In this way, I am able to observe a broader segment of Russian civil society, including both actors that are targeted by donors and those that exist outside the world of donors.

Democracy Assistance: A New Area of Policy Analysis

Democracy assistance comprises only a small portion of all Western foreign aid programs to Russia and other countries, but democracy assistance generally and civil society assistance specifically have grown steadily as a proportion of foreign aid spending since 1990. Analysts have acknowledged that accurate estimation of foreign aid spending devoted to democracy is extremely difficult, largely because few states or nongovernmental donors classify their democracy promotion activities under a unified category of assistance, and donors vary a great deal in how they classify aid that would be widely identified as part of democracy assistance (Perlin, 2003, p. 13). Estimating civil society assistance expenditures within the broader category of democracy assistance is yet another, even more difficult step.

We can gain some insight into the growth of democracy assistance and civil society expenditures by governments from data gathered by the OECD. According to the OECD, in 2002 foreign aid expenditures by developed states' governments for promoting "government and civil society" overseas totaled approximately US$4.5 billion, or 7.8 percent of official bilateral development assistance. This compares with approximately US$1.8 billion, or just 3.2 percent of total official bilateral development assistance in 1996 (the first year in which the OECD separated the category of "government and civil society" assistance from other development categories), and assistance from multilateral organizations in this category has grown similarly, from 2.3 to 8.2 percent of official development assistance (OECD, 1997, 2003). It is important to note, though, that various kinds of aid for government reforms, which most analysts would not characterize as promoting democracy per se, fall under this category of "government and civil society," such as technical reengineering of government agencies in terms of efficiency or international standards. Other authors, as well as myself, have made rough estimates of the share that democracy assistance occupies in official (government-funded) international development assistance. The available figures are inconsistent in terms of years covered and method of calculation, but they give a rough idea of the magnitude of funds expended by donors in this area. They are all somewhat different since analysts must make judgment calls regarding what should be counted as democracy assistance. For example, U.S. assistance to Russia under the Freedom Support Act (FSA) includes funds that are dedicated partly to democracy assistance and partly to market reforms and other programs, and civil society development specifically falls under several different line items. Based on the OECD data, George Perlin estimates that democracy assistance ranges between 6 and 11 percent of individual states' international development budgets (2003, p. 13). Mendelson and Glenn found that 2.8 percent of all U.S. assistance to Russia and 19 percent of all EU assistance to Russia was devoted to democracy assistance during 1990–1999 (2002, p. 5). I estimate that between 1990 and 2002, the total amount of U.S. government assistance to promote democracy in Russia was roughly $860 million.[13] During the period 1991–2001, the EU's Technical Assistance to the CIS (TACIS) program spent somewhere in the area of 750–800 million euros on democracy programs in Russia (European Commission, 2001). In the particular area of civil society assistance, it becomes even more difficult to estimate donor expenditures, since civil society is often folded into more general funding categories, such as democracy, governance, and human rights. Sarah Henderson has estimated that the U.S. Agency for International Development (USAID) alone spent approximately $92 million on civic initiatives and NGO support programs in Russia from 1992 to 1998 (Henderson, 2003).

In tandem with the growth of democracy assistance as a component of Western states' foreign aid budgets, scholars and policy analysts have begun to treat it as a significant topic of research. It can now be said that some general points of consensus are emerging from studies of democracy assistance. Researchers have examined the impact of democracy assistance in newly democratizing regimes in all relevant regions of the world: Africa, Asia, Latin America, the Middle East, and Eastern Europe/Eurasia (Henderson, 2003; Mendelson and Glenn, 2002; Mendelson, 2001; Burnell, 2000; Carothers, 1999; Ottaway and Carothers, 2000).

Most authors in this growing field concur on several points that this book reinforces: that democracy assistance tends to be structured as a universal template that donors assume to be equally applicable in any democratizing environment; that it is implemented in a manner that is too directive and closed to influence from actors in local contexts; and that it often supports very narrow constituencies of Westernized intellectuals, to the neglect of the vast majority of the public in countries that receive assistance. Most authors also argue that democracy assistance can only hope to improve democratic practices in very small ways and cannot decide the course of a nascent democratic regime.

In accordance with the point that democracy assistance tends to be too far removed from the desires of local actors in democratizing countries, this book adds the finding that foreign assistance to NGOs has a significant impact on the success of those NGOs only when it is directed at organizations that pursue norms that are broadly embraced in the local society. When the opposite is true, the results of assistance in terms of successful NGO mobilization and achievement of goals in society are likely to be negligible. In addition, assistance must be combined with a local political atmosphere that either openly supports or, at worst, benignly neglects independent citizen activity in order to have a sustained positive influence on the development of individual NGOs. Despite these limitations to democracy assistance, most authors, including myself, agree that democracy assistance is a worthwhile enterprise in which established democratic states should engage. Democracy assistance already provides a crucial lifeline to help proponents of democracy to continue working in many transitional local contexts around the world. If it were structured to be more effective along the lines suggested by myself and others, then its positive impact on direct recipients of funding and society more broadly would increase in significant ways.

Research Variables and Choice of Cases

Having laid out many of the major theoretical and practical questions surrounding civil society and the role of NGOs in its development, we now shift to the more specific design of the study: competing factors considered in explaining NGO development, cases chosen, and methods employed.

NGO DEVELOPMENT

NGO development is the phenomenon to be explained in this study, and my focus on two NGO subsectors calls for further clarification of how I define each group. The definition of "women's organization" is somewhat broader than that which is typically assumed in Western contexts. These are often understood in Russia to be any organization made up of exclusively women members, whether they work on an issue directly regarding women or on such areas as social services or cultural activities. Women's organizations in this book are defined as those that are formed and run by women (comprised of, with few exceptions, exclusively women members) and concern themselves with issues that, under existing social structures, disproportionately affect women. Thus, in some cases, they may focus on lobbying for or voluntarily providing services and family benefits, rather than on a specific issue concerning women as a target group. Examples of such organizations would include Mothers Against Narcotics (*Materi protiv narkotiki*) in St. Petersburg, which counsels parents of drug-addicted children, or the group Faith, Hope, and Love (*Vera, nadezhda, liubov'*) in the small city of Staraia Russa, which provides help to families with disabled children. The crucial defining factor is that in each case, they define themselves as a "women's organization" due to their work in a sphere of responsibility that is typically placed upon women. Many Russian women's organizations also work on issues—such as domestic violence, gender analysis, women in business, and women's political leadership skills—that are more familiar to Westerners who are accustomed to a feminist women's movement.

NGOs in the soldiers' rights subsector typically consider themselves to be part of the Russian human rights movement. Some analysts consider the soldiers' mothers' organizations to be "women's organizations"; however, interviews with the soldiers' mothers and leaders of women's organizations suggested that the soldiers' mothers do not consider themselves to be part of a movement to advocate for women's interests and instead view themselves as human rights proponents. For example, soldiers' mothers have allegedly made statements that dismiss the problem of violence against women in comparison with the problem of conscript abuse in the army.[14] Although I chose to focus on soldiers' rights organizations, in many cities I did interview and become familiar with leaders of human rights NGOs in other issue areas, such as those that focus on protecting journalists, victims of political repression, and the disabled.

The two particular areas of women's organizations and soldiers' rights organizations were chosen for a number of reasons. Women's organizations came naturally to mind, first, because I had already spent a great deal of time researching the Russian women's movement in previous work. The very idea of studying the influence of foreign funding on Russian NGOs was sparked for me as I attended a conference of Russian gender studies scholars in 1997, at which several of the attendees loudly voiced their concerns about the effects that foreign funding was having on the Russian women's movement. I knew from reading and direct experience that the transnational connections of Russian feminists, at least in Moscow and St. Petersburg, were significant, and I wondered about the nature of those organizations that were not in contact with transnational actors, due to either lack of desire or lack of knowledge. At least one groundbreaking scholarly work, by Valerie Sperling, had confirmed that the international environment is an important factor affecting the post-Soviet Russian women's movement and called for further study of these issues (Sperling, 1998, pp. 264–65). One of the areas of strategic focus for Western donors among Russian NGOs has been women's issues, and several donors, such as the Global Fund for Women, Soros Open Society Institute, and the Canadian Embassy, have programs dedicated specifically to funding women's NGOs.[15] Thus a great deal of opportunity for investigating transnational influences on civil society was possible through studying transnational actors' interactions with the Russian women's movement.

However, I was also aware that the women's movement had some characteristics that perhaps made it atypical of many other Russian NGO subsectors. I was acutely aware of the fact that the women's movement has few followers or even sympathizers in Russian society. The word "feminist" is a highly negative term, even among most activists whom Westerners would undoubtedly call "feminists" according to parameters that are familiar to them. As one women's NGO in the Siberian city of Tomsk notes, "Inequality of women in Russia is not perceived as overt discrimination, which, according to general opinion, does not exist in our country" (ICIWF, 1999b). Dismissive attitudes toward the idea that women constitute a viable interest group exist even among female staff members in the Russian offices of foreign donors. For example, a staff member in the Moscow OSI Civil Society program once stated to me that "civil society groups must be those that represent everyone in all of society, and therefore women's organizations are not part of civil society."[16] Moreover, many typical Russian citizens also suspect that more conventional women's organizations in fact do nothing useful; for example, those that conduct activities such as charity, social services, or women's business support. A Western grant officer at the Ford Foundation's Moscow office stated that he frequently found himself defending grants to women's organizations against the complaints of Russian female employees in his office.[17] This problem of low domestic popularity was likely to affect outcomes in NGO development among women's NGOs and might have little to do with foreign donors' assistance, yet it would be closely correlated with donors' involvement. This characteristic led me to seek out another NGO subsector for comparison that also had relationships with foreign donors, but would likely display greater public acceptance.

I found this subsector in the area of human rights work that deals with the rights of soldiers. These organizations range from those that offer simple humanitarian assistance and demand that the Russian army provide adequate living and working conditions for its soldiers, to antimilitary or pacifist organizations that assist conscripts in avoiding military service and spend most of their time advocating passage of a federal law on alternative service and reform to a professional army. The most numerous organizations within this subsector, called Committees of Soldiers' Mothers, boast representation in nearly every major city of Russia and are extremely popular and well known among the Russian population. Arguably, they are the best-known and most widely respected type of NGO in Russia, with public opinion polls consistently showing their name recognition among citizens in the range of 70 to 80 percent (Gerber and Mendelson, 2003, p. 5; MosNews, 2005). Many other, more radical antimilitary organizations are less widely known and even suspiciously regarded by Russian citizens. However, their ultimate goal of a smaller, professional army is welcomed by a solid majority of Russians.[18] The issue of conscription and military service conditions is one that touches virtually every family in Russia in which there are male sons, and citizens typically have high regard for organizations that attempt to deal with these problems.

How can we measure NGO development among these NGOs and others? Although it is considerably less difficult to define for research purposes than the broad concept of civil society, NGO development is still not simple to operationalize. Since I am concerned ultimately with the relationship of NGO development to political behavior and regime democratization, I sought to define it in terms of organizational characteristics that most authors would agree contribute to an active civil society that encourages democratic governance. For individual NGOs, these elements include well-organized work toward focused goals in pursuing some collective purpose; autonomy from state manipulation of activities (although a certain amount of state funding is not excluded); knowledge of, communication with, or even collaboration with other NGOs working on similar issues; outreach to the public constituency to which the NGO's activities are relevant; and, where appropriate to the organization's concerns, turning to state and government institutions to advocate improved public policy. For the overall NGO sector in each region examined, elements of general sectoral development include the degree of NGO voice and influence in public affairs and politics and the existence of actually working NGO associations or networks. Improvement or growth in these individual and sectoral characteristics constitutes NGO development in a particular location. I consider these elements of NGO development to fall into two general categories: *internal development and professionalization* of individual organizations and the NGO sector as a whole (including development of management skills, definition of goals, attainment of autonomy, and networking among NGOs); and *external mobilization* (including development of societal constituencies and interest articulation to the state, growth of public support, and increase in the size of the NGO community working on an issue). Throughout this book, when I discuss NGO mobilization, I am referring to the publicly palpable aspects of NGO activity.

I argue that foreign donors on the whole have focused heavily on internal development and professionalization of the Russian NGO sector, but have largely ignored external mobilization.

A final element of NGO development, which is shaped by both internal professionalization and external mobilization, is the material sustainability of NGOs. Are organizations able to continue their activities in the long term, or will they collapse if a single source of material resources—whether the state, an individual benefactor, or the foreign donor community—withdraws its support? This is a serious problem for most NGOs in Russia today. Very few have developed long-term reliable and diverse sources of funds. With many foreign donors expecting to exit Russia in the next five to ten years, NGOs that rely exclusively on foreign assistance are in a highly unsustainable position unless they develop sources of support from domestic actors. Foreign donors have been complicit in the failure of NGOs to attain some degree of sustainability—despite their repeatedly voiced concern with the problem—because they have failed to encourage NGOs to mobilize externally to develop domestic supporters in their communities.

The density of NGOs in terms of sheer numbers of organizations was also taken into account as one means, albeit unreliable, of concrete comparison among regions. These figures are not emphasized as the most revealing indicator of NGO development, because accurate counts of NGOs that are comparable across regions are extraordinarily difficult to obtain. Many organizations remain hollow, with few members or even a single person forming several organizations (sometimes dubbed NGIs, or "nongovernmental individuals"), mostly as a result of foreign donors' preference to grant funds to many different organizations over time (Henry, 2001, pp. 7–8). Large numbers of officially existing NGOs in Russia are in fact inactive or defunct, and many active organizations choose not to register officially with the Ministry of Justice. Registration is an expensive and time-consuming exercise, and in recent years, some NGOs have been denied registration for reasons that are ostensibly legal but appear in reality to be political, disproportionately among environmental and human rights groups that voice opposition to the Putin government (Information Center of the Human Rights Movement and the Center for Development of Democracy and Human Rights, 2000; Pustintsev, 2001; Henry, 2001, p. 21; Goble, 1999).

It was also not possible to obtain alternative counts of active NGOs that were comparable across regions. Nonetheless, in Chapter Four, I use the official and unofficial counts of NGOs in the seven cities studied as an indicator of NGO development, since together these estimates do provide a limited sense of the density of NGO activity in each city.

FOREIGN ASSISTANCE, LOCAL POLITICAL ENVIRONMENTS, AND FRAME RESONANCE

Exposure to foreign democracy assistance, local political environments, and normative frame resonance are the major factors examined as influencing NGO development. The factor of greatest interest, foreign assistance, includes transnational interactions that are both material and ideational in nature. The foreign donors involved with Russian NGOs include mostly the official international aid agencies of foreign states, development agencies of intergovernmental organizations such as the United Nations and the European Union, and Western NGOs that carry out material assistance or training. The latter often implement programs that are subcontracted by foreign state aid agencies.

Of course, in addition, Russian NGOs sometimes develop relations with foreign organizations or individuals for the purposes of information exchange or transnational mobilization on certain issues. One example of this kind of relationship is the Network of East-West Women, a transnational organization with over 2,000 members that links women's organizations from Western countries with those of the post-Communist region. Other examples are information exchanges that have been formed between Russian human rights NGOs, such as the Soldiers' Mothers of St. Petersburg or Moscow Memorial, and Western human rights organizations, such as Human Rights Watch, Amnesty International, or the U.N. Committee Against Torture. In this book, I do not discuss the transnational actors involved in such informational or coalitional relationships for the simple reason that they are not intentionally engaged in the process of NGO development. That is, their contribution is not aimed in any organized way at assisting the development of Russian civil society. Rather than "teaching" or "developing" Russian NGOs in specific ways, they are collaborating with Russian NGOs as more or less equal partners.

Material forms of foreign assistance to Russian NGOs include mainly grants but also contributions of other resources such as office space, equipment, and Internet access. Ideational forms of influence include mainly international travel experiences and training seminars for NGOs organized by transnational organizations. At an aggregate level, it was possible to observe patterns across regions and NGO subsectors that seemed to correlate with levels and types of foreign assistance. Through the process of detailed discussion with and observation of NGOs and their members, it was possible to determine with some confidence whether activists' thinking or behavior had been affected by contacts with foreign donors. For example, did they discuss concepts or mention projects during interviews or in their organizational literature that were specifically traceable to their trainings and/or grant projects with donors?

A major competing domestic factor affecting NGO development, and the one considered in detail in this book, is the local political environment. The concept of "political opportunity structure," developed in social movement theory, includes opportunities and constraints for activities that consist of the arrangement and extent of openness of political institutions, alignments of relevant political elites, the state's capacity and propensity for repression, and the presence or absence of movement allies in the state or government (McAdam, 1996, p. 27). Sidney Tarrow defines political opportunities as "consistent—but not necessarily formal, permanent, or national—dimensions of the political struggle that encourage people to engage in contentious politics" (1998, pp. 19–20). Several existing studies of transnational influences on NGO development have tried to gauge the impact of foreign donors on the NGO sector, but without considering the extent to which variations in domestic political opportunity structure also affect local NGOs (Mendelson and Glenn, 2002; Richter, 1997; Henderson, 2003). Some analyses, particularly the internal policy evaluations by foreign donors themselves, have tried to judge their success in affecting the behavior of various levels of Russian government toward NGOs through training and advocacy programs

(USAID, 1999a). However, the impact of foreign assistance on the development of Russian NGOs in combination with helpful or discouraging local political factors has not been systematically researched.

In this book, I make such an attempt by examining how NGO development differs across regions. Specific aspects of local political contexts taken into account include the presence or lack of material support for NGOs from regional governments (such as grant programs, social contracting, or office space); elements of institutionalized dialogue with NGOs (such as committees for relations with NGOs, active "public chambers" of NGO consultation with government, or municipal resource centers); the existence of widely acknowledged NGO allies in the regional administration; the presence or absence of an open conflict between regional and city governments that affects NGO relations; and any clear evidence that the administration either threatens NGOs for maintaining "wrong" positions or plays favorites with a few select NGOs. Chapter Four discusses in detail how these various aspects were measured and weighted.

A second domestic factor considered is the normative or "frame" resonance of transnational concepts. Like political opportunity structure, this concept is also drawn from social movement theory. Frame resonance is introduced as an intervening factor that affects the type of impact that transnational influences have on NGO development. Social movement theorists argue that, in order to succeed, movement activists must depict or "frame" their issues in terms that resonate both with target audiences' experiences and with their extant beliefs (Snow and Benford, 1992). While such theorists have traditionally used the concept of frame resonance to analyze the influence of domestic social movement organizations on the norms and beliefs of the broader public, in this book, frame resonance is applied to foreign donors to assess the extent to which the concepts they promote are compatible with historically developed norms and beliefs in Russian society. I employ the concept of issue framing on a Russia-wide basis, rather than regionally, since it is assumed that regional differences in domestic norms and beliefs regarding the NGO issues examined in the book are not significant enough to warrant separate consideration.

Utilizing Cross-Regional Comparisons

Chapter Four includes a cross-regional analysis comparing the seven cities chosen for study: Moscow, St. Petersburg, Ekaterinburg, Izhevsk, Vladivostok, Khabarovsk, and Novgorod. These cities exhibit varying levels of foreign assistance and, not surprisingly, variations in many additional factors that might conceivably affect NGO development patterns—including level of urbanization (city size), economic wealth, education, and degree of military "closedness."

Level of urbanization is one of the most important socioeconomic factors emphasized in studying citizens' political activism and is arguably a major component of modernization processes that create fundamental changes in social structure (Durkheim, 1960; Janos, 1986). The usual assumption is that large cities provide more opportunities than rural areas for individuals to associate with a critical mass of like-minded people, and they also allow individuals to remain more anonymous and less monitored in their activities by those around them.

We have little reason to suppose that the widely found correlation between urbanization and social movement activism does not hold in post-Soviet Russia as well. Until very late in the Soviet regime, the state maintained undeniably significant constraints on free association among citizens that precluded this kind of automatic relationship (Fish, 1995, pp. 19–20). However, by now, over a decade since the breakdown of these mechanisms of control with the end of Soviet rule, associational dynamics traditionally connected with the greater socioeconomic diversity in urban areas are likely to apply to some extent in Russia as well.

Unfortunately for a researcher interested in pinpointing the influences of transnational actors on NGO mobilization, transnational actors have tended to concentrate their attentions more on larger population centers than on smaller, more remote ones. The danger for the study was that, in the likely event that larger cities would have larger and more sophisticated NGO movements than smaller cities, it would be difficult to separate the influences of urbanization as a background factor from the specific influences of foreign donors.

In order to avoid this outcome, I included large cities that have been disproportionately ignored by foreign donors as well as smaller cities that have been targets of focus for them. The latter category of city was easier to locate than the former, because a few donors have experimented with a pilot technique of concentrating resources in a few cities that they believe hold promise in terms of economic potential and local political climate. The city I chose in this category, Novgorod-the-Great—with a population of only 230,000, by far the smallest of my study—was just such a target of foreign assistance. Novgorod was the first Russian city chosen as a site for the Regional Initiative of the U.S. Department of State.[19] It was more difficult to find large cities that have been overlooked by foreign donors. However, I succeeded in locating a number of medium-sized cities (in the range of

600,000–700,000 population), of which one (Izhevsk) has been relatively ignored, while two others of the same size (Khabarovsk and Vladivostok) have been targets for foreign assistance. In the course of research, I did find that urbanization shaped NGO development in some ways, principally indirectly by affecting the strength of the local political environment's influence on NGOs.

Fortunately, one other common factor explaining variations in civic political activism—levels of education—does not vary as much across post-Soviet Russia as in most Western countries. It is well known that the Soviet Union had an especially developed education system that provided postsecondary education to a large percentage of the population across the country. Many of the best-educated specialists were concentrated in elite industrial regions, such as those engaged in military production, while many areas, namely agricultural and basic-industry locations, remained relatively undereducated, despite the broad system of education. However, differences in educational levels among the regions I studied were fairly small, with the proportion of the population attaining mid- or higher-level education only varying by only about 8 percent outside the two vast cities of Moscow and St. Petersburg.[20] As it turns out, these differences did not correlate clearly with differences in NGO development. Moscow and St. Petersburg, with up to 16 percent higher levels of education in their populations, did have more diverse NGO populations than the other smaller regional cities, but there was no correlation between levels of education and activism of the NGO community in the other five regional cities.

Literature on democratization has also argued that in societies with higher levels of economic wealth, citizens are more likely to push for and sustain civil liberties and democratic governance (Lipset, 1959; Przeworski and Limongi, 1997; Bunce, 2000). Indeed, if we extrapolate that this would predict livelier civil societies in wealthier contexts—particularly because from a social movement perspective, more income and spare time provides resources to support civic mobilization—this expectation seems to bear out in the wealthiest Russian regions. Moscow, in particular, has a wealthy population with lower than average levels of unemployment than other regions, and it also has one of the largest and most sophisticated NGO communities in the country. The study included cities with a range of economic wealth, with Moscow, Khabarovsk, and St. Petersburg at the higher end of the per capita income range and Izhevsk and Novgorod falling at the lower end. It turned out that economic wealth did seem to help NGO mobilization in various regions, but the poorest regions did not have the least developed NGO communities.

An additional factor that researchers of political activism in Russia have described as important is the level of a region's military production or military strategic importance, which affects the degree to which a city has been closed to access by foreigners and even Russian citizens (Fish, 1995; Zaslavsky, 1982). It was very common in the Soviet Union for the state to restrict the movement of people into and out of cities considered sensitive due to the presence of military production or bases. Cities were subject to varying levels of "closedness"—with some cities involved in nuclear production so closed that even Soviet citizens experienced very restricted entry and exit privileges, and many more were completely closed to access by foreigners.

While the urbanization factor may be growing stronger in affecting Russian social activism, the opposite is likely to be true regarding the significance of formerly closed cities. The importance of military production and related control over workers is nowhere near as great today as it was during the Soviet and immediate post-Soviet period. First, most of the closed cities, with the exception of a few highly sensitive locations, became open during the 1990s. Second, military enterprises for the most part today have far less financial capability to provide the material fringe benefits that they provided during Soviet times, and they have lost to private sources any monopoly on these goods and services that they once had.[21] And third, there are more numerous and more lucrative opportunities outside military enterprises today for the "best and brightest" of the Russian educated elite than there were in the past. In short, the threat that military enterprises once posed to their employees is drastically less serious today than it was during the Soviet era.

Nonetheless, it seems reasonable to expect that sociopolitical mobilization in cities that were opened up to the outside later than others would remain affected for some time by the inertia of fear in public consciousness. The cities I chose for study do vary in levels of historical closedness and military production. Izhevsk, for example, maintains erratic but significant restrictions on foreigners' access to the city to this day, and Vladivostok was highly restricted to foreigners until 1994. In fact, I found that the most influential aspect today of a city's former levels of openness/closedness is the amount of contact that Russians in a particular city have with foreigners. It seems no longer to be the case that a history of closedness affects NGO activism to a significant extent through domestic control by enterprises and the state over workers, but rather that it impedes transnational influences on NGO development.

Limits of the Study and Methods

Because research into the detailed behavior and attitudes of NGO activists, government actors, and foreign donors requires intensive interviewing and local observation, it was impossible during this project to make the dozens of cross-regional comparisons that a fully representative research design would demand. I instead used the case study approach to make controlled comparisons across seven regions of Russia. First, by employing controlled comparisons across cities with similar characteristics, according to Mill's "method of difference"—varying one factor among transnational exposure, local political environment, and city size, while holding the remaining factors fairly constant—I attempted to ascertain the relative effects of transnational interactions and local political environments on NGO sector development. The limitations of this method of cross-case comparison are well known, and the most serious was noted by Mill himself: cases almost inevitably vary in numerous respects other than the variable under examination (Mill, 1973).

Similar modesty is warranted in interpreting the book's conclusions from the comparisons across NGO subsectors. My argument regarding the compatibility of foreign donors' norms with domestic norms must at this point be viewed as requiring further testing. Comparison of two NGO subsectors, while fruitful for generating plausible hypotheses, cannot comprise a strong test of such hypotheses. In order to test and strengthen these hypotheses, future examination of further NGO subsectors will be necessary.

Field Research and Evidence

I conducted the primary field research for this book between July 1998 and August 2000. It consisted largely of semistructured interviews with leaders and members of Russian NGOs, relevant representatives of foreign assistance organizations that work with women's and human rights NGOs in Russia, and officials in Russian federal, regional, and city administrations who are responsible for working with NGOs. In the cases of Moscow and St. Petersburg, where there were roughly a hundred (in Moscow) and fifty (in St. Petersburg) active women's organizations, I was not able to interview them all. In the other cities examined, however, it was possible to conduct interviews with nearly all known women's organizations. Soldiers' rights organizations were far fewer in number, and I was able to interview nearly all relevant NGOs in that subsector. I could not fully ascertain whether I was reaching all organizations in the area, despite use of numerous sources of contact information. Even in regions where NGO resource centers exist, often the information is out of date and incomplete. I also interviewed representatives of most major foreign donor and Russian government organizations relevant to women's and soldiers' rights NGOs. In total, the study consisted of 205 interviews with 208 subjects in 163 organizations (117 of which were with Russian NGOs or resource centers, and the remainder of which were with Russian government officials, foreign donors, or other foreign organizations). For information on interview questions and techniques used, refer to Appendix 2.

Aside from conducting interviews, I gathered primary literature from organizations about their activities and programs, media articles regarding NGOs, copies of government laws and policies regarding NGOs, and secondary analyses of the NGO sector and transnational assistance in Russia. These also enter the analysis. I used some basic Russian statistical sources on regional demographics and official NGO registration to explore socioeconomic factors affecting regional variations in NGO development, and to gain comparative data in terms of organizational numbers. While these official statistics are flawed—especially as concerns numbers of registered NGOs—they at least offer some standardized measures that can be compared across regions, and they are the only available statistics that do so.

The book makes use of a database I created of ninety interviews with eighty women's and soldiers' rights NGOs that were conducted between March 1999 and August 2000.[22] The database does not include the interviews conducted during an initial plausibility probe for the study from July to September 1998, during which the questions asked were slightly different and interviews were not audiotaped.[23] The database allowed me to code and search interview transcripts in order to make extensive and complex comparisons of organizations by category and region, according to such characteristics as funding sources, activities, relations with foreign assistance organizations, and relations with the state. These findings are included in the empirical data of Chapters Three and Four.

CHAPTER 2

Introducing the Protagonists: Russian NGOs and Foreign Donors

IT WILL BE HELPFUL for our purposes to begin with a broad understanding of the preexisting status of civil society in Russia, and what that meant both for the starting point of post-Communist Russia's NGO sector and for the spectrum of actors and approaches involved in foreign assistance to Russian NGOs. This chapter introduces the context in which independent organizations began to emerge in Russia during the late 1980s and early 1990s, prior to the involvement of most foreign donors. It also outlines the range of foreign donors, both governmental and nongovernmental, that were involved in promoting Russian civil society during the 1990s and draws distinctions among them in terms of the strategies they were employing.

Civil Society and NGOs Before Foreign Assistance

While it is undeniably true that civil society was weak and lacked autonomy in the Soviet Union, it is simplistic to argue that there was no civil society before the collapse of Communist power. Many authors have pointed out that volunteerism has a strong history in Russia (Conroy, 2005; CAF International, 1997; Ruffin, McCarter, and Upjohn, 1996). Indeed, in the prerevolutionary era, thousands of self-help and charitable organizations existed in Russia. Ruffin argues that "the fact that the Soviet government had to exert so much brutal force in order to wipe out these groups in the 1920s and 1930s attests to their vitality" (Ruffin, McCarter, and Upjohn, 1996, p. xi). Nonetheless, even in the prerevolutionary period from the late seventeenth to early twentieth centuries, the Russian voluntary sphere tended to be centralized, heavily guided by government or the church, and primarily occupied by the wealthy and the intelligentsia (Conroy, 2005; CAF International, 1997, pp. 2.1–2.3). It did not have the autonomous and decentralized qualities that we associate with liberal civil societies in the West today.

During the Soviet era, the state did not suppress civil society uniformly at all times. A small sector of volunteer associations sprouted up for a brief period during the "Khrushchev thaw" of the late 1950s and early 1960s (CAF International, 1997, pp. 2.1–2.5; Ruffin, McCarter, and Upjohn, 1996, p. xi). Ann Phillips (1999), in writing about Central-Eastern European civil society, testifies to the enormous amount of organizational experience that Soviet-bloc citizens did in fact acquire, even if it was carefully state directed (see also Henderson, 2003, p. 95). While citizens of Eastern European satellite states experienced greater freedoms than citizens of the Soviet Union itself, Phillips' point is well taken. Indeed, in the Soviet Union, as in Eastern Europe, "outside the explicitly political sphere, many civic organizations existed that provided arenas where membership was self-selected based on interests . . . even if they lacked full autonomy" (Phillips, 1999, p. 74). Communist-era sport clubs, hobby clubs, and women's organizations are some examples of these kinds of nonautonomous but nonetheless interest-based organizations (Evans, 2005a).

Many of these organizations continued into the post-Communist period in essentially the same form and with most of the same members as in the Soviet period. As we will see in my analysis of women's organizations, many of these organizations conduct useful work, primarily of a charitable sort, in Russian civil society. The break with the Communist past, both in terms of ideas and the specific individuals inhabiting governmental and nongovernmental institutions, was much less clean and more complicated than most analysts admit (Henry, 2005), and Phillips notes that "reluctance or unwillingness to appreciate the complex mixture of positive and negative components of the socialist experience has informed western democratization strategies" (1999, p. 75).

Despite the existence of interest-based, state-initiated groups in the Soviet Union, all attempts at independent organization were strongly discouraged until the perestroika period in the late 1980s, especially if they carried any politicizing potential. Indeed, as Fish states, by the Brezhnev era, mass terror techniques were no longer necessary to maintain official repression against non-state forms of association. Rather, harassment of independent organizing efforts "became an automatic, reflexive, institutionalized bureaucratic response to any organized expression of social autonomy" (Fish, 1995, p. 31).

The tragic histories of the few thousand Russian citizens who actually attempted to organize independent oppositional or human rights groups have been vividly documented by several authors (Reddaway, 1972; Rubenstein,

1985; Parchomenko, 1986; *Maria,* 1981; Dyukova, 1998; Applebaum, 2003).
Arrests, labor camps, psychiatric hospitals, and exile were several of the techniques that the Soviet regime frequently used to quell such impulses. For
example, Soviet authorities severely punished a late-1970s attempt by women
to organize an independent journal and discussion club in St. Petersburg.
Numerous women associated with the *samizdat* journals *Woman and Russia*
and *Maria* were expelled permanently from the Soviet Union, and a few were
sentenced to hard labor camps.[1] This repression, after several years, effectively
deterred women's independent organizing until the late 1980s.

Beginning in 1985, certain sections of the Communist party began to
admit the appropriateness of societal diversity at a theoretical level, signaling
the opening of limited tolerance of informal, non-state citizen activity (Fish,
1995, p. 32). By 1987, informal groups with semipolitical agendas began to
form, albeit tentatively, including the organization that eventually became
the unionwide human rights group Memorial. Another major organization,
the Moscow Helsinki Group, which initially formed in response to the 1975
signing of the Helsinki Declaration and closed down in 1982 as a result of
severe state repressions against it, announced its revival in 1989 (Moscow
Helsinki Group, n.d.; Laber, 2002, pp. 182, 249–50). In 1988, as Fish documents, informal groups (*neformaly*) of citizens outside state organizations
began to form in great numbers. However, they were truly informal, with
fluid memberships and loose organizational structures. Most of them disappeared with the collapse of the Soviet regime, since most discussed perestroika reforms and regime alternatives—topics that became obsolete with
the dismantling of Soviet power—and their members held diverging opinions beyond such questions. Soviet authorities accepted the existence of
informal groups that kept discussions within the bounds of supporting perestroika. Yet any groups that tested the accepted boundaries of political discussion—such as the Democratic Union, a group composed of advocates of
multiparty liberal democracy—were seriously punished through persecution,
police raids, and sometimes imprisonment (Fish, 1995, pp. 33–34).

According to most Western observers of their activities, the informal dissident and pro-democracy activists of the Soviet era formed the main core
of independent citizen activity that could have been expected to develop and
expand in post-Soviet Russian civil society. However, these dissidents were
specifically concerned with human rights issues, and those that remained in
the 1990s were mostly isolated within the human rights movement.
Although they continue to feature prominently within that movement—
with figures such as Liudmila Alekseeva, of Moscow Helsinki Group, and
Sergei Kovalev, a founder of Memorial and later liberal politician in the

1990s—with few exceptions, former active dissidents have not played a major role in other parts of Russian civil society.

Many of the most active human rights advocates that I encountered in my research did, in fact, have roots of participation and protest that extended back to dissident activities. Several other contemporary activists had been anxious to become involved in independent activities in Soviet times, but saw no safe way to do so publicly. Nearly all of the former dissidents I encountered were leaders of soldiers' rights organizations, rather than women's organizations (with the exceptions of a few feminist leaders in Moscow and St. Petersburg). This pattern makes sense, given the dissidents' main concern with problems of human rights violations by the state, as opposed to more socially conditioned issues of discrimination or unequal opportunities in certain population categories.

Perhaps the major problem impeding former dissidents' impact on the post-Soviet NGO community is the fact that, once the Soviet regime had collapsed, there was little that tied the dissidents to one another in their aims, and even less that connected their grievances with the concerns of average Russian citizens (Gessen, 1997, p. 18; Kagarlitsky, 2002, Ch. 2). They lacked the focus and outreach that would allow them to develop into meaningful organizations in post-Soviet civil society. The ongoing endeavors of many former dissidents—such as revealing the histories of Soviet repression or drawing parallels between Soviet human rights violations and those of the current regime—appear anachronistic or irrelevant to most Russians, particularly those under age thirty, who see today's problems as very new and different from those of the past (Kagarlitsky, 2002, p. 57). Masha Gessen, in her analysis of how the Russian intelligentsia became "dead again," cites two prominent Russian scholars as praising "the demise of what they dubbed 'literary political delusions' and promis[ing] that soon Russia would rid itself of the dysfunctional intelligentsia in favor of a productive class of intellectual professionals" (Gessen, 1997, p. 18). The extent and speed of this erosion of the dissidents' relevance reflects the revolutionary change that took place at the end of the Soviet Union: as McFaul (1996) argues, it entailed an unprecedented simultaneous dismantling of the state, the political system, and the economic system.

The near absence of former dissidents in most NGO movements is not the only surprising outcome in post-Soviet civil society. It also seems counterintuitive that Russian citizens should exhibit such low levels of civic involvement, now that freedoms of speech and association exist. Several Western authors in the late Soviet period argued that socioeconomic developments in the Soviet Union—education, urbanization, and diversification of skills—were creating a middle class of sorts that might ultimately lead to a more politically active and less submissive population (Ruble, 1987; Starr, 1988; Bialer, 1988; Hough, 1990). Indeed, during the period just prior to the Soviet collapse, around 1990–91, large numbers of Russians participated in informal groups and frequent rallies demanding democratic reforms (Fish, 1995, pp. 44, 49). But following the years of initial tumult during the regime transition, Russian citizens have not become the civic activists that many predicted, despite the opening of opportunities for independent participation in society and politics. James Alexander has noted that "[f]rom a Western perspective, it is ironic that a more open political process did not generate greater participation" (2000, p. 151).

Instead, a number of factors have weighed negatively upon citizens' willingness to participate in public affairs since the collapse of the Soviet regime. Some Russians have taken the removal of state-mandated participation in public affairs (through activities like the Pioneer and Komsomol organizations, or *subbotnik* days to clean the neighborhood) as a welcome opportunity to withdraw from them and focus on their private affairs (Howard, 2002, pp. 161–62). During the Soviet period, "voluntary" activities often involved little choice. But the low level of Russians' interest in politics is also prompted by the sense that politics has always been dishonest and farcical in Russia. If Soviet politics was tainted by a restrictive ideology and special privileges for loyal party functionaries, post-Soviet politics is dirtied by corruption and suspicious business connections. The continuing economic crisis and "lumpenization" of Russian society have also distracted and discouraged Russians from political participation (Kubicek, 2000, p. 17). Masha Gessen states: "The high of glasnost and perestroika was followed by a brief plateau of self-satisfaction followed by a nightmare of inflation, destruction, depression, bureaucratic battles, aggressive alienation, a morbid festering national identity crisis and frightening, impenetrable apathy" (1997, p. 17). In that sense, the late perestroika period was a brief interlude of optimism, and many of those who earnestly believed in the promise of democracy and a prosperous market economy are now discouraged by Russia's failure to develop into such a society within a short period of time.

Moreover, Russians are fairly suspicious of the motives behind some NGO activities. Many believe that NGO leaders misuse or misappropriate resources, and this belief was only exacerbated by scandals revealing the widespread use of veterans' and sports NGOs by criminal and commercial organizations for tax evasion purposes in the mid-1990s. Sixty-five percent of respondents in a 1994 poll of Muscovites believed that "charitable organizations are a cover for dubious activities" (CAF International, 1997, p. 2.25). A more recent poll by the Russian ROMIR agency showed that only

23 percent of respondents were willing to support the charity activities of NGOs, while 64 percent were not willing to do so (ROMIR, 2000b). Several other studies and specialists have noted the prevalence of Russian citizens' suspicions that any donations to organizations would be improperly used (Bredun, 1999, p. 41; Validata/Yankelovich, 1995).

Thus, while it is inaccurate to claim that civil society is something entirely new to Russian citizens, the 1990s following the Soviet collapse was a period when the independent voices of protest and dissent from the late Soviet era largely receded from public activism. Some former dissidents and nonconformists from the Soviet period continue their activism. However, most of the individuals who populate Russian NGOs today are either those who were members of Soviet official organizations and continue their organizational activities in similar organizations, or those who are new-style professionalized NGO activists, trained mostly by foreign donors. Bahry and Way note that people who belonged to the CPSU tend to participate in all kinds of conventional political activities, including public organizations, at substantially higher rates than the rest of the population (1994, p. 351). This lack of citizen interest in participating in public activities has made foreign donors' lack of attention to the mobilizational aspects of NGO development even more detrimental than it might have been in another, more participatory civil society such as those existing in many Latin American countries (see Howard, 2003, p. 65, for comparative data).

We can conclude, then, that NGO development prior to 1990 was virtually nonexistent in the Soviet Union, since organizations independent of the Communist party could not exist legally until then. Organizations that existed formally lacked autonomy, while those that were independent lacked the freedom to mobilize publicly. Moreover, the dissidents, as the primary autonomous underground movement, lacked professionalization (in fact, they resisted it and still resist) and organizational specialization. As we shall see in Chapter Three, soldiers' mothers' organizations constitute an exception to the rule, as one of the few autonomous NGO networks that was developed informally during perestroika, mobilized public protest, and has actually grown in strength in the post-Soviet period.

We now turn to examine how assistance from foreign donors has affected the development of these new organizations. It is important to emphasize, as the funding profiles of NGOs in later chapters show, that domestic sources of funding for Russian NGOs have been scarce, although they are slowly growing. Overall, approximately two-thirds of the NGOs interviewed in the study had received foreign funding of some kind, while only one-third had not. Only twenty (17 percent) of the women's and soldiers' rights NGOs interviewed existed solely on domestic sources of funding, while an additional five (7 percent) had no funding at all. Over 40 percent received most of their funding from foreign donors.

Several reasons explain the bleak domestic philanthropy situation in Russia. Donations to NGOs by individuals are especially rare, due to the atmosphere of distrust of NGOs noted above, a lack of a tradition of regular charitable giving by citizens, high levels of poverty in the general population, and perhaps most notably, the absence of any tax privileges for charitable donations. Survey research conducted by the VTsIOM agency in several Russian cities has found this latter fact to be the primary reason why private sector businesses in Russia have been reluctant to donate funds to Russian NGOs, followed by a lack of trust in NGOs' honesty (Krestnikova and Lyovshina, 2002, p. 9).

Foreign Donors: Many Strategies, One Vision

The first foreign donors began to operate in Russia in the late perestroika period. Among the initial pioneers were the MacArthur Foundation and foundations funded by George Soros. Once the Soviet Union collapsed in 1991, dozens of government foreign assistance agencies, international organizations, private foundations, and Western NGOs quickly began to establish granting and technical assistance programs for Russian NGOs.

Anglo-American and continental European foreign donors adopted similar aims regarding Russian civil society. Despite significant differences in the political systems and models of democracy that exist in their countries of origin, donors largely converged to promote a unified and rather limited definition of the essential players and roles of civil society, focusing on advocacy NGOs as the main component. The greatest differences among donors arose in more tactical matters: the specific priorities they selected in promoting NGO development, how programs were implemented in practice, and what proportion of assistance they chose to devote to civil society development.

CONSENSUS IN DEFINING CIVIL SOCIETY AND ITS ROLES

Given the wide range of domestic values in continental European and Anglo-American countries, one might expect that foreign donors would differ in their approaches to developing Russian civil society and specifically NGOs. A natural expectation might be that Anglo-American donors (from the United States, Canada, and Great Britain) would be more likely to promote a liberal, oppositional model of NGOs as an antidote to state excesses, and encourage NGOs to minimize their interactions with the Russian state. In contrast, we might expect that continental European donors, proceeding from a more communitarian notion of appropriate relations between civil society and the state, would encourage Russian citizens and organizations to work closely with Russian state institutions and pursue avenues of cooperation with them. We might also expect that American donors would be more concerned with increasing the number and variety of Russian NGOs than European donors are, given American pluralist political culture. European donors might not focus on strictly *non*governmental organizations at all, and instead include institutions that are state supported but autonomously managed as a significant part of civil society. This is indeed what I expected to find in my research. What I found, however, was that in the area of civil society assistance, there was very little difference among continental European, British, and North American donors in the models they promoted.

What was striking in assistance to civil society was the degree of similarity among donors' philosophies, rather than the differences. Thomas Carothers has made the same observation regarding foreign donors as concerns democracy assistance overall (1999, p. 12). In the specific area of civil society assistance, the similarities are even more striking, since most donors have equated civil society development with the development of independent nongovernmental organizations. Van Rooy argues that "what has happened in much of the policy writing on civil society is a misappropriation of the idea of terrain into a simpler sphere, and final simplification into a neat circle drawn around organizational types" (1998b, p. 21). For nearly all donors, civil society has become a discrete sphere of nongovernmental associations, sharply separated from the state and the market (Van Rooy and Robinson, 1998; Carothers, 1999; Carothers and Ottaway, 2000).

In other areas of economic and political assistance to Russia, distinct differences between EU and American donors appear in terms of their willingness to work with the state. While the EU structured most aid through "government-to-government relations," U.S. assistance involved "almost exclusively the 'private' sector" (Wedel, 1998, p. 37). But in the specific realm of assistance to civil society, European and American donors have not differed significantly in their approach to the state. Despite the varying political cultures of their countries of origin, both have advocated a basically liberal, "constructive dialogue" model according to which NGOs should be autonomous from the state and receive their material resources chiefly from non-state sources, but should engage in constructive conversation with the state. That is, NGOs should advise and advocate in public policy issues, and oppose decisions that they consider wrong. As such, donors from both continents have promoted neither a strictly adversarial form of liberal civil society nor a communitarian one.

Further similarities stand out when we compare the ways in which foreign donors have defined their goals in relation to civil society. The following quotes, from a range of Anglo-American and continental European donors, both governmental and nongovernmental, indicate how similarly they have defined the composition and proper functioning of civil society. All have argued that their goal is to strengthen civil society in order to promote democratization, and they have done so by supporting the development of NGOs that work to increase citizens' participation in public or political life.

USAID: Increased citizen participation in political and economic decision-making is a key component of Russia's democratic transition . . . Civil society activities help empower non-governmental organizations to ensure that citizens can articulate their opinions and influence decision-makers through collective action (USAID, 2000b, Activity Data Sheets).

European Commission: The Democracy Programme's . . . general objective is to promote the concept of democratic society governed by the rule of law . . . In particular, it aims to support: increased knowledge of democratic practices at local and national level; the work of non-governmental organisations which promote pluralist democratic societies; the transfer of specific expertise and technical skills concerning democracy and the rule of law to professional groups and associations in these countries (EC, 1996, p. ix).

Ford Foundation (USA): This [civil society, local governance, and community development] program seeks to empower citizens, united in associations or organizations, to undertake initiatives that would promote the civic interests of their members, strengthen their local communities, and stimulate participation in local government (Ford Foundation Moscow Office, 2001).

Westminster Foundation for Democracy (UK): The development of civil society enables wider citizen participation in influencing social, cultural and economic policy, an alternative to the ballot box as well as a means of involvement between elections . . . NGOs play a key role in creating civil society . . . WFD's emphasis within the sector is on NGOs of a civil and political nature (WFD, 2001a).

While the definition of civil society and the basic goals that donors pursue with regard to it have been fundamentally similar, some definite differences were encountered among donors in terms of how their civil society assistance programs were structured and how their strategies had evolved over the years. The next section presents an overview of the wide spectrum of foreign donors providing assistance to Russian NGOs.

DIFFERING FOREIGN DONOR STRATEGIES

During the 1990s, foreign donors varied considerably in the degree of emphasis they place on civil society development as a portion of their overall political assistance (often called "governance aid"). Unfortunately, since most government assistance agencies do not break down their foreign assistance expenditures into categories that specifically indicate funding for civil society development (as opposed to democratic reform as a whole), it was difficult to estimate accurately the amounts being directed toward NGO development.

We can draw some broad comparisons among government donors in terms of their relative emphasis on civil society in their development programs. This chapter considers in detail the approaches of the United States and the European Union as the largest donors of civil society assistance. It also examines Great Britain, Canada, the Netherlands, and Germany as smaller donors with varying strategies.

The British government traditionally has devoted only a small portion of its political assistance to civil society development and has instead emphasized reforming government and state institutions. The United States is by far the largest absolute donor to civil society in Russia and worldwide has devoted approximately one-third of its political aid to this sector (Van Rooy and Robinson, 1998, p. 60). Canada's overall assistance budget to Russia has been fairly small, compared to the contributions of the major state players, yet its relatively high emphasis on grants to NGOs made the Canadian government a visible donor in the Russian community. The Embassy of the Netherlands was a frequently mentioned donor by NGO activists in the study, and like the Scandinavian countries other than Finland, it has contributed one of the highest proportions of GNP to overseas development assistance.[2] The Netherlands is known for dedicating a high share of its overall overseas democracy promotion budget to NGOs (as opposed to government), relative to most other government donors (Landsberg, 2000, p. 120). Germany is unique as a foreign government donor in that nearly all of its NGO development funding is channeled through foundations, or *Stiftungen*, that are closely associated with particular German political parties. Most of the German foundations' assistance was directed toward political party development and electoral improvements, rather than NGO development, but some, such as the Heinrich Böll Foundation, were heavily involved in funding NGOs.

By all accounts, the proportion of general democracy assistance directed to civil society development has increased steadily since the early 1990s (Van Rooy, 1998c; Carothers and Ottaway, 2000; Carothers, 1999a). Around the mid-1990s, foreign donors quickly began to amend their democracy assistance strategies for regions all over the world to include specific civil society development programs (Carothers and Ottaway, 2000, p. 6; Van Rooy and Robinson, 1998, p. 55; Hearn and Robinson, 2000, p. 244). The trend was led by the U.S. government, which indeed was the earliest strong proponent of encouraging market and democratic reforms through non-state institutions.

The U.S. government focus on NGO development in Russia began with initiatives like the Eurasia Foundation's small grants program in 1993 and USAID's Civic Initiatives Program in 1994. The United States continues to be by far the largest contributor of assistance to civil society. Yet other donors caught on quickly, with the EU increasing its emphasis on civil society after a major policy review in 1997, and virtually every foreign donor implementing specific NGO programs by the late 1990s.

Why this enormous surge in the popularity of civil society occurred in the donor community and why there are striking similarities in the models of civil society that different donors adopted are questions that deserve further research. But it is clear that part of the reason for the sudden turn toward assistance through NGOs is a reaction to failures that donors experienced in channeling most of their initial democracy assistance through government institutions and personnel. Several authors have noted this reasoning (Carothers and Ottaway, 2000, pp. 7–8; Hearn and Robinson, 2000, p. 244), arising from the specific problems of government resistance to democratic reforms, bureaucratic inertia, and significant corruption leading to misuse of funds. Foreign donors initially saw civil society as a possible solution to these problems, both because they viewed it as a potential wellspring of public scrutiny and reform of government institutions and because—correctly or not—they perceived NGOs as being more honest and transparent than government institutions.

In the late 1990s, the U.S. government embarked on a process of shifting assistance resources more to NGOs and away from Russian government agencies. With President Clinton's launch of the Partnership for Freedom program in 1997, funding for democratic reform initiatives increased, and in particular, the USAID strategy shifted from a prior focus on macro-level institutional and policy reform through grants mainly to U.S. contractors, to a greater emphasis on local-level civil society and thus on strengthening Russian NGOs as a route to reform (Sakwa, 2000, p. 295). The 1998 financial crisis in Russia and simultaneous allegations that Russian government officials had misused foreign aid and loans further contributed to USAID's conscious decision to shift as much assistance as possible away from the central government (USAID, 2000b).

While civil society development has been a rapidly growing category in Western states' foreign assistance programs, it still comprises only a very small portion—generally under 10 percent—of overall foreign assistance budgets. As mentioned in Chapter One, funding to Russia in other areas of assistance— for example, in economic reforms or nuclear security—has been vastly greater than that devoted to civil society. Of course, aid to civil society specifically is only a portion of all democracy assistance, which typically also includes assistance aimed at such constituencies as elected officials, mass media, political parties, local governments, the judiciary, and law enforcement.

In addition to the variations in donors' overall emphasis on civil society as a priority, significant variations also occurred among donors in the mechanisms they used in NGO development programs and where their priorities lay. I have broken down these differences into four categories, all of which concern mechanisms and tactics of implementing NGO development assistance.

First, most donors predefined their funding priorities for Russian NGOs fairly strictly in a top-down manner and changed their priorities over time, while some defined their funding priorities more broadly and selected projects on a demand-driven basis. Top-down determination of priorities allows for more donor control over the use and results of funding, but it discourages NGOs from reaching out to constituencies of citizens and developing responses to pressing problems in society. It is worth noting that the individuals who staff the offices of foreign donors can vary considerably in their sensitivity to the preferences of Russian NGOs. As a result, within the broader top-down or bottom-up framework of donor strategies in supporting Russian civil society, shifts in local office management can temporarily affect donor-granting tendencies.

Second, foreign donors differed in their relative emphasis on building the general infrastructure of the NGO sector versus supporting projects to work on specific social or political issues, with American organizations typically favoring the former, and European organizations the latter. While, theoretically, a focus on specific social and political issues would create more incentives for NGOs to engage in external mobilization and perhaps improve NGO sustainability by building constituencies of supporters, in reality even those donors that focused on specific issues placed less emphasis on NGO outreach to society than they did on the internal professionalization aspects of NGO development.

Third, donors differed in the types of NGOs they tended to support. Most donors focused more on advocacy or human rights questions than on less controversial but pervasive socioeconomic welfare issues. Small, private foundations generally supported more radical, controversial causes than large foundations or government donors. Overall, though, donors devoted little attention to ensuring that the advocacy groups they supported had significant public support or that NGOs were working to develop societal constituencies. This pattern, over time, has hampered the ability of NGOs to develop sustainable forms of resource mobilization.

Fourth, donors varied in the extent to which they concentrated their funds in particular organizations or regions. They differed among themselves and across time in whether they spread their support broadly and thinly—that is, to as many different organizations in as many locations as possible across Russia—or narrowly and intensely—possibly giving large institutional grants to small numbers of NGOs and/or concentrating on particular cities or regions. Some donors preferred to support an NGO's entire range of activities and overhead expenses by funding an organization long term, while the vast majority only gave grants for specific projects for limited periods of time. Both approaches have pros and cons. Virtually any NGO leader would like to have the comfort of knowing that his or her organization has secured sufficient funding for several years in order to be spared the constant cycle of small-grant proposals to donors and thus be able to concentrate on developing a sustained program of activities. Yet the more donors concentrate their grants in large institutional chunks or particular regional locations, the fewer NGOs they can support and the less diversified NGO funding sources are likely to be.

While the programmatic differences between the two largest government players in Russian NGO development—the USA and the EU—were rather small, the variations among the smaller players were more noticeable. By far, the largest amount of foreign assistance to Russian NGOs has come from the United States, mostly in government funding, but also significantly from nongovernmental foundations. Thus it is the American version of NGO development assistance, with its relatively strict predefinition of specific priorities and emphasis on infrastructural development, that has dominated the community of donors.

The following discussion draws distinctions among donors in these four respects and covers donor initiatives and the range of approaches that donors have exhibited in operating their programs up through the year 2000. For more specific information on major donors' programs at the time of the study, refer to Appendix 3. Another useful description of donors' NGO development programs can be found in Henderson (2003, Appendix D).

Top-Down Versus Bottom-Up

One of the major criticisms that Russian NGO activists and Western analysts have made of the U.S. government's approach to Russian civil society is that program priorities have been shaped far too rigidly from above by Washington, based on conditions that exist in the United States and the demands of the U.S. Congress (Henderson, 2003, pp. 85–87). This approach has not left much room for Russian activists to suggest ideas for their own projects based on the problems they feel are most pressing in their communities. This criticism has emerged not only in Russia; all over the world, in countries as diverse as South Africa and Romania, the USAID approach has been accused of being unresponsive to local problems (Ottaway, 2000, p. 99; Petrescu, 2000, p. 226). In a 1999 report by USAID that evaluated its assistance to NGOs in post-Communist countries, the agency admitted that its strategic development style of choosing specific issues to focus on "inevitably follows the agenda of foreign donors and may not reflect local priorities" (USAID, 1999a, p. 32).

The German *Stiftungen* receive their funding from the state budget, and the amount that each foundation receives depends on the size of its affiliated party in the parliament. The *Stiftungen* are much more closely affiliated with their respective political parties than the American party-affiliated foundations, National Democratic Institute (NDI) and International Republican Institute (IRI). They depend on good relations with their parties in order to remain well funded, and their programs are thus closely associated with the various parties' foreign policy perspectives (Mair, 2000, pp. 130–31). This traditionally has rendered the *Stiftungen* both strongly directive in their programming, as much American official assistance is, and more firmly ideologically oriented. During the Cold War, multiple conflicting priorities emerged among the *Stiftungen* in their international work due to the fairly close ideological dependence of the foundations on their parties (Mair, 2000, p. 132). Even in the late 1990s in Russia, NGOs that had been funded by multiple *Stiftungen* reported distinct ideological preferences among them. Boris Pustintsev of the St. Petersburg human rights organization Citizen Watch (*Grazhdanskyi kontrol'*) recalled his experience this way:

One of the leftist foundations met with us . . . and we proposed to them that we work on improving access to government information . . . on rights of specific groups, like soldiers, children, refugees . . . and the representative said 'Very interesting—tell me, couldn't you be interested in the theme of the workers' movement in Russia?' Even though we do not really have a workers' movement in Russia! . . . So it's very politically directed.[3]

Indeed, the ideological leanings of the *Stiftungen* were visible in the human rights and women's organizations I visited. Overwhelmingly, those that had received German funding had obtained grants specifically from the Green Party's Heinrich Böll *Stiftung*, which emphasized "women's emancipation, ecological and human rights issues" (Mair, 2000, p. 134), rather than from the other parties' foundations.

Nonetheless, although the German *Stiftungen* traditionally operated according to their political value orientations and lent long-term support to like-thinkers overseas, they gradually changed their strategy through the 1990s. They began to give small grants to large numbers of NGOs, in the process becoming less partisan in their value orientations and thus less distinct from other foreign donors in their approach (Mair, 2000, p. 140).

Netherlands government assistance illustrates the opposite approach to that of German and American government assistance programs. The MATRA Projects Programme, the largest component of the Netherlands' program of partnerships between Dutch and Russian organizations, emphasized that "the demand for the project should come from the recipient country and there should be clear support for the project in that country" (Netherlands Ministry of Foreign Affairs, 2000). The MATRA program did not include any specific priority areas in its criteria, and it stressed that funded projects must have clear results in serving the interests of specific citizens. This explicit focus and the absence of strategic funding objectives was a rare example of a demand-driven program orientation. The benefit of this kind of strategy was that truly needed projects were likely to be funded and to have noticeable impact for citizens at local levels. On the other hand, in the emphasis on producing "concrete, material results," the program was likely to discourage projects such as voter education or human rights awareness campaigns, which aim chiefly at changing the consciousness of large numbers of people and rarely deliver measurable results.

The EU's programs exhibited a mix of strategies. The targeted projects of the European Initiative for Democracy and Human Rights (EIDHR), for example, were designed in a top-down manner with specific areas of focus defined in each year, while the EIDHR micro- and macro-projects had less specific guidelines. Canada's programs also included a mix of designated project priorities (such as focusing on women's rights, human rights, and elections) and funding that was open to proposals from Russian NGOs. Great Britain's programs were not highly specific in their substantive priorities, but their strong focus on infrastructural projects to improve the NGO community as a whole entailed substantial project limitation by the donor. Overall, USAID strategic objectives and the EU targeted projects program were the most donor-driven in predefining strategic objectives for grant recipients in Russia.

Although donors have felt that they have more control over the outcomes of assistance expenditures when they specify the exact results they want from a grant, there have been some disadvantages to such a top-down approach. Donor-driven agendas for project grants often do not result in sustained positive change, as illustrated in the poor results generally achieved when donors to Russian NGOs have mandated the creation of NGO networks in a particular issue area.

I encountered a total of seventeen Russia-wide networks or organizations formed among NGOs, including those that existed within the framework of a single organization. Five of the networks were initiated largely through projects sponsored by foreign donors. Several of these transnationally sponsored networks had large memberships with broad geographic coverage. Yet despite frequent communications for information exchange among members, the networks tended not to be closely knit, thus their impact on NGO collaboration was not terribly high.

Among those networks that began without foreign donor participation, the umbrella organization was the most frequent—with a head office in Moscow and regional divisions across Russia—although their structure varied tremendously. For example, the Union of Women of Russia (UWR) largely maintained its Soviet-era hierarchy of a national head office and *zhensovety* that existed at the regional, city, neighborhood (*raion*), and sometimes factory levels. *Zhensovety* were originally created by Khrushchev to be the monopoly Soviet organizations for women, and they persisted as a network into the post-Soviet era (see Chapter Three for this history). Priorities in the post-Soviet UWR network were mostly formed in Moscow and communicated to the regions; however, both the Moscow and regional offices insisted that local divisions chose which programs they wished to follow closely and discerned details of implementation on their own. On the other hand, the group Memorial and the human rights network Union of Committees of Soldiers' Mothers of Russia had less hierarchical structures of largely independent local organizations.

In virtually all of the networks that were not formed by foreign donors, each regional organization carried the same name and, to some extent, could be considered a division of a single organization. Several of these networks—such as the Union of Committees of Soldiers' Mothers of Russia and many divisions of Memorial—became frequent foreign-funding recipients after their founding in spite of being formed entirely without foreign donor participation. In contrast, the networks that were both transnationally funded and founded tended to be much looser and composed of preexisting, separate organizations. All of the networks encountered in the study that were initiated as part of a foreign grant project had this character. Three of them—the Information Center of the Independent Women's Forum (ICIWF), the Consortium of Women's Nongovernmental Organizations (formerly the NIS-US Consortium), and the Russian Association of Crisis Centers for Women—were nationwide networks.[4] Two others, the League of Women Voters in St. Petersburg (unrelated to the American League of Women Voters) and an NGO Association in Khabarovsk, were local-level associations.

With the exceptions of the Association of Crisis Centers and, possibly, the League of Women Voters, the unity and effectiveness of these networks were relatively low. The ICIWF and the Consortium did provide ample information by e-mail to their subscribers regarding such topics as the work of different women's NGOs around Russia, grant opportunities, and legislative initiatives. The Consortium, which is the largest umbrella association of autonomous women's NGOs in Russia, also offered some small grants to member organizations for such purposes as gaining Internet access and publishing books. Occasionally, the Consortium held events and training seminars attended by members from different regions, but typically its events were attended mainly by Moscow member organizations. The ICIWF maintained a huge list of subscribers to its regular e-mail bulletins and printed journals, but the number of network members who joined actively in programs was small.

In this sense, both the Consortium and the ICIWF were fairly unidirectional networks, with information running from Moscow to the regions. Dozens of women's organizations reported to me that they found the information sent by these networks to be very useful, but the networks did not involve much in the way of active work or dialogue among organizations. NGOs tended to join these networks for the goods they provided and not necessarily to participate actively in a program or agenda. The mobilization potential of the networks was thus doubtful, had the headquarters or regional members suddenly wished to organize a campaign.

Having said this, there were numerous instances in which the Consortium and the ICIWF asked their members across Russia for letters of protest or suggestions on amendments to public policy proposals on various issues. Unfortunately, it was difficult to ascertain in any detail the volume and quality of response that these calls elicited. But such attempts were still Moscow-centric and sporadic exceptions to an otherwise relatively passive network.

The Khabarovsk NGO Association, by virtually all accounts, was dead at birth. The goal of founding an association of NGOs was part of a foreign-funded conference on NGO development in Khabarovsk in early 1999.[5] By late 1999, the association had fallen apart as a result of quarrels over leadership control, only six organizations remained nominal members, and a disgruntled pretender to the leadership was founding a competing association. I learned of this situation from several sources, but one remaining member of the dwindling association stated to me: "It was just done as a grant requirement and is not a real working association. The problem is power and money between [the two competing leaders]."[6]

The League of Women Voters in St. Petersburg had a membership of approximately eighty organizations in the city—largely women's NGOs and political parties interested in monitoring election violations or promoting female electoral candidates. The League also had sister organizations in several cities of the northwest region of Russia. Especially around election periods, this network organized candidate meetings and discussions, with active participation of the member organizations.

The Russian Association of Crisis Centers for Women, formed in 1994, has been one of the most tight-knit and effective NGO associations in Russia. It has held frequent conferences and workshops to train NGOs in crisis center work, compiled data for studies of violence against women in Russia, and consistently grown over time as it provides assistance to more and more women's organizations in various regions that are establishing new crisis centers. Thirty-four NGOs from regions across Russia, stretching from Moscow to Norilsk in the far north to Irkutsk in Siberia, were members of the Association by 2002.

Why such different outcomes in the depth of network collaboration between, on the one hand, the Consortium, ICIWF, and the Khabarovsk NGO Association and, on the other hand, the Association of Crisis Centers and the League of Women Voters, even though all were largely initiated by foreign donors? In the first three instances, formation of an association or a representative national network was an explicit condition or end goal of a foreign grant. It must be noted clearly that the Independent Women's Forum was by no means initiated by a foreign donor. It was a loose coalition of activists, informally developed during the two Independent Women's Forums held in 1991 and 1992, and these forums were entirely domestically inspired. The forum itself was never officially registered. Later, in 1994, a small group of participants from the forum founded the Information Center of the Independent Women's Forum (ICIWF), and through foreign grants ICIWF founded a larger network of women's information centers. The ICWF, Consortium, and Khabarovsk NGO Association were founded with pressure under grant projects to have broad regional representation, or as many members as possible. There was a lack of early participation by the broad membership in developing network goals, and hence, the quality of those members' subsequent participation was low relative to that in the other two networks.

The Association of Crisis Centers was also founded under foreign grant support, but the situation differed in that the idea for the Association had sprung up spontaneously during an overseas training internship in 1994, and the founding parties had specific goals in mind.[7] The expansion of the Association was gradual, with new member crisis centers applying at their own initiative, a requirement of recommendations from two existing association members, and formal principles to which new members had to agree.[8] The League of Women Voters, although founded under foreign donor sponsorship, also was not exposed to pressure from funders regarding membership or regional breadth. It, too, was founded with specific goals in mind: to train and support female electoral candidates and to promote voter education and information in the immediate region.

The conclusion to be drawn from these different organizational patterns is that when NGO networks or associations are founded as an explicit condition or goal of foreign grants, their effectiveness is less likely, especially over time as foreign donor funding may dissipate. These networks, in contrast to indigenously developed ones, are in a sense forced together rather than built through members' perceptions of a common purpose. As a long-time feminist activist, Marina Regentova, described the problem in relation to the Consortium: "The Ford Foundation had a desire to unite all women's organizations to do a single huge project. The NIS-US Consortium . . . came out of this attempt. Entirely different people were thrown together."[9]

Although foreign funding in some instances has been instrumental, at a surface level, in founding and expanding networks of communication and collaboration among NGOs, these networks can be fairly hollow and not extend significantly beyond information sharing. In a detailed report on the influences of foreign-funded information networking projects on Russian women's NGOs, Tina Nelson stated that "despite the significant benefits of being connected, such as feeling part of a larger community and gaining information about grants and conferences, it is clear that the women's networks which have been developed are not being exploited to their full potential for membership-building, outreach and advocacy" (Nelson, 2000, p. 14).[10] While information sharing in itself is a useful resource for NGOs for learning about the existence and techniques of similar organizations, or about funding opportunities, its actual effect on NGO collaboration should not be exaggerated.

Infrastructure Versus Specific Social Issues

Government donors have varied considerably in their focus on general NGO sector infrastructure—such as professional training for NGOs of all kinds, the creation of NGO networks, and support for NGO resource centers—as opposed to focusing on NGOs that work in specific priority issue areas. Several donors have shifted their emphasis over time from one end of the spectrum to the other.

In U.S. government assistance, increasingly in the late 1990s, USAID's strategy emphasized the need for sustainability in the Russian NGO sector. In keeping with this, the agency began to concentrate on projects to develop the infrastructural aspects of the NGO sector more than on individual organizations' projects to work on particular social or political issues. USAID argued that this approach would increase the ability of NGOs to sustain themselves in the future, when donors eventually retreat from Russia. The strategy consisted of programs to professionalize NGO management, build institutional support mechanisms such as Russian NGO resource centers, improve NGO fundraising techniques, and create a legal environment that would permit organizations to survive autonomously (USAID, 1999a, pp. 8–10).

British government assistance has also focused heavily on these infrastructural aspects of the Russian NGO community, while other government donors have been more inclined to favor grants for specific projects. British assistance almost exclusively emphasized infrastructural development in the NGO sector, including transfer of management skills, lobbying for improved legislation to govern NGO activities, and forming transnational partnerships among NGOs. The British government devoted very little attention to the kinds of specific issue projects and organizational maintenance grants that dominated many other donors programs. In this sense, the British approach strongly resembled that of USAID.

Echoing government priorities, U.S. granting organizations that received a large portion of their funding from government agencies, such as Eurasia and IREX, focused heavily on infrastructural development and professionalization of Russian NGOs, and less on specific social issues. For example, by 2000, Eurasia was focusing on promoting the financial and organizational management skills of Russian NGOs, increasing their local fundraising abilities, and improving the legal and regulatory environment that affects NGOs (Eurasia Foundation, 2000a).

In contrast to the U.S. government and government-funded programs, official EU assistance programs tended not to focus on supporting concrete infrastructural development of the NGO sector in Russia. For example, NGO management training and the development of resource centers scarcely appeared in EU assistance projects. Instead, projects focused on supporting NGO work on concrete social or political issues, especially human rights. The Canadian government also placed less emphasis on infrastructural assistance and more on assisting NGOs with specific issue areas, as did many small private granting organizations, such as Mama Cash in the Netherlands and the Global Fund for Women in the United States.

Even with this attention to concrete social issues, however, throughout the 1990s donors were much more focused on professionalizing and developing the internal networks of groups that worked on these social issues—such as by building networks, creating websites, distributing information, or holding conferences of specialists—than they were on encouraging NGOs to work directly with significant numbers of affected citizens. A few figures from the interviews illustrate this tendency. Among NGOs that had received funding from foreign donors, only 11 percent had ever engaged in basic charity work (versus 50 percent of non-foreign-funded NGOs), 11 percent (versus 27 percent) had organized public celebrations or exhibitions, and 15 percent (versus 23 percent) had conducted social service consultations for citizens. Meanwhile, 13 percent of foreign-funded NGOs had conducted NGO management training courses (versus zero non-foreign-funded groups), and 54 percent (versus 15 percent) had engaged in information production such as websites and newsletters.

Types of NGOs Supported

One common criticism of American assistance is that it has focused far too narrowly on particular kinds of professionalized advocacy NGOs and ignored many service-oriented NGOs that do valuable work in their local communities. As a response to this criticism, in its 1999 report, USAID argued that it had moved in recent years to shift its focus "from an emphasis on supporting only 'advocacy' NGOs to supporting a broader range of groups that increase citizens' ability to participate more fully in their communities" (USAID, 1999a, p. 16). My own observations did not indicate a great deal of change in focus—at least so far—in USAID's program implementation from advocacy NGOs to community-based service-provision NGOs in the women's and human rights sectors. Service-provision organizations with close links to their communities still tended to be funded much less frequently than Western-style advocacy organizations. Part of the reason for this was that many basic charity organizations were able to raise funds and access material resources from local Russian businesses and government agencies, while advocacy NGOs such as human rights groups and women's NGOs, with rare exception, were not. However, it should be noted that many of these traditional service-provision organizations, such as *zhensovety*, could benefit from training in areas like public awareness campaigns and strategic planning, which only Western donors offer and which could help them transform into more effective advocates for their constituencies.

The kinds of organizations that received grants through programs of the European Union did not differ visibly from those funded by USAID. They were mostly rights–advocacy NGOs, with the occasional service-provision NGO in the mix, such as a society of trustees of penal institutions (European Union, 1999). However, EU-sponsored projects tended to emphasize human rights protection and civic education projects more than USAID-sponsored projects did. One substantive priority in the EIDHR program that stood apart from USAID assistance was that of encouraging civilian monitoring of security structures. This may be due to Europe's history of difficulties with civil-military relations in countries such as Spain and Greece. At any rate, USAID did not focus on these issues in any formal way. Another difference was a priority on initiatives aimed at ending the death penalty; this is a clear policy stance of the European Union, and, given American domestic politics, obviously not a priority that U.S. assistance policies could ever include.

Like U.S. and EU programs, many Canadian government-sponsored programs focused on rights-advocacy NGOs. These included the Canadian Fund for Support of Russian Women, launched in 1999, which focused specifically on promoting gender equality through women's NGOs, and the Elections Fund, supporting NGOs working for free and fair elections. However, one of the NGO programs in particular, the Canada Fund, differed from most other programs in its emphasis on socioeconomic development rather than civil and political rights.

In contrast to both governments and large, private foundations like OSI and the Ford Foundation, small, private granting foundations typically promoted more controversial goals, such as lesbians' rights and ending "oppressive traditional norms" (see Appendix 3). Nongovernmental sources of assistance to Russian NGOs from continental European countries in particular tended to be small foundations rather than large ones. Part of the reason for small foundations' more radical objectives is that they are usually funded neither through government sources, which place all kinds of restrictions on program content, nor by large family endowments. Family endowments also tend to limit themselves to funding fairly mainstream activities, due to their historical mandates, board composition, and in the United States, certain tax-related restrictions. Since the 1969 Tax Reform Act was passed, only nonpolitical organizations have been eligible for tax-deductible grants in the United States; that is, the recipient organization cannot be "political" in the sense of engaging in direct lobbying or supporting political candidates (Judis, 1992, p. 19).

Broad and Thin Versus Narrow and Intense

Many foreign donors working in Russia began with an approach of spreading their resources very thinly, supporting large numbers of NGOs with small amounts of seed funding in order to assist as many activists as possible in the sector. Over time, though, a definite shift occurred, so that most decided to choose strategically which NGOs, regions, or issues deserve focus and to support those priority organizations and areas intensely. The logic was that large amounts of resources are needed in order to make progress in civil society development, and that resources are more effective when concentrated in areas where they can make a difference.

One prominent example was USAID's change in strategy in the late 1990s. USAID decided to shift programs gradually "from their early concentration on broad support to NGO sectors as a whole to keener attention on specific topical issues and social problems" (USAID, 1999a, p. 32). This contrasted with the agency's philosophy of the early 1990s, in which it tried to assist as many NGOs as possible in Russia, through exchanges, trainings, and small grants programs in order to increase the number of organizations and develop the management skills of activists in the NGO sector as a whole.

The U.S. Regional Initiative (RI) Program, an interagency program of the U.S. government, is a major example of this general shift in approach from an early strategy of spreading resources as broadly as possible (and perhaps too thinly to create a visible impact) to one of concentrating on the most promising assistance targets. It is also an example of the attempt to shift resources to regions outside Moscow.

Launched in 1997, the RI (originally called the Regional Investment Initiative) was coordinated by the U.S. Department of State and mainly executed by USAID and its subcontractors, but also with the participation of agencies like USIA and the Overseas Private Investment Corporation (OPIC). The RI aimed to concentrate U.S. assistance in specific Russian regions in which regional governments and investment climates are particularly encouraging for reform. While most of RI's resources and strategic decisions focused on economic reforms and improvement of trade and investment climates, part of the initiative also promoted civil society and democratic reforms. Three of the regions of focus in this study, Novgorod, Khabarovsk, and Vladivostok, have been RI locations, the latter two combined within the RI Russian Far East location.[11] Novgorod was chosen for its pro-reform and pro-investment regional government, and Khabarovsk and the Russian Far East appear to have been chosen because of their strategic importance in terms of proximity to the United States and economic potential in natural resources. No other foreign governments have attempted to concentrate their assistance on "promising" regions to quite this extent.

The Canadian strategy in assistance to NGOs changed somewhat over the years, according to Solveig Schuster, the embassy's first secretary for Canadian cooperation programs. Whereas the strategy in the early 1990s was to spread assistance as far as possible in the Russian NGO community, and to disallow repeat grants to organizations, the later strategy was one of concentrating on a limited number of successful NGOs. By 2000, the strategy rested somewhere in the middle. Schuster stated that many donors had gone through this process of choosing one extreme strategy, then the other, and settling eventually on a compromise position between scattering assistance extensively and investing intensively in a small number of areas. She called it "a herding instinct" among donors: "We all make the same mistakes."[12]

Considerable differences were seen among the private foundations in terms of their organizational focus and strategies in Russia. Both the MacArthur and Ford foundations had only one Russian office, located in Moscow. The Ford office decided to concentrate its resources on Russia, while MacArthur's Moscow office tried to cover the whole former Soviet Union as much as possible. In contrast, the Open Society Institute, until its closure of Russian foundation offices in 2003, had an extensive network of representatives in most major cities around Russia. As an indication of the breadth of this network, only one of the cities in my study, Khabarovsk, did not have a local OSI representative, and in another city, Izhevsk, the OSI representative was the only local representative of any foreign granting organization.

Ford and MacArthur gave much larger grants to NGOs than did OSI and Eurasia, but they awarded far fewer grants. Ford in particular was trying to make sustained investments in worthy, preferably Russia-wide NGOs, in the hopes of creating a noticeable impact with limited resources. Its grants usually exceeded fifty thousand dollars and frequently exceeded one hundred thousand dollars. MacArthur grants were also large, typically exceeding twenty thousand dollars and often reaching into the hundreds of thousands. In contrast, OSI and Eurasia have traditionally tried to spread their resources widely to an extensive number of organizations. OSI's grants to Russian NGOs were often less than ten thousand dollars and did not exceed twenty thousand dollars. The Eurasia Foundation stood somewhere in the middle; its Russian field offices awarded civil society grants with an average value of twenty thousand dollars. Its Washington office administered larger "partnership grants" with the intention of transferring skills from U.S. partners to Russian organizations, which averaged one hundred thousand dollars in value (Eurasia Foundation, 2000a).

Nearly all foreign donors who work with Russian NGOs were using the approach of granting funds for NGO activists to conduct particular projects within a specified time period. The reason for this approach was that it was easier for donors to spread funds more broadly in the NGO sector and to monitor the outcomes from their grants when grants were given for defined projects rather than general organizational costs. The problem with this approach, however, was that NGOs had to fundraise constantly in order to keep their income streams flowing and remain in operation, and they were typically forced to misappropriate some of those funds by spending funds granted by donors for specific projects on administrative costs such as office rent and staff salaries. The need for perpetual fundraising through applications for specific project grants detracted many NGOs from being able to develop sustained program concentrations. Some NGOs have shifted their programmatic focus in sync with changes in donor priorities. For example, a palpable increase occurred in the number of women's NGOs working to battle domestic violence and, later, away from this to focus on preventing trafficking of women across borders. These shifts coincided with changes in the priorities specified in foreign donors' requests for grant proposals. Larisa Korneva, a leader of a St. Petersburg crisis center that specializes in legal assistance to victims of violence, stated:

Trafficking now is the big thing. At one time it was domestic violence, when Mrs. Clinton came here . . . They started to fund [programs against] violence, so we all began to work on violence [between 1997 and '99]—who in the world didn't work on violence then? There was a huge conference in Russia on violence against women, and all these organizations attended that had never had anything to do with violence.[13]

Yet a few donor organizations—most prominently the German *Stiftungen*—traditionally supported entire organizations for extended periods of time. Until the late 1990s, the *Stiftungen* typically cultivated deep and long-term connections with a few core partners, often supporting organizations' entire programmatic and maintenance needs for many years. After that, though, they shifted their approach to work with a wider variety of partners, funding smaller projects on an ad hoc basis (Mair, 2000, p. 138). Thus, unlike most donors—who tended to shift from a policy of thin but widespread distribution of support for NGO activists to concentration on a select number of successful organizations—the *Stiftungen* made the opposite shift.

The *Stiftungen* initiated this change in response to a difficult problem: when massive resources are invested in single organizations, all of the investment is lost if that organization collapses or fails to work well. While this shift is understandable, Mair argued that it placed the *Stiftungen* in peril of losing the comparative advantage they possessed as donors who allowed their grantees to work fairly autonomously for long periods of time on continuing programs rather than short-term projects.

Choice of Strategies and Effects on NGO Development

In the early 1990s, as the Soviet Union crumbled, Western governments and nongovernmental organizations saw an unprecedented opportunity to push Russian society in a firmly democratic direction. Some limited networks of civic organization persisted from efforts to oppose the Soviet regime as well as monopoly networks that were created by the regime itself to represent groups in society. Virtually all foreign donors—both providers of funding to Russian NGOs and implementers of training—acted on the same basic assumptions concerning the role of civil society in democratization and the key importance of advocacy NGOs in defining civil society. However, some differences emerged in the more detailed objectives and tactics that foreign donors pursued in their assistance to Russian NGOs. Some, such as the U.S.

government and the Soros Foundation, specified narrow program objectives, assuming that donors can pinpoint what is needed in Russian civil society based on the structure of NGO sectors in Western countries and experience gleaned from past assistance programs in Russia and other areas of the world. Others, like the European Union and the Canadian government, launched programs with broader and vaguer mandates, believing that Russian NGOs would submit ideas for projects that were needed locally and that, in the end, the overall results of these projects would contribute to larger developments in Russian civil society. There are problems with each approach, as donors are now well aware. When program priorities are too specifically defined, there is a great risk that they will be irrelevant to the local areas in which they are implemented. In contrast, if donors do not outline any clear objectives, their programs may not show any identifiable results in the end.

Yet the definitions of civil society and the broad goals that foreign donors of all stripes have pursued in Russia are strikingly similar, despite varying political cultures and institutions in their countries of origin. All have employed a concept of civil society defined largely by nongovernmental advocacy organizations, and their aim has been to broaden and deepen citizen participation in politics and public affairs. In fact, as the following chapters will show, with some exceptions, these efforts have not been successful in promoting the end goal of an NGO sector that includes more citizens in public life and the political process. This has been a pattern in foreign assistance to civil society not only in Russia, but all over the world, as many authors have pointed out in other studies (Carothers, 1999; Ottaway, 2000; Quigley, 2000; Van Rooy and Robinson, 1998).

CHAPTER 3

A Tale of Two Sectors: The Mixed Success of Foreign Assistance Across Issue Areas

DESPITE INTERACTIONS with foreign donors that are similar in kind and intensity, the two Russian NGO subsectors of soldiers' rights and women's organizations have developed in strikingly different ways. Soldiers' rights organizations are extremely well known and respected in Russian society, although they began as a small protest group and were treated initially with suspicion by the Russian government and military. Women's organizations began similarly as small and unpopular groups, but remain marginal to this day. Why is this so?

Compelling factors, connected with norms in Russian society (both culturally specific to Russia and more universal), help to explain the differences in mobilizational success between the two NGO issue sectors, despite similar types and amounts of foreign assistance. Norms refer to widely shared concepts of appropriate behavior. Some problems have prompted incredibly strong mobilization by citizens in Russia and all around the world. Often, cases of successful transnational mobilization occur in issues concerning the physical abuse of innocent people, which confront a nearly universal norm against violations of human physical dignity (Keck and Sikkink, 1998, p. 27). We see this kind of successful mobilization in the problems of mistreatment of soldiers and domestic violence in Russia.

Yet some problems in Russian society have prompted successful NGO campaigns in Western contexts but still have not resulted in effective Russian mobilization, despite foreign assistance to organizations that pursue them. In these cases, specific domestic norms are the likely explanation. For example, in the area of women's rights, discriminatory hiring and firing practices clearly exist in Russia. A quick perusal of job advertisements in virtually any Russian newspaper—specifying the sex, age, and even details of the personal appearance desired of applicants—confirms this. Studies also show that Russian women are not paid equally with men for performing similar work. These are the kinds of issues that sparked a powerful feminist movement in most Western countries; yet in Russia, we do not see significant mobilization or popular support for NGO efforts to organize around such issues. One of the puzzles about Russian gender politics is that Russian women are highly educated, and the vast majority work outside the home. Trends of increasing education levels among women and their entry into the paid workforce are widely argued to have played a crucial role in sparking feminist opinions and the development of Western-style women's movements (Della Porta and Diani, 1999, p. 231); yet the same processes in Russia and the Soviet Union did not bring about the same outcome. We can only explain this striking difference in women's activism by tracing the historical development of Russian ideas on women's rights, equality, discrimination, and feminism, which differ strikingly from the ideas about women and gender roles that Western donors generally promote.

A Normative Explanation for Mobilization

This chapter explores the reasons why some NGO issues, combined with foreign assistance, have resulted in effective mobilization to solve problems and increase public awareness, while mobilization around other issues has failed thus far despite assistance from foreign donors. I argue here that where foreign assistance is employed to promote norms that are universally embraced around the world, it is highly likely to lead to a successful NGO movement. While such a movement in most cases can be built gradually by local activists without the help of foreign donors, foreign assistance creates the material opportunities for NGOs to work on a grander scale and thus to grow a movement more quickly than would otherwise be the case.

In contrast, when foreign assistance is employed in pursuit of norms that are not universal and are specific to other societal contexts, it will fail to spark an NGO movement, regardless of the amount of funding foreign donors devote. In fact, foreign assistance may succeed in creating a plethora of NGOs purporting to pursue the norms that donors promote; however, they will ultimately lack public outreach efforts and will not attract significant public support.

Of course, other factors influence the effectiveness of donors' NGO development efforts, such as the local political opportunity environments that NGOs encounter, as I argue in the next chapter. Social movement theorists also have examined such factors as the severity of grievances and resource mobilization, yet underlying all other factors are the societal normative contexts that either aid or hinder NGO mobilization. Moreover, these are often nationwide in nature, shaped by historical developments that members of a society all share. In contrast, local political opportunity environments can vary tremendously across a country, particularly in an enormous federal state such as Russia.

The success of mobilization is measured in accordance with the mobilizational aspects of NGO development outlined in Chapter One. I do not consider public policy change as a major indicator of mobilizational success for a number of reasons. First, independent NGOs have existed openly for only fifteen years in Russia, and observers widely acknowledge that the Russian NGO sector as a whole continues to have relatively little impact on public policy (Lambroschini, 2000b; Mendelson, 2000). As this chapter shows, both women's and soldiers' rights movements have had only minor influences on public policy outcomes. In fact, given the institutional changes being implemented in Russia at the time of writing, discussed in Chapter Five, I fully expect that influence to decrease over the foreseeable future. Second, often social movements (such as the women's movement) focus not only on public policy change as goals but also on social and cultural change (Giugni, 1999, p. xxiii). And finally, it is often difficult to assess the precise role of NGOs in bringing about policy changes that are desirable to them. Clearly, though, where such changes do occur and can be linked to NGO campaigns, they are a clear indicator of the success of an NGO movement.

However, more important measurable aspects of mobilizational success are the growth of public awareness and support for NGOs, since this bodes well for the future abilities of NGO activities to influence public policy and change social behavior. These aspects of mobilization can be shown through survey data on attitudes toward the organizations, numbers of citizens who turn to the NGOs for assistance, and the volume and nature of media coverage of the movements. Unfortunately, because of reasons mentioned in Chapter One, growth in numbers of NGOs themselves cannot be considered an accurate indicator of movement success. Membership size, too, is a poor measure of relative NGO success in Russia, since Russian NGOs tend not to focus on increasing their members, and active membership is almost universally small (Henderson, 2003, p. 113; Henry, 2005, p. 214).

SUBSTANTIATING THE EXISTENCE OF SOCIETAL NORMS

Many norms-based explanations for outcomes have rightly been criticized for lacking convincing evidence for why particular norms are crucial in certain circumstances, when other explanations might be more easily provided (Checkel, 1998). Moreover, norms-based explanations often fail to account for the origins of norms and suffer from a lack of independent evidence to substantiate the salience of a particular norm or idea (Kowert and Legro, 1996). Arguments concerning norms and political culture have also been attacked for dealing poorly with the presence of competing norms that may be significant in a particular society. After all, members of a society are never unanimous in their beliefs, and individuals in any context have numerous cultural identities upon which they can draw (Laitin, 1986, 1988; Tarrow, 1992).

In this chapter, I argue for the crucial salience of societal norms and show that other major alternative explanations from social movement theory are insufficient to account for the outcomes among Russian women's and soldiers' rights NGOs. When similar NGOs use different kinds of arguments to battle serious problems in society, they experience strikingly different degrees of success. This suggests that prevalent norms surrounding the issues and strategies pursued have more impact than even the severity of the problems NGOs address, the NGOs' organizational resources or skills, or any significant differences in the political opportunity structures they face.

My argument about the importance of congruence between transnational norms and domestic norms addresses *necessary* conditions, rather than *sufficient* conditions, for successful mobilization by NGOs involved with transnational actors. That is, a whole host of problems may impede NGO success in working on certain issues, even when there is normative support from domestic constituencies. For example, NGOs may lack material resources or face political obstacles in their attempts to change public policy. Conversely, even under favorable conditions, when NGOs face a resistant domestic normative context it is highly unlikely that they will succeed in producing change—unless they can connect their arguments with existing norms by using widely accepted principles to express their demands.

Social movement theorists such as Douglas McAdam, David Snow, and Sidney Tarrow have long argued that the "frame resonance" of particular ways in which social movements depict issues is critical to their level of success (McAdam and Rucht, 1993; McAdam, 1996; Snow and Benford, 1992; Tarrow, 1992). For example, scholars have demonstrated the importance of a discourse of individual rights and opportunities in the United States (Snow and Benford, 1992, p. 145; Tarrow, 1992, pp. 189–90) and of working-class rhetoric in Italy until recently (Tarrow, 1992, pp. 192–96). Social movements are especially successful when they manage to depict certain issues within the same ideational frame as other issues in which social movements have already won changes in public policies or public opinion. The most often-cited example is that of how the women's movement became particularly successful when activists framed their demands in similar terms as the African American civil rights movement—with emphasis on the rights of all individuals to equal opportunities (Della Porta and Diani, 1999, p. 78; Gelb

and Palley, 1987). This approach to understanding social movement mobilization has not often been employed to understand the patterns of success
and failure in transnational actors' attempts to promote social movements
overseas, however.[1]

My argument should not be mistaken for a view that norms are static. A
key characteristic of norms is that they are socially constructed and thus tend
to develop and change over time as new events and information affect the
ways in which people understand the world around them. Social movement
theorists recognize that interpretative cultural frames can be changed
through the collective action of social movements themselves over time
(Della Porta and Diani, 1999, p. 69; Tarrow, 1992; Checkel, 1998). Sidney
Tarrow has stated appropriately that "at best, political culture provides leaders with a reservoir of symbols with which to construct a cognitive frame for
collective action" (1992, p. 177). Hence, I do not preclude the possibility that
foreign donors, over a long period of time, can influence domestic norms
concerning women and human rights by supporting NGOs that work in
these issue areas. Nonetheless, when NGO campaigns are framed in particular ways that are compatible with existing norms in society, they will succeed much more quickly than campaigns that may be supported by foreign
donors but conflict with prevailing local norms.

ALTERNATIVE EXPLANATIONS

How do we know that varying normative contexts rather than some
other factor explain the different mobilizational outcomes among women's
and soldiers' rights NGOs? We can rule out other factors that scholars typically raise as affecting NGO mobilization. Social movement theorists focus
mainly on three factors, other than normative frame resonance, in accounting for mobilizational success: the existence of grievances among identifiable
groups in society (do serious problems exist?); the ability and success of
movements in mobilizing material and human resources; and the political
opportunity structure in which movements operate.

Grievances

The problems that both the women's and soldiers' rights movements in
Russia address are undeniably serious and widespread. Soldiers' rights organizations have become incredibly popular in part because of the frequent
incidence and acute nature of the problems they address. Virtually every family in Russia must deal with the issue of male conscription, and there is indis-
putable documentation of the abuse and neglect that take place in the armed
forces. The problems of physical abuse that soldiers' rights organizations
address are more obviously acute than many women's issues aside from vio-

lence against women, yet abundant sources—including official government sources—show that problems such as discrimination against women, disproportionate female unemployment, and sexual harassment are rampant phenomena in Russia and have seriously damaged the careers and quality of life of huge numbers of women. In sum, there is no shortage of documented grievances around which either women's or soldiers' rights NGOs could mobilize.

Resource Mobilization

Women's and soldiers' rights organizations have experienced similar types and levels of interactions with foreign donors. In fact, in terms of their frequency of foreign funding and degree of dependence on such funding, the two subsectors exhibited strikingly similar profiles. The proportions of foreign funding in each NGO subsector were very similar, as shown in Table 3.1.

Soldiers' rights organizations were certainly no wealthier than women's NGOs, and in regions outside Moscow and St. Petersburg, they tended to be considerably poorer. Many NGOs were reluctant to reveal the amount of funding that they received from various sources, although others did so willingly, but it was possible to find out their primary sources of financial support.

This history suggested that, if anything, women's organizations had received more funding than soldiers' rights organizations in total dollar figures. For instance, up to the end of the field study period, the largest soldiers' rights organization, the Union of Committees of Soldiers' Mothers (UCSMR) had received grants totaling approximately US$200,000 from the Swiss government, the Right Livelihood Foundation, and the Ford Foundation. The largest autonomous women's umbrella organization, the Consortium of Women's Nongovernmental Organizations, on the other hand, had received far more funding (a total figure was not available) from USAID, Soros' Open Society Institute, the Ford Foundation, the MacArthur Foundation, the U.S. Information Service, the International Research and Exchanges Board (IREX), and a few other small foreign donors. Similarly, two other major women's organizations, the ICIWF and MCGS, had received more foreign funding than either UCSMR or the Soldiers' Mothers of St. Petersburg (SMSP). For both sets of NGOs, though, foreign funding occupied a similar position in terms of its weight in the subsectors' overall funding profiles. Table 3.1 shows that the organizations interviewed in the two subsectors had very similar proportions of NGOs reporting any foreign funding, as well as those reporting primary reliance on foreign funding.

Moreover, the two subsectors did not differ significantly in terms of the length of time that they have been receiving foreign funding. The median

TABLE 3.1. Foreign funding levels in women's and soldiers' rights NGOs.

Level of Foreign Funding	Women's NGOs (n=60)	Soldiers' Rights NGOs (n=14)
Recipient of foreign funding	67% (40)	64% (9)
Nonrecipient of foreign funding	33% (20)	36% (5)
Primarily foreign funded	40% (24)	50% (7)
Little or no foreign funding	60% (36)	50% (7)
Exclusively foreign funded	15% (9)	29% (4)
Frequently foreign funded	25% (15)	21% (3)
Occasionally foreign funded	27% (16)	14% (2)
Exclusively domestic funded	27% (16)	29% (4)
No funding	7% (4)	7% (1)

(and also the average) year in which organizations had received their initial foreign grant was 1996 among women's NGOs and 1995 among soldiers' rights NGOs.

NGOs in both the soldiers' rights and women's movements also had received only small amounts of domestic-sourced funding. Approximately one-quarter of both soldiers' rights and women's rights NGOs in the study received funding only from domestic sources (the discrepancy between this proportion and the figure for "nonrecipient of foreign funding" in Table 3.1 is due to the existence of some NGOs with no funding of any kind). However, contributions from domestic sources in all cases were very small if in cash form and were usually in-kind donations—most frequently, office space or event facilities—from government agencies or private organizations. In general, as acknowledged by other authors on Russian NGOs, the domestic funding scene was incredibly small (Sperling, 1999; Henderson, 2003, p. 92).

In the forms of support that involve transferring ideas rather than material resources—through training, information exchanges, and overseas travel opportunities, for example—frequencies of transnational interactions within the two sets of NGOs were slightly different. In training interactions and travel opportunities, women's organizations had somewhat denser relations with foreign donors than did soldiers' rights NGOs. But the differences were slight, and as Table 3.2 shows, soldiers' rights NGOs were more frequent participants in cases that involved dialogue rather than foreign training or material assistance (such as submitting reports to international organizations) and membership in transnational organizations.

TABLE 3.2. Nongrant forms of transnational interactions among women's and soldiers' rights NGOs.

Type of Nongrant Transnational Interaction	Women's NGOs (n=60)	Soldiers' Rights NGOs (n=14)
Overseas Travel		
Conferences	48% (29)	29% (4)
Short internships	47% (28)	36% (5)
Long internships	8% (5)	7% (1)
Locally Based Interactions		
Training seminars	57% (34)	43% (6)
Visits and information exchanges	32% (19)	21% (3)
Membership in transnational organizations	3% (2)	14% (2)
Submission of reports or cases to international organizations	2% (1)	21% (3)

NOTE: Percentages and quantities indicate the proportion of organizations that have ever engaged in these activities.

In terms of nongrant interactions with transnational actors, the greatest differences between women's and soldiers' rights NGOs were in the frequencies of attending transnational training seminars and overseas conferences. An important factor explaining the relatively high proportion of women's NGOs whose members had attended overseas conferences is that a considerable number of them attended the 1995 NGO Forum on Women in Beijing. This was a major international focal event for women's NGOs with no comparable event of similar magnitude in the area of soldiers' rights.

Finally, there is little basis for thinking that soldiers' rights leaders were more skilled or entrepreneurial than the leaders of women's NGOs. In fact, as shown in Table 3.2, women's NGOs had received even more training from transnational actors in how to manage and promote their organizations than had soldiers' rights NGOs. In addition, many women's NGOs that were not actively involved with foreign donors were led by women who had acquired a great deal of organizational experience and powerful government contacts during the Soviet era.

Political Opportunity Structure

Explanations that examine the overall political situation for each set of NGOs are unsatisfactory insofar as soldiers' rights organizations have in fact faced a more difficult political opportunity structure than women's NGOs nationwide. Soldiers' rights NGOs aim to change military institutions, which are notoriously resistant to change, closed to public input, and in Russia have little effective legislative oversight (Caiazza, 2002, pp. 111–13). Women's NGOs have at least managed more often to find allies, albeit ephemeral, in decision-making institutions such as the federal Ministry of Labor and Social Development and legislative committees of the State Duma, as well as local government structures (Sperling, 1999, pp. 129–43).[2]

Moreover, the Russian military is well known for its continuation of the Soviet management principle of *edinonachalie,* or one-person command, under which the commander of a military unit is responsible for undertaking all disciplinary actions within the unit (Ministry of Defence of the Russian Federation, 1993). As a result, commanders of individual units possess an extraordinarily high level of control over the troops they lead, making the Russian army unusually decentralized in its processes for investigation and rulings on internal legal problems (Vallance, 2000). Thus, policy change in the Russian army is not easily implemented at the government level, and in fact, discipline of widespread Russian military practices such as *dedovshchina,* an extreme form of hazing in which senior soldiers abuse first-year recruits, is quite decentralized.

The following sections examine NGO activism in several of the issues that soldiers' rights groups and women's groups address: mandatory conscription and physical abuses in the army, employment discrimination and sexual harassment against women, and domestic violence. Foreign donors have heavily supported NGOs that work in all of these areas; yet Russian NGO mobilization on these issues has encountered dramatically varying levels of success due to the different normative contexts that surround each issue.

Soldiers' Rights Issues—A Response to Brutality

Among soldiers' rights NGOs, we find compelling evidence of the importance of widespread domestic norms in determining the varying success levels of different issue campaigns. These organizations experience great popularity and even some policy successes when they call for military reforms by protesting physical abuses and deprivation of soldiers in the Russian army. However, when they oppose conscription based on antimilitarist or pacifist principles, they are much less successful.

The issues of military conscription and army service conditions affect virtually every family in Russia. All men, upon reaching age eighteen, must serve two years in the Russian military or find a legal way to avoid such service for the ensuing decade. With no shortage of active conflict zones in

Russia over the past ten years, concern surrounding this state duty is understandably high.

SOLDIERS' MOTHERS' ORGANIZATIONS

The first committees of soldiers' mothers were formed in Russia in 1989, near the end of the Soviet war in Afghanistan, in protest of the Soviet army's decision to draft male students enrolled in postsecondary educational institutions.[3] The approximately three hundred soldiers' mothers who participated in that campaign succeeded in overturning the policy. They held their first national conference in June 1990. At a forum in September 1990, the soldiers' mothers first declared their demand for "radical military reform" in the Soviet Union. They have not achieved this goal in any significant way, but they have made military reform a topic of serious discussion that the Russian government has had to acknowledge and appear to act upon, even while very little serious progress is made because of staunch resistance in Russia's powerful and enormous military sector.

By the time the Soviet regime collapsed, the soldiers' mothers had already secured a few small political victories, including formation of a presidential commission to investigate the deaths of soldiers during peacetime. Soldiers' mothers sat as members of that commission, and their work resulted in guarantees of pensions for deceased soldiers' parents and personal insurance policies for conscript soldiers. In addition, the soldiers' mothers succeeded in their demand for a revision of the list of illnesses for conscripts and military personnel that can qualify service conditions or exempt draftees from service.

The mothers initiated consideration of a draft law on alternative service in the Supreme Soviet; however, this Soviet-era law was never passed (Obraztsova, 1999, p. 2). Soldiers' rights organizations continue to be confounded in their quest for a suitable alternative service law. In mid-2002, a law on alternative service finally passed by a slim margin in the Russian State Duma (AFP, 2002; Bivens, 2003). Yet this law was greeted with great disappointment by soldiers' rights groups and liberal politicians, since its provisions included an exceedingly long alternative service term (ranging from 36 to 42 months depending on type of service), discretion to military commissions in deciding whether to grant alternative service in each draftee's case, and unclear (and potentially onerous) service conditions (AFP, 2002).

Yet also in 2002, Ida Kuklina, a member of the Coordinating Council of the Union of Committees of Soldiers' Mothers of Russia (UCSMR), the largest association of soldiers' mothers' groups, was invited to join the Russian Presidential Commission on Human Rights. This was an important signal of the presidential administration's understanding of the power of the soldiers' mothers' organizations and also provided the UCSMR with a high-level forum at which to articulate its complaints on soldiers' rights issues.

Initially, the soldiers' mothers were perceived by many Russians to be a marginal and emotionally unstable group of women. They soon garnered a great deal of popular support, however, and are now widely known, receive ample positive media attention, and are respected—if not always liked—by the government. Committees of soldiers' mothers are found in nearly every major Russian city today. They assist thousands of conscripts, active soldiers, and families annually in various areas ranging from reestablishing contact between soldiers and their families and walking families through the process of legally avoiding the draft to investigating instances of murder and suicide in the military.

In November 2004, the soldiers' mothers founded their own political party, called the United People's Party of Soldiers' Mothers, with plans to compete in the 2007 federal Duma elections. This represents no small feat for the movement, since registration of a political party requires 10,000 members as well as at least 100 members and representative offices in each of at least half of Russia's eighty-nine regions. It remains somewhat unclear what the party's platform will be, although its leaders have mentioned the goals of abolishing the compulsory draft system, creating a better benefit and care system for soldiers returning from war, and negotiating a peace settlement in Chechnya (Yablokova, 2004; MosNews, 2005).

The soldiers' mothers at first did not oppose military conflicts as such; they instead protested the ways in which their sons were being treated in the Soviet military and the unreasonable risks to which they were being exposed during service. The UCSMR has stated its position, which reflects the position of most soldiers' mothers' organizations, as follows: "From the very beginning the soldiers' mothers have said: a degraded, beaten, hungry, and rights-deprived soldier can protect neither the state nor its citizens, since he himself is in need of protection" (Obraztsova, 1999). In fact, in times of peace in the post-Soviet Russian armed forces, unbelievable numbers of Russian conscript soldiers die during military service. According to the UCSMR and other human rights organizations, peacetime deaths among Russian conscripts total between three and five thousand each year (Obraztsova, 1999, p. 2; Hall, 2001). The most common reasons for these deaths are beatings, harassment leading to suicide, intolerable living conditions (cold, hunger, and lack of hygiene), denial of necessary medical treatment, and excessive labor. Aside from this, the UCSMR estimates that 30,000 Russian soldiers are beaten by their officers or fellow soldiers every year (RFE/RL, 2001c).

Although their early concerns and accomplishments mostly surrounded the mistreatment and deaths of soldiers in peacetime, the soldiers' mothers' organizations have been busiest and have experienced their greatest surges in membership during times of military conflict. Initially, the movement expanded in connection with Soviet-era internal conflicts in locations such as Nagorno-Karabakh, Georgia, Northern Ossetia, and Tadzhikistan. But the greatest increase in their activities and popularity occurred during the first Chechen war in 1994–96. They protested both the excessive killing and terrorization of Chechen civilians and the involvement of their unprepared sons in the war. They called upon the country's leaders to cease military means of settling the conflict (Kuklina, 1997, p. 101). Among other activities, they expended a great deal of energy arranging for mothers of soldiers being held prisoner in Chechnya to travel there and beg the release of their sons. They sought remedies in thousands of cases of active soldiers experiencing problems such as abuse or neglect, and for those who were drafted illegally despite medical problems. They also defended conscientious objectors, draftees whom the military formally considered to be criminals evading service. According to UCSMR records, the numbers of appeals for help from soldiers and their families increased fivefold from 1994 to 1995, and the number of draftees seeking assistance in avoiding service more than doubled.[4] It was during the first Chechen war that the soldiers' mothers acquired abundant expertise in defending conscientious objectors in the courts system.

While the least radical soldiers' mothers' organizations lobby to merely ensure that soldiers receive proper food and clothing during service and their legally due social benefits following service, the more radical organizations have opposed Russian military operations in Chechnya. Virtually all of the soldiers' rights organizations call for military reform to a professional army and an end to conscription, although some committees of soldiers' mothers merely passively articulate this position, while others actively lobby politicians and hold public demonstrations on the issue. Many, especially in larger cities, frame their work in terms of individual human rights protection, rather than limiting themselves to securing legally due social services. This is especially true of the soldiers' mothers' organizations in Moscow and St. Petersburg.

Most of the day-to-day work of the soldiers' mothers' committees—especially busy during the spring and fall draft seasons—involves individual consultations with draftees and their parents concerning their rights in the draft process, as well as responding to letters from families in distant locations concerning these and other questions. The UCSMR reported that 40,000 soldiers and parents turned to their committees across Russia in 2002 (UCSMR, 2003).

Organizations of soldiers' mothers are renowned not only within Russia but also internationally as human rights advocates and reliable sources of information about violations of soldiers' human rights and crimes against civilians during war. The UCSMR has delivered reports twice to the U.N. Commission on Human Rights and in 1996 received the Right Livelihood Award, which is informally known as the Alternative Nobel Peace Prize.[5] In November 2004, Human Rights Watch recognized Natalia Zhukova, head of the Committee of Soldiers' Mothers in Nizhnii Novgorod, with a large public event to honor her efforts (Human Rights Watch, 2004a). The Soldiers' Mothers of St. Petersburg (SMSP) have given reports to the European Commission, the European Parliament, and Amnesty International. Several soldiers' mothers' organizations around Russia contributed large amounts of information for a 2004 Human Rights Watch report on Russian army conditions (Human Rights Watch, 2004b).

A separate organization for soldiers' parents deals specifically with "the rights and interests of parents whose sons have died in the army in peacetime on the territory of Russia and the CIS, as a result of crimes, unsanitary living conditions, and an abnormal psychological climate" (Mother's Right Foundation, 1999). This Moscow organization is called "Mother's Right" (*Pravo Materi*). Most of its activities are directed toward investigating soldiers' deaths that occur during peacetime military service, demanding delivery of remains to parents for burial, and securing legally due monies for burial, pensions, and insurance. The idea for the organization began in 1985 when its leader, journalist Veronika Marchenko, published a story on some terrible instances of soldiers' peacetime deaths through the practices of *dedovshchina*.[6] Marchenko began to receive letters and telephone calls from dozens of parents who had similar stories. In 1990, she invited fifteen mothers of soldiers killed in peacetime to come to Moscow and conduct a demonstration in front of the Central Military Prosecutor's office (Right to Life and Civil Dignity, 1999, p. 3). Soon afterwards, Marchenko created a formal organization to deal with these instances and seek legal redress for the military's negligence and refusal to pay benefits due to the parents by law. Today, Mother's Right consults with parents, takes their cases to court, and publishes data on the deaths of soldiers.

Another network of soldiers' mothers' committees around Russia cannot truly be called nongovernmental, as it has been established by the Russian military. Nongovernmental committees of soldiers' mothers call these committees "twin committees" (*komitety-dvoiniki*). They are a source of concern to the independent soldiers' rights groups, since their role is chiefly to ensure that all young men serve their two years, even when issues such as abuse of soldiers or chronic health problems are involved (Kuklina, 1997, p. 100; CSMR, 1999). Rather than assisting soldiers in defending their legal rights, these committees cajole mothers into forcing their sons to serve, and their work with soldiers mainly consists of visits to entertain them and distribute gifts. Often these pro-military committees are headed by the wives of military division commanders and, in the words of one member of the UCSMR, they "remain in Soviet times" (Kuklina, 1997, p. 100).

This kind of attitude was visible during an interview with the chair of one of the twin committees in a St. Petersburg House of Officers (*Dom ofitserov*). A distraught mother had come to the committee to seek help in removing her eighteen-year-old son from his current division. The son had been sent into active fire in the North Caucasus without any training whatsoever and was experiencing severe beatings from his commanding officer. The chair of this government-sponsored Soldier's Mother Committee, a *blokadnitsa* who had defended Leningrad during the World War II blockade of the city, made the following retort: "This often happens to kids because they are homesick. At home everything was good, but he goes down there and everything's different . . . He can get used to all of that. I lived through the entire blockade in Leningrad. I was hungry, cold, shot at, and everything, but I survived."[7]

Since mothers and conscripts are frequently confused by the organizational name "Soldier's Mother," they often turn to the twin committees for help and leave convinced that there is nothing that can be done to help their situation. Note that throughout this book, discussions of soldiers' mothers' committees refer specifically to nongovernmental committees, and not to the committees established by the military.

OTHER SOLDIERS' RIGHTS ORGANIZATIONS

Many other Russian human rights NGOs also advocate the rights of soldiers and draftees and tend to be more radical in their aims and methods than most of the soldiers' mothers' organizations.

The Antimilitarist Radical Association (ARA) in Moscow advocates similar goals to those of the soldiers' mothers: facilitation of the right to refuse military service, reform to a professional army on a volunteer basis, civilian control over the military, and demilitarization of Russian society more generally. ARA was formed in 1995 by Russian members of the Transnational Radical Party, a UN-accredited transnational political party with headquarters in Italy, in part as a reaction to the first Chechen war in 1994–96. It has set as its main goal the passage of a satisfactory Russian law on alternative service.

ARA's goals and methods contrast to those of most soldiers' mothers' organizations in that it minimizes individual consultations with draftees and instead focuses on political lobbying and mobilizing public opinion in favor of legislation allowing refusal of military service. As Nikolai Khramov, ARA's

Russian secretary and de facto leader, states: "Our mandate is not the defense of concrete individuals' rights in each concrete situation. Of course we work on this as needed, but generally we define ourselves as a political organization. . . . So we are a lobby group in fact."[8] The chair of the organization is Valerii Borshchov, a former Duma deputy (1994–99) from the liberal Yabloko party, who has strongly supported passage of an alternative service law. ARA frequently holds public demonstrations at which it distributes materials and petitions related to its campaign. The organization also operates an e-mail listserv, to which over one thousand people subscribe (ARA, 2000).[9] In 1998, ARA had 238 members in forty-nine cities across Russia.

A similar organization—and one that cooperates closely with ARA—is the Ekaterinburg Movement Against Violence (EMAV). It conducts weekly individual consultations with draftees and soldiers and regularly manages court cases for those who have refused military service. It is no coincidence that EMAV's techniques strongly resemble those of the Soldiers' Mothers of St. Petersburg: EMAV leader Gleb Edelev visited SMSP some years ago specifically to study its methods. Despite the tactical difference between ARA and EMAV concerning work on individual cases, the philosophies of the two organizations are identical. EMAV especially resembles ARA in its frequent use of public demonstrations. In fact, since the second Chechen war began in 1999, EMAV has held weekly demonstrations in the center of Ekaterinburg. EMAV was formed in 1994 by a number of activists from the Ekaterinburg Democratic Union—one of the major pro-democratic political coalitions in Ekaterinburg during the late perestroika and early post-Soviet period. EMAV has only a few dozen active members.

CLEAVAGES DIVIDING THE SOLDIERS' RIGHTS MOVEMENT

Entirely united social movements simply do not exist, and soldiers' rights NGOs are no exception. The major issues of disagreement have been (1) whether soldiers' rights NGOs emphasize human rights education over efficient case processing, (2) whether their philosophy includes pacifism— opposition to all military operations and the army in general—or merely the concept of reforms to create a professional army and phase out conscription, and (3) the extent to which they concentrate on avoidance of conscription through legal medical and family reasons versus the constitutional right to conscientious objection and alternative service. As in other social movements, frictions have also arisen from the competing ambitions of individual leaders.

Variation exists among committees of soldiers' mothers in terms of how radical their aims are and how friendly they should be with the state.

Nonetheless, very few organizations in the study completely rejected cooperation with the state in pursuing their goals, and aside from the enmity
between nongovernmental soldiers' rights organizations and the twin soldiers' mothers' committees described earlier, this difference was not a source
of significant conflict among organizations. Some, such as the SMSP and
Mother's Right, adopted an adversarial stance and were more suspicious of
government. For example, most of Mother's Right's activities involved court
cases against the state, and its press secretary expressed the extent to which
Mother's Right perceives itself as a direct adversary to the state. In response
to an interview question about where Mother's Right obtains all of its information about deaths of soldiers, she replied that "of course" they receive all
information from parents and citizens, rather than the state. She responded:
"How could it be any different? We're fighting with the state, we judge the
state."[10] Nonetheless, Mother's Right did distribute its information publications to members of the State Duma and since 1994 had worked closely with
several Duma committees in trying to make improvements to Russian legislation that affects the families of deceased soldiers (Mother's Right, 2001).
Committees of soldiers' mothers in more provincial locations such as Izhevsk
or Khabarovsk tended to cooperate fairly extensively with the military committees (*voenkomaty*) and regional or city administrations. Even so, this dis-
tinction among organizations is not dramatic—all of the soldiers' mothers'
organizations that worked on conscription issues sought some means of dialogue with the state, and none of them perceived its role as one of "helping"
the state. It is worth noting that in the intervening years since the interviews,
the soldiers' mothers' groups that had tried to work cooperatively on policy
change with the central government, such as the UCSMR, have lost most of
their friendly networks in the Duma and the presidential organs as the Putin
administration has consolidated its power and decreased receptiveness to
critical NGOs (U.S. Helsinki Commission, 2004; MosNews, 2005). The
UCSMR has become more fervent and vocal in its opposition to the continuing conflict in Chechnya and begun to work independently with
Chechen rebel leaders to seek a peace agreement.

　More serious differences exist among soldiers' mothers' organizations regarding the extent to which they view their role as one of teaching ordinary
citizens to defend their own rights. Is it preferable to educate citizens in
human rights or to work toward quick and effective solutions to their problems? This has probably been the greatest difference hindering cooperation
between the UCSMR and SMSP. While the two organizations have cordial
relations and attend the same conferences of soldiers' mothers, in interviews
the SMSP complained that the Moscow UCSMR had little lasting impact on
citizens who appeal to the organization, since UCSMR volunteers simply

heard their stories and took care of their problems for them. In contrast, as a condition of assisting soldiers, the SMSP obligated soldiers (or their parents) to attend its training session on how to defend one's case in avoiding military service and required that they write their own case documents. The organization assisted applicants with questions, gave them armloads of information, and helped them in any resulting court cases, but according to Elena Vilenskaia, co-chair of the SMSP, "our motto is for people to help themselves." The goal is for the relatives and friends who accompany a draftee to learn skills and principles that will allow them to defend their rights in other areas of life.[11] In fact, the SMSP leaders specifically refused to call themselves a "committee" because of the word's association during the Soviet period with hierarchy and passive requests by citizens to arbitrary authorities.[12] The UCSMR, in contrast, accused the SMSP of dropping its clients midway through the process, rather than ensuring that draftees' cases reach a successful conclusion.[13]

Soldiers' rights organizations also disagree over how much army reform and demilitarization is necessary in Russia. Most soldiers' mothers' organizations are not opposed to wars or military actions in general, although the SMSP is the most pacifist among them. The SMSP argues for nonviolent methods in all areas of life and extends its philosophy even to aspects of family life. Soldiers' rights organizations other than soldiers' mothers' groups tend to adopt a more radical antimilitary stance. Organizations such as ARA and EMAV argue against violent means in all areas of life, such as the prison system and the environment, and their approaches more closely approximate a pacifist philosophy. ARA, for example, emulates the Gandhian philosophy in its activities.[14]

ARA and some other organizations disagree in principle with the soldiers' mothers' focus on assisting draftees to avoid conscription based on medical problems rather than working with draftees to refuse service based on their constitutional right to alternative service. The right to alternative, civilian forms of service is in fact included in the Russian Constitution, but the problem for conscientious objectors has been that the Duma, until mid-2002, had not passed any federal law specifying forms or mechanisms of alternative service.[15] In fact, most soldiers' rights organizations have lobbied for passage of a reasonable federal law on alternative service. The version that the Duma finally passed in mid-2002 included conditions of service that soldiers' rights organizations consider "punishment" for avoiding military service rather than an equitable alternative: serving for three to three-and-a-half years (instead of the usual two) in potentially very difficult and undefined circumstances, such as on military bases (AFP, 2002; Bivens, 2003).[16] It took until 2002 to pass an alternative service law at all, and that bill was passed by only a slim margin, since military leaders largely oppose it, arguing that it harms Russia's military readiness (Right to Life and Civil Dignity, 1999, p. 3).

While the disagreements described above hinder cooperation among soldiers' rights organizations, they are not severe, and the organizations do cooperate with one another on various initiatives, such as legislative lobbying and acts of protest. The truly devastating cleavages that exist derive from conflicting leadership ambitions and, to some extent, battles for control over foreign funding.

A huge conflict occurred within the soldiers' mothers' movement in 1996, between the head of the Committee of Soldiers' Mothers of Russia (CSMR), Maria Kirbasova, and the other CSMR leaders, including Valentina Melnikova, who have since formed a separate national organization, the UCSMR. This split immediately followed the Swedish Right Livelihood Award Committee's selection of CSMR to receive an "alternative Nobel Prize" for peace in 1996. Some regional CSM leaders blamed the split on disputes over dividing the prize money. However, senior members of both the Russian Committee of Soldiers' Mothers (RCSM), headed by the former leader of the CSMR, Maria Kirbasova, and the newer Union of Committees of Soldiers' Mothers of Russia (UCSMR), led primarily by Valentina Melnikova, claimed that the prize money was not the immediate cause of the organizational split. Yet both sides attributed some role to the money, which amounted to over eighty thousand dollars.[17] They mostly concurred with the assessment of one leader in the RCSM, that the breakup of the organization was due to "money and hunger for power," which created a huge amount of bad blood between the two ambitious leaders (although the two sides disagreed over who was more unreasonably ambitious). This conflict resembled others that have occurred in Russian NGOs in the wake of a sudden influx of foreign funding (see, for example, the section on Ekaterinburg's Urals Association of Women in Chapter Four).

Because the original CSMR was a national umbrella association, the conflict resulted in the split of the Russia-wide network of regional Committees of Soldiers' Mothers into two camps—those loyal to Kirbasova and those loyal to Melnikova. Some committees, such as the Khabarovsk CSM, have managed to remain above the fray of the conflict and maintain cordial relations with both associations.[18]

While conflicts between organizations did not seem to occur appreciably more in either of the NGO issue sectors examined in this book, there seemed to be a difference between women's and soldiers' rights NGOs in terms of the kinds of disagreements that tended to arise. Distinct ideological disagreements seemed to be at stake in hindering collaboration among soldiers' rights NGOs more often than among women's NGOs. Open conflicts among women's NGOs instead centered more often around issues of leadership ambitions, perceived "ownership" of a certain issue area, and distribution of foreign grant funds (with the exception of the major split in the CSMR over the Right Livelihood Award prize money). This difference is partly due to the fact that the major ideological split in the Russian women's movement—between state-supporting official organizations and independent feminist groups—already took place in the late 1980s and early 1990s. The depth of these differences and the fact that they crystallized some years ago led to a situation in which there was no longer major ideological conflict because, in most cases, the organizations from different camps simply did not communicate with one another.

Another reason for more divisive philosophical differences among soldiers' rights organizations is that they focus on a very narrow issue area, in which differences of opinion arise more clearly. Women's organizations, by contrast, work on a tremendous variety of issues. They largely agree on the basic goal of improving women's status in society, and organizations that work in different issue areas (for example, domestic violence versus women's business development) may have no grounds for ideological disagreements. As a result, to the extent that they have clashed with one another (or even encounter one another at all!), conflicts have emerged more frequently over resource competition.

SUCCESS AND CONDITION OF THE MOVEMENT

The soldiers' mothers' organizations are extremely well known, respected, and popular in Russia (Malyakin and Konnova, 1999; Politkovskaya, 1999). They are one of the few kinds of NGOs that most Russians have heard of and can recall by name. One large recent survey found that 81 percent of Russian respondents were familiar with the activities of the soldiers' mothers, and the vast majority took a positive view of their activities, while only small minorities of respondents were familiar with the work of other major Russian human rights NGOs (Gerber and Mendelson, 2003, p. 5). The soldiers' mothers are well respected by other NGOs and better respected by government officials than most other NGOs. They have grown from small, weekly protest gatherings of thirty to forty mothers in Moscow in 1989, into cohesive networks of hundreds of committees, covering nearly every Russian region. As discussed earlier, soldiers' rights organizations receive tens of thousands of requests for help from Russian citizens every year, and most of them conduct regular consultation sessions with draftees, soldiers, and their families.[19] It is customary for soldiers' mothers' organizations to have lines of people waiting outside their doors for help. They appear often on television programs and constantly provide interviews and information at the request of Russian journalists.

Soldiers' rights NGOs are not only popular and widely known among regular citizens, but they have attained concrete victories in their public policy campaigns and in relations with the military. Several organizations have begun to win court cases regularly, in cases of draftees refusing to serve based on their right to alternative service. Military draft commissions have begun to recognize medically based refusal cases more frequently and no longer dare to bend the conscription regulations in cases overseen by some soldiers' mothers' organizations such as the SMSP. As Elena Vilenskaia of SMSP states, "Earlier, we got no responses from our applications to the draft commissions. Now, we are getting responses and court cases. We have taught the bureaucrats to read the laws, and this is very important."[20] For the first time in 1999, Moscow City courts began to accept lawsuits filed by soldiers and parents of deceased soldiers against the military in cases of illegal conscription.[21]

Even though soldiers' rights groups have been unhappy with the alternative service law that the Russian government passed in 2002, it is notable that the goal of "military reform" has been an openly stated part of the Russian government's policy plans since the mid-1990s. This is an enormous change in the government's official stance since the early 1990s, when, as Valentina Melnikova of the UCSMR states, "the phrases 'military reform' or 'professional army' were considered crimes" (Caiazza, 2002, p. 139). Military reform has been transformed rapidly from a highly controversial and politically impossible goal into one that government officials frequently articulate (however little has actually changed). This is in no small part due to the success of the soldiers' rights movement in building public support for an end to conscription.

Foreign donors have assisted many soldiers' rights NGOs in their activities to defend the rights of Russian army conscripts. At various times, donors such as the European Union's EIDHR grants program, the Ford Foundation, and OSI have made such organizations a priority in their granting programs. Foreign assistance to soldiers' rights NGOs, in the forms of project grants, seminars, and overseas exchanges, has not distracted them from conducting grassroots work with citizens, and neither has it led them to adopt projects outside the scope of their original fundamental aims. In contrast to phenomena that researchers have observed in many other NGO subsectors, such as women's and environmental organizations (Sperling, 1999; Henry, 2001), foreign grant incentives have not led to the proliferation of new soldiers' rights NGOs willing to shift their focus with the changing priorities of foreign donors. Instead, foreign assistance has merely strengthened soldiers' rights organizations by giving them more resources with which to work. Certain normative reasons, both specifically Russian and more universal, explain why these organizations have remained focused in their work, engaged in public outreach, and developed an enormous degree of popular support.

THE NORM OF BODILY HARM AS AN EXPLANATION FOR SUCCESS

Many of Russians' concerns about mandatory service in the contemporary Russian army result from frequent reports of beatings, torture, and neglect of conscript soldiers, especially under the common hazing system of *dedovshchina*. In addition, since the two military campaigns in Chechnya during the 1990s, even more Russians worry about the high likelihood that their sons will be sent, poorly trained, into heavy fighting in the Caucasus region.

The situation for conscripts has deteriorated considerably since the collapse of the Soviet regime. Although a great deal of Russian pride in the military remains, citizens are becoming increasingly aware of the extent of physical abuse and abysmal conditions that exist in today's armed forces. In the post-Soviet economic environment, there have not been enough government resources to maintain soldiers adequately, and many commanding officers hire their soldiers out as laborers or withhold provisions intended for soldiers in order to earn extra money for themselves unofficially. Because of Russia's low birthrate and poor standard of living, there are not enough healthy young men to fulfill the military's conscription targets.[22] Due to increasing awareness of the dangers of army service and available strategies for avoiding it, fewer and fewer eligible draftees actually end up being conscripted: in the spring of 2004, only 9.5 percent of those of draftable age were conscripted, compared to 54.6 percent in 1988 (see Ministry of Defence of the Russian Federation, 2004; Yegorov, 2000). As a result of this shortage, during the first and second Chechen conflicts, young conscripts frequently were sent into active battle with inadequate training. One 1999 newspaper article estimated that every fourth new draftee was being sent to fight in Chechnya (Yermolin, 1999).

According to evidence available from opinion polls, Russian citizens are largely opposed to mandatory military service. In a poll conducted by the VTsIOM agency in 2001, 69 percent of respondents claimed that they were unwilling to serve and would not allow their relatives to be enlisted. The same poll found that 84 percent of Russians believe that the nation should have a professional army composed on a contract basis rather than by mandatory draft (*Russia Journal*, 2001). In their 2002–3 Russia-wide survey of 2,408 respondents, Gerber and Mendelson found that only 30 percent of respondents believed that Russia should maintain a conscript army (Gerber and Mendelson, 2003, p. 3). After the first war in Chechnya, in 1997, the Defense Ministry conducted a poll among fresh recruits and found that only 10 percent expressed a "positive attitude" toward army service (Semyonov, 2000).

Here, a widely accepted norm against violations of physical dignity plays a large role in explaining Russians' opposition to current conscription conditions and the enormous popularity of soldiers' rights NGOs. Keck and Sikkink posit that this norm is nearly universal: "Not all cultures have beliefs about human rights (as individualistic, universal, and indivisible), but most value human dignity" (1998, p. 205). Case studies on transnational campaigns against antipersonnel land mines, torture and disappearance of political dissidents, violence against women, and rainforest destruction have shown how campaigns frequently succeed when they are framed in terms of physical harm to innocent victims.[23] It is precisely through appeals to human dignity and opposition to physical abuse that soldiers' mothers have been so successful in attracting public support.

Some might argue that in fact it is not the nature of the problem that soldiers' mothers' groups pursue, nor the way in which they frame the problem, that has led to their success. It could be argued instead that soldiers' mothers have become so popular because of the vast amount of basic needed services they provide for soldiers and their families: securing benefits, distributing goods for soldiers, making contact between families and soldiers, and helping soldiers to avoid illegal conscription. It certainly seems true that, in the Russian context, service provision organizations are more accessible and appreciated by citizens than organizations in the human rights or women's rights sphere. The same point could be made about crisis centers for women, discussed below. Yet if it is the service provision aspect of soldiers' mothers' work that is so crucial, then why are vast numbers of women's organizations that provide important services, such as *zhensovety*, not as popular as the soldiers' mothers' groups? The service provision aspect does play a role in the soldiers' mothers' popularity; however, the popularity of service provision organizations varies significantly depending on the societal norms surrounding the NGOs involved.

In contrast to campaigns that focus on physical harm to innocents, Keck and Sikkink have shown that NGO campaigns often fail when they are framed in terms of norms that are not universally accepted (for example, discussing environmental issues in terms of conservation or biodiversity rather than human suffering), or when the norm against bodily harm competes with strong local norms (such as national pride in the issues of female genital cutting in Africa or veiling in Muslim countries) (Keck and Sikkink, 1998; Keck, 1995). In a similar way, there are limits to Russian citizens' support for soldiers' rights NGOs. Beyond concrete instances of bodily harm, a norm of respect for the army and Russia's status as a strong military power complicates popular attitudes toward conscription. Objection to military service for reasons of conscience is a far less accepted action in Russia than objection on the basis of likely physical abuse.

ANTIMILITARISM AND PACIFISM AS NORMATIVE BARRIERS TO MOBILIZATION

Soldiers' mothers' organizations are often noted as one of the strongest NGO movements in Russia. Yet outside the circle of soldiers' and human rights NGOs, and especially beyond Moscow and St. Petersburg, very few people know of other soldiers' rights organizations such as ARA (Malyakin and Konnova, 1999). Caiazza states in her study of soldiers' rights groups that "ARA had relatively little political capital. Its public membership and support were minimal" (Caiazza, 2002, p. 151). Even the secretary of ARA, Nikolai Khramov, noted that "politically, we are marginal."[24] Both the soldiers' mothers' organizations and others such as ARA pursue largely the same goal: the end of a conscription-based army. Yet NGOs that focus on the constitutional right to conscientious objection are regarded with much more suspicion by Russians than those that focus on rampant physical abuse as the basis for demanding an end to conscription.

Here the work of social movement theorists on issue framing is important. While many soldiers' mothers' organizations in fact oppose militarization in general and, for example, oppose the Russian army's interventions in Chechnya, they pursue their goal of army reform by using a more accepted tactic: exposing physical abuse and lawlessness in the army. Most of their work consists of using legal means to obtain exemptions from army service for draftees as a way of preventing physical mistreatment, and initiating petitions and court cases in individual soldiers' cases of abuse, death, or unlawful conscription. In contrast, those soldiers' rights NGOs that pursue a campaign for army reform based on principles of nonviolence and antimilitarism have been far less resonant with the Russian population.

The low level of policy success (in terms of winning actual court cases) of soldiers' rights organizations that focus on conscientious objection—compared to those that concentrate on more pragmatic ways of avoiding conscription—is largely due to the fact that existing laws in Russia make other approaches far easier to pursue. Specific laws and regulations exist that exempt draftees from service under particular medical, educational, or family circumstances, and there is a recognized process for pursuing draftees' rights under such circumstances (although note that in mid-2006, some of these provisions were under threat of cancellation). In contrast, the mechanism for alternative service was not specified in Russian law at all until mid-2002. Even so, that law leaves service provisions unclear and potentially onerous (AFP, 2002).

Moreover, as concerns an eventual end to conscription through transition to a professional army, there has been a great deal of disagreement in the government and the military over whether and when reform will be possible. In spite of a 1996 election campaign promise by Boris Yeltsin to end conscription by 2000 and the Russian government's formal commitment to reform to a professional army, no such reform has taken place. Within the Russian political and military elite, including ministers of defense Igor Sergeev and Sergei Ivanov, the prevailing view has been that Russia cannot afford a professional army until it becomes a wealthier country, able to pay enough professional soldiers.[25] This is despite several observers' claims that a smaller, professional army would in fact cost less than a conscript army, due to reduced training time and costs (Lambroschini, 2000a). Thus, a significant part of the explanation for the limited public policy success of NGOs pursuing the right to conscientious objection and alternative service is that the political opportunity environment is hostile. Nevertheless, political barriers do not account for the low level of citizen mobilization around antimilitarist principles. The small number and size of these kinds of soldiers' rights organizations, as well as the relatively low degree of impact they have in society compared to the soldiers' mothers' organizations can be explained by the conflict between their principles and widespread norms in Russian society.

Counterbalancing the norm against bodily harm is a widespread norm of support and even glorification of the armed forces, largely springing from memories of the strength of the Soviet army. This explains the rejection of openly pacifist ideas, despite broad support for efforts to end conscription or to make army service more humane. While Russians believe that individual human rights abuses of soldiers are wrong, they do not oppose war or the army as a whole. Many Russians view the army as "a necessary instrument for personal development" (SMSP, 1996; LaFraniere, 2001; Hoare, 1998).

The enormous number of Russian adults who have undergone military service or are employed by military institutions contributes to a common attitude of strong support for the military. The proportion of the Russian population included at any one time in the armed forces is staggering, according to both official and independently compiled figures. Various counts place the size of the Russian armed forces, including the Defense Ministry and other forces, between five and six million people—approximately 3.2 percent of the Russian population (Felgenhauer, 2000; Ivankovskaia, 2001; RFE/RL, 2001a). Not many studies have been conducted to pinpoint the reasons for Russian citizens' growing resistance to fulfilling military service.

One of the few existing large surveys finds that, among the 72 percent of respondents who would not want one of their relatives to serve in the army, by far the most common reasons are the possibility of death in a conflict (44 percent), *dedovshchina*, or hazing (35 percent), and poor physical conditions (23 percent). Pacifism or opposition to militarism did not appear as a reason at all (VTsIOM, 2002).[26] Gerber and Mendelson (2003, p. 6) found in their large survey that 94 percent of respondents believed officers who tolerate *dedovshchina* should be prosecuted. Recently in the city of Ryazan', the human rights organization Memorial organized a focus group study to design a public relations campaign and found that "people react badly to posters showing how many schoolbooks one tank shell would buy, because they do not think the army should be kept short of funds, but that they are moved by images of soldiers' suffering" (*Economist*, 2004).

Attitudes on other issues reinforce the argument that significant proportions of Russians espouse pro-military, rather than antimilitary, ideas. Respect for the military remains high, even though there are serious doubts about mandatory conscription. Gerber and Mendelson (2003, p. 2) found that, while confidence in the Russian military has waned significantly in the post-Soviet era, approximately half of their survey respondents continue to have partial or complete confidence in the army. Over two-thirds of respondents believed that military spending should be increased in Russia (Gerber and Mendelson, 2003, p. 6). The ongoing *New Russia Barometer* surveys find that, consistently throughout the 1990s, the military received higher levels of trust from respondents than any other state institution, despite a campaign in Chechnya that has dragged on miserably since 1999 (Rose, 1999, p. 21). Another example of positive views of military authorities comes from a poll by the ROMIR agency in October 2000, in which 31 percent of respondents agreed that military leaders generally (not naming specific candidates) would make better governors than civilians, and only 10.1 percent thought that they would make worse governors (ROMIR, 2000a). All of these data concerning attitudes toward the military suggest that among most Russian citizens, opposition to conscription is based not on a philosophical objection to military values, but on concerns about the dangerous conditions of service in the current army.

These normative distinctions suggest a prediction regarding the future fate of the United People's Party of Soldiers' Mothers. If the party focuses its platform on fighting *dedovshchina* in the Russian military, I expect that it will win a significant number of votes in the next Duma elections in 2007, perhaps even enough to cross the new 7 percent vote threshold for winning seats in the Duma. Yet if it expands its platform to include demands for an alternative service law or negotiations to end the conflict in Chechnya, the party will have only a negligible following. This is predicated on the condition that the party is not run into the ground prior to the election by onerous legal and fundraising regulations.

Soldiers' mothers' NGOs and other soldiers' rights NGOs alike have worked fairly intensively with foreign donors, receiving funding and training and participating in conferences and information exchanges. Yet those that work for reform of the Russian army chiefly by exposing physical abuses and informing conscripts of their legal rights in the draft process tend to be better known and more successful than organizations that promote antimilitarist and pacifist principles in a more general sense. This is despite the significant transnational support that both kinds of organizations have received and despite the fact that they advocate essentially the same end goals. The key difference between the two groups of NGOs is in the normative frames that they use to pursue their goals, with soldiers' mothers using the horror of physical abuses, and other soldiers' rights groups employing the philosophy of nonviolence and antimilitarism.

It is worth noting here that the universality of the norm against bodily harm may also affect the way in which foreign donors behave toward soldiers' rights NGOs. Foreign granting agencies tend to be particularly moved by pleas for resources from NGOs that seek to prevent or document such violations, as opposed to many other NGO projects that are less universally understood. As a result, grant program officers may well try more assiduously to find ways of fitting soldiers' rights project proposals into their specific grant programs, rather than requiring soldiers' rights NGOs to modify their own programs to fit changing grant mandates. They may feel uncomfortable in suggesting to soldiers' rights NGOs that they should shift their focus to conform with transient granting priorities.[27]

While there is no direct evidence to prove this potential exceptionalism of soldiers' rights NGOs in their relations with foreign donors, the comment of one officer in charge of NGO assistance at the Canadian embassy in Moscow suggests that the soldiers' mothers are particularly revered: "It's very sacrosanct; as a government you can't criticize them. It's like criticizing motherhood itself or something."[28] The director of the Strategiia Center in St. Petersburg, which administered a grant program for NGOs funded by the Danish government, similarly stated that the SMSP is a formidable organization: "they are strong, they are angry, and they should be . . . the government doesn't like them, but it respects them."[29]

Indeed, the difference between women's and soldiers' rights NGOs in their nongrant interactions with transnational actors, displayed earlier in

Table 3.2, is an indicator that foreign donors have not perceived soldiers' rights NGOs as neophytes in need of training to the extent that they have with women's organizations. Soldiers' rights NGOs—given their frequency of reports to international institutions, membership in transnational organizations, and relatively less common exposure to training seminars—seemed to be treated more often as expert partners than as trainees in their transnational relations. Among those soldiers' rights NGOs that are transnationally active, ideational exchanges more frequently consisted of speaking tours in Europe than attending NGO training seminars.[30]

On the whole, even though the soldiers' mothers groups are more renowned than other soldiers' rights NGOs, both kinds of organizations have experienced greater popular support than most women's NGOs. This is also despite similar levels of foreign assistance and because of normative resistance to ideas of feminism and gender discrimination in Russia. In fact, the combination of domestic rejection of Western donors' ideas and heavy investment of resources into women's NGOs by foreign donors, has exacerbated the distance between women's NGOs and grassroots concerns in Russia.

Women's Organizations—Struggling from the Margins

There is abundant and incontrovertible evidence that the status and opportunities of women were and continue to be much poorer than those of men in the former Soviet Union (see Zakharova, Posadskaya, and Rimashevskaya, 1989; Pilkington, 1992; Fong, 1993; Funk, 1993; Ayvazova, 1998). In numerous areas, such as hiring practices, media portrayals, and treatment by law enforcement institutions in cases of domestic violence, women face blatant gender stereotypes and discrimination. On a multitude of fronts, including unemployment levels, salaries, domestic workloads, and representation in positions of power, women are much worse off than men. Reproductive health has always been an enormous problem, with abortions being the major form of birth control.

Despite all of these problems, there is not a strong women's movement in Russia today. The Russian public is far less aware of the work of women's NGOs than they are of soldiers' rights NGOs. Women's NGOs also have not managed to have the same impact on public policy decisions and public attitudes that soldiers' mothers' groups have. Small and very gradual improvements are taking place in the political clout and media treatment of women's NGOs. But the improvement of their public reputation is painfully slow.

Like all forms of independent organization in the Soviet Union, women's NGOs were not permitted to exist until the very last years of the regime. A huge network of official women's organizations or "women's councils" (*zhensovety*) existed throughout the country at all levels—from republic to oblast, city, neighborhood (*raion*), and even factory levels—with the official Soviet Women's Committee (SWC) at the top of the hierarchy. Yet the role of these organizations was not principally to advocate for social and public policy change to improve the status of women.

As numerous authors and interview subjects have reported, the two basic roles of the SWC and the *zhensovety* were to support the goals of the CPSU with regard to women in the domestic arena and to glorify the Soviet state's record of promoting women's equality in the international arena. Domestically, Soviet leaders were concerned about two serious problems with which the roles of women were closely connected: a shortage of labor to keep the economy growing, and an alarming decline in the birth rate (Lapidus, 1978; Buckley, 1989). The state needed women to be active participants in the Soviet economy but at the same time needed them to produce children, and the SWC and *zhensovety* were vehicles through which state authorities could respond to these dual pressures. However, the international role of the central SWC was far more important than its domestic role throughout most of its history (Racioppi and See, 1997).[31]

The *zhensovety* had been created under Khrushchev's leadership in the late 1950s and 1960s. They continued to exist, but were only minimally active, during the Brezhnev period. In 1986, at the 27th Party Congress, Mikhail Gorbachev called for a major revival of the *zhensovety* and for their structure to become unified under the national-level Soviet Women's Committee (SWC). The *zhensovety* were to work on resolving barriers to women's full equality with men in politics, the workplace, and daily life. Gorbachev expressed the wish to ensure that "questions directly concerning women's interests would not be solved without their participation and without their decisive judgement" (cited in Buckley, 1989, p. 199). Reportedly, by 1988 there were 236,000 *zhensovety* in the Soviet Union, involving 2.3 million members (Buckley, 1989, p. 210). To this day, the network of these organizations remains enormous and relatively intact at the municipal and regional levels. Many of the factory-level councils have disappeared due to a lack of willing participants and a shortage of material and moral support from factory managers.

Yet, as Mary Buckley shows, even after their renewal during perestroika, the *zhensovety* were not politically assertive. They largely acted as "tame 'helpers' of the CPSU" (1989, p. 217). While they conducted a great deal of useful social work with women and children in their local communities, most displayed a lack of initiative and waited for party superiors to give them commands. Most of the *zhensovety* that have survived to this day continue to adopt this basically subordinate attitude, despite the breakdown of authoritarian rule. Some, however, have managed to become fairly politicized and independent in their activities. For example, among the organizations in this study, the city *zhensovety* in Vladivostok and Izhevsk displayed some rebellious tendencies, and other authors have documented the autonomous forms of activism that some *zhensovet* leaders pursued in the late Soviet and post-Soviet periods (Sperling, 1999, pp. 23–24; Browning, 1987, pp. 97–117). At the national level, the SWC did grow more outspoken in the late 1980s regarding the "unsolved" nature of the "woman question" in the Soviet Union. It turned its attentions somewhat away from international propagandizing to concern itself with the very real problems of Soviet women at home, including the low numbers of women in leadership positions and female unemployment caused by economic restructuring (Racioppi and See, 1997, p. 77).

In 1990, as the Soviet Union was breaking apart and the CPSU monopoly on organizations was removed along with material support for those organizations, the SWC ceased to exist as an organization with networks extending throughout the Soviet Union and became instead the Union of Women of Russia (UWR). Although the UWR was now officially non-governmental, it kept most of the same leaders at all levels and retained its governmental and international contacts and free office space. Thus, it possessed major institutional advantages over smaller independent women's organizations, which were just beginning to form. These advantages were, and continue to be, a source of suspicion and jealousy from other Russian women's organizations.

Women's independent mobilization and their formation of non-state organizations began very tentatively in the late 1980s and early 1990s, starting with the formation of small, informal feminist organizations. These began to operate openly beginning in 1990, when NGOs became legal. They included, for example, SAFO (the Free Association of Feminist Organizations) and LOTOS (League for Emancipation from Societal Stereotypes), many of whose members continue to be active figures in the women's movement.[32] In the early 1990s, Russian women began to form other organizations, not necessarily feminist in orientation, to try to cope with the developing economic crisis and problems of women's unemployment in the transitional economy. NGOs proliferated to help women retrain for new careers or establish their own businesses.

Undoubtedly, two crystallizing early moments in the development of Russian women's NGOs were the First and Second Independent Women's Forums, which took place in the small city of Dubna, near Moscow, in 1991 and 1992. Many of the activists of the nascent Russian women's movement became acquainted with one another and began to work together at the first

Forum in Dubna.[33] The organizers of the First Independent Women's Forum worried about how state officials would react; it was still a time, prior to the Soviet collapse, when freedom of speech was uncertain. Indeed, uniformed police stood in the room while the Forum took place (Sperling, 1999, p. 107). Aside from fear of overt state repression, the organizers of the Forum were also plagued with state attempts to discredit the gathering. Prior to the Forum, the widely read newspaper *Moskovskii Komsomolets* reported that the conference was a meeting of "overexcited lesbians" (cited in Sperling, 1999, p. 106).

Yet, in retrospect, the two Forums in Dubna were blessed with material advantages of the Soviet period that no longer exist for NGO activists. The gathering required very little money to organize, as women of the relatively progressive city *zhensovet* in Dubna managed to arrange a free conference hall and organizers secured donations of supplies (such as food and office materials) from their institutes.[34] Moreover, long-distance telephone calls and postal costs to inform invitees, as well as train tickets for two hundred participants to attend from twenty-five Soviet cities, were far more affordable in 1991 than they are today. Zoia Khotkina of the Moscow Center for Gender Studies (MCGS) recalled that "it was all done on the solidarity of women alone. That's how it was in 1991; now, it's impossible to work like that."[35]

The two Dubna Forums were extremely important for creating links among women's organizations and for establishing contacts that would lead to an e-mail information network in later years under the auspices of an NGO called the Information Center of the Independent Women's Forum (ICIWF).[36] It was the first meeting ever to gather together nongovernmental women activists from across Russia. Among activists, having attended one or both of the Forums in Dubna is a badge of honor of sorts to this day.

Analysts contributing to a recent directory of women's organizations in Russia estimated that in January 1998 no more than two thousand nongovernmental women's organizations existed in Russia. They argued that, given the total number of NGOs registered in Russia in 1998, women's NGOs comprised only 0.5 percent of the overall NGO sector (Abubikirova et al., 1998, p. 10). Far more NGOs in Russia work in areas of sports and culture, ethnicity, the arts, the environment, issues dealing with children, the elderly, veterans, and disabled persons.[37] Nonetheless, it is important to note that this number of women's NGOs has emerged from only a few dozen independent organizations that existed in 1991. A "boom" in the creation of new women's organizations took place in the mid-1990s; at the time of the study, the rate at which new women's NGOs were forming appeared to be slowing down (Abubikirova et al., 1998, p. 12).[38]

CLEAVAGES DIVIDING THE WOMEN'S MOVEMENT

Some major divisions among women's organizations in Russia have impeded the development of active coalitions on issues. One deep rift, especially in Moscow and St. Petersburg, has been between organizations led by women who were active in Soviet organizations and those that emerged as independent, nongovernmental organizations during or after perestroika. Leaders of newer organizations resent the historical institutional advantages that the successor NGOs of Soviet organizations possess, and they harbor bitter memories of the ways in which state ideologues largely disguised or ignored the real problems of Soviet women, in favor of promoting Communist party goals.[39] In turn, former Communist organization members resent this lack of respect from younger activists, stating that they have always conducted an enormous amount of work to help women. Some have even openly voiced the opinion that feminist activists who initially worked in the SWC out of necessity, and later rejected that organization to form their own independent groups, are "turncoats" and not trustworthy.[40]

This rift, as I experienced in my field research and as reported by Sperling (1999, pp. 239–41), was much more intense in Moscow and St. Petersburg than in smaller cities, where a great deal more unity prevailed between traditional *zhensovet* organizations and newer, independent women's groups. This was partly due to the fact that the political process of transition from Communism to a democratic regime in Russia was less dramatic and divisive in most regional locations than it was in Moscow or even St. Petersburg. Aside from Ekaterinburg, the other regional cities in my study did not witness massive demonstrations or conflict during the transition period of 1990–93.

Another, more subtle rift among women's organizations is between those whose passionate activists fought to establish themselves in the volatile perestroika period and those that formed more recently, in the mid- to late-1990s. Here, the hostility comes nearly completely from the side of the older NGOs. They are proud of having fought for the right to organize and having overcome adversity to create their organizations. They sense that many latecomers to the women's movement are mercenaries—often forming organizations to attract foreign funding or because they have nothing else to do with their time—rather than dedicated activists.

A definite contributing factor to these conflicts has been the presence of foreign funding. Organizations that have their roots in former Soviet official organizations have experienced great difficulties in attracting foreign grants, which fuels their resentment toward newer women's organizations. Similarly, and more sharply, longer-existing women's NGOs that fought for every crumb prior to the arrival of foreign donors have felt hostility toward those organizations that simply "fell into" foreign grants from the moment they were established, and they therefore have doubted the authenticity of those activists' work. This foreign-funding factor also goes a long way in explaining why the conflicts and competition among women's organizations have been so much deeper in Moscow and St. Petersburg than anywhere else: in other areas of Russia there has simply been much less funding to fight over, and thus the stakes have been much lower.[41] NGOs in the less populous regions tended more often to work not as paid professionals but as unpaid volunteers in their spare time, and for many, foreign funding had not even entered their minds as a potential source of money.

The Russian mass media have shown very little interest in the concerns and activities of women's NGOs, in great contrast to the ample, positive media exposure enjoyed by soldiers' mothers' organizations, for example. Elizabeth Waters has pointed out that, even in the late Soviet period, women's issues were peculiar in their absence from Russian media reports, when other issues such as environmental problems received serious coverage (Waters, 1989, p. 15). Political scientist Svetlana Ayvazova reports that "the mass media publicize neither the aims and achievements of women's nongovernmental organizations, nor their values and norms. This seriously complicates both dialogue of these organizations with society, and their dialogue with the state, and decreases their chances of receiving approval from society" (1998, p. 131). Only sporadic serious treatment of women's issues has occurred in the Russian media, such as a biweekly column by the sympathetic journalist Nadezhda Azhgikhina in the popular newspaper *Nezavisimaia Gazeta*.[42] Some positive articles in *Segodnia* newspaper appeared in the past, and recently, television documentary programs and even police drama series have aired on the problem of domestic violence.[43] Aside from these exceptions, most media references to women's organizations are made in an ironic and misunderstanding manner. Elena Ershova of the Consortium in Moscow stated that the weakest point of the Russian women's movement is the position of the Russian mass media. She argued that "if we are going to influence the public, we need to influence the media, but the media is very patriarchal."[44]

When we look at particular issues pursued by women's NGOs, we find that despite similarly high levels of foreign assistance, NGOs that work on certain issues, such as domestic violence, have engaged in far more outreach to average citizens and have inspired more public awareness and support than NGOs that work on battling other problems, such as employment discrimination and sexual harassment. Foreign donors have offered a great deal of support to Russian NGOs to promote women's rights. The most active donor in this area has been the U.S. government, which devoted considerable resources, especially during the Clinton Administration under Madeleine Albright's tenure as secretary of state, to "promoting human rights and, in particular, combating violence and discrimination against women" (Human Rights Watch, 1997; USAID, 2000b). Other foreign donors were focused heavily on women's issues at the time of the study. The German Heinrich Böll *Stiftung*, affiliated with the Green party, and one of its ancestors, the *Frauenanstiftung* of the German Women's party, placed a great deal of emphasis on women's issues. The Canadian embassy in Moscow also had a grant program specifically for women's NGOs, and nongovernmental foreign foundations such as the U.S.-based Global Fund for Women and the Dutch organization Mama Cash were devoted solely to funding work on women's issues and had funded many Russian organizations.

The weak results of foreign assistance to Russian women's NGOs are due largely to Russians' widespread rejection of feminist principles. Domestic violence is one of the few issues in which women's NGOs have managed to mobilize as a strong movement and to make some significant headway in changing societal understandings of the issue. This, I argue, is because domestic violence, like abuses of soldiers, is also an issue of bodily harm and physical dignity.

EMPLOYMENT DISCRIMINATION AND SEXUAL HARASSMENT

NGO efforts in the areas of employment discrimination and sexual harassment in the workplace are examples of foreign donor–supported activities meeting resistant domestic norms. In cases like this, the efforts of donors to encourage domestic NGO mobilization have met with very little success, despite the existence of major problems in society.

Abundant evidence from Russian official sources, women activists, and observers from outside Russia shows that employment discrimination against women and sexual harassment in the workplace are rampant phenomena. Occupational segregation and a sizable male-female wage gap are obvious problems that exist now and also existed during the Soviet period. Female employees dominate in low-paid industrial and social service sectors such as health, education, and light industry (Fajth, 2000). According to one measure used by UNICEF, Russia has the highest level of occupational segregation among all of the post-Communist countries. Nearly half (45–47 percent) of Russian women or men would have to change occupations in order to equalize gender representation in each occupation, compared to 30–40 percent in most other countries in the post-Communist region (UNICEF, 1999).

As in most Western countries, substantial differences exist between the earning levels of men and women in Russia. Rather than improving in Russia, though, the disparity is worsening over time. In the early 1990s, women's salaries were on average 60–70 percent of men's, but by 1999 they had dipped to just 56 percent of men's (Baskakova, 2000, p. 63; ICIWF, 2001b).[45] Some estimates put women's current average income levels even lower, at 40–50 percent of men's (Azhgikhina, 2000). Not only is this because of the usual contemporary reasons for such disparities in the West—that is, that women work in lower-paying occupations than men—but it is also because men and women are in fact paid unequally for doing the same kind of work (UNICEF, 1999, p. 36). Yet the rallying cry of "equal pay for equal work," so resonant in North America in past decades, is barely audible outside the walls of a few NGOs' offices.

There are compelling indicators that women face discrimination in employers' layoff decisions. Inspections conducted by the Russian Labor Inspection organs (*Rostrudinspektsii*) in 1994–96 showed that increasing numbers of labor law violations were occurring through illegal dismissals of women during periods of pregnancy and childcare leave. The inspections also showed that the tactic of sending workers, predominantly female, on forced leave without due compensation had become a "massive phenomenon" among employers as a means of pressuring women to quit on their own volition (Baskakova, 1998, pp. 52–53). According to the Federal Employment Service of the Russian government, in 1995 women constituted 62.2 percent of the total registered unemployed population in Russia (Government of the Russian Federation, 1995; ICIWF, 2001b). By 1999, this figure had increased to 70 percent (ICIWF, 2001b). There is also frequent discrimination in hiring processes. As noted at the beginning of this chapter, Russian job advertisements commonly detail the desired sex, age, and even physical description of job candidates (Bridger, Kay, and Pinnick, 1996, p. 80; Khotkina, 1996b, p. 17). Typical examples, cited by Bridger, Kay and Pinnick (1996, p. 80) are:

SECRETARIES REQUIRED; ATTRACTIVE GIRLS WITH OFFICE EXPERIENCE, AGED 18–22, AT LEAST 168 CM TALL.

SECRETARY/PERSONAL ASSISTANT REQUIRED WITH KNOWLEDGE OF ENGLISH, PRETTY GIRL UNDER 25.

In the recent context of a weak economy and the disproportionate location of women in low-status occupations, women have been especially vulnerable to sexual harassment from their employers. According to the small amount of research available, sexual harassment is extremely widespread in Russia: one survey conducted by the Moscow Center for Gender Studies found that one in four respondents had been subjected to sexual harassment in the workplace (Vandenberg, MacGrory, and Kochkina, 1996, p. 126). The

Moscow NGO Diana, which has documented complaints about sexual harassment, claimed in 1996 that "in 35 percent of the private firms in the capital, the main step on the professional ladder for women is in bed" (Khotkina, 1996b, p. 17). These figures must be viewed as preliminary and likely inaccurate, since they have involved small samples in select areas. However, one clue to the frequency of the problem is that in the "seeking work" announcements of newspapers, women's entries often specify "without intimate relations."[46]

Low Mobilizational Success

Some of the most prominent, heavily foreign-funded women's NGOs in Russia have taken up the issues of sexual harassment and labor discrimination, including the Consortium, MCGS, and the ICIWF. Foreign organizations and Russian NGOs have organized international workshops and seminars on the problem of sexual harassment, including one hosted by the ABA-CEELI office in 1995 and several at MCGS. Women's NGOs have also briefed government officials on the extent of employment discrimination and harassment in the Russian labor market, and recommended legislative and oversight strategies to tackle the problem. Women's NGOs have worked with the Duma Committee on Women, Family, and Youth and the Committee on Social and Religious Organizations to lobby for legislative change on labor and employment issues as well as tax law, reproductive rights, family policy, and demographic issues (Consortium, 2004a).[47]

Foreign donors such as USAID and the Soros Open Society Institute, as well as transnational NGOs such as the Network of East-West Women (NEWW), have supported "gender expertise" projects to analyze Russian labor legislation and its differential impacts on women and men. Much of this lobbying activity has focused on bringing Russian legislation into accordance with the language of international agreements regarding women's rights (Richter, 2002, p. 40). The deputy head of the Department for Family, Women, and Children within the Russian Ministry of Labor and Social Development, Olga Samarina, was noted by both women activists and Samarina herself to be an ally of women's NGOs in working to bring Russia's labor laws into accordance with the UN's 1995 Beijing Declaration.[48]

Russian governmental commitments and institutions to promote the status of women, developed especially following the Beijing World Forum on Women in 1995, have been mostly declaratory, with no significant allocation of resources. One example is the federal law "On State Guarantees of Equal Rights and Freedoms of Women and Men and Equal Guarantees of Their Fulfillment," which basically detailed gender equality guarantees already implied by the Constitution and easily passed in its first reading by the State

Duma in April 2003. Formal mechanisms exist, largely to comply with commitments made by the government during the Beijing World Forum on Women in 1995, such as the governmental Commission on Advancing the Status of Women; the Presidential Commission on Women, Family, and Demography; the Duma Committee on Women, Family, and Youth; and the Department for Family, Women, and Children within the Ministry of Labor and Social Development. Yet, as Elena Ershova of the Consortium notes, aside from the formal existence of these official bodies, "there is not a single kopeck in the [state] budget dedicated to improving women's status. That means that everything looks well resolved on paper, but in reality, there are practically no concrete solutions."[49]

Indeed, most legislative initiatives promoted by women's organizations that would cost money, challenge power bases, or otherwise require changes to existing institutions have failed miserably. Some partial victories affecting legislation have prevailed. Notably, the Consortium of Women's Nongovernmental Organizations claimed that as a result of several meetings between women's NGO leaders and the head of the Russian Pension Fund between 2001 and 2003, Russian pension legislation was modified to include women's years of maternity leave in their employment record accumulating state pension funds. In addition, the Consortium argued that women's NGOs were influential in amending two clauses of the new Russian Labor Code draft among many for which they had lobbied throughout the 1990s.[50] These dealt with restrictions on women's labor in heavy or dangerous types of work (women's organizations requested a specific list of professions where female labor would be restricted, rather than a general ban), and employment protection for pregnant women and mothers of children under 1.5 years of age (Consortium, 2004b).[51] The Consortium also claimed that, during the development of the Code, the government heeded the wishes of women's NGOs for the inclusion of fathers and other family members as allowable candidates for parental leave, in addition to mothers.[52] Unfortunately, women's organizations did not succeed with the many other amendments that they wished to have included in the Labor Code (Consortium, 2004b).

These employment-related issues have been part of the broader agenda of breaking down gender discrimination and stereotypes that transnational actors have supported among women's NGOs in Russia. That agenda has also included activities such as efforts to improve media images of women, decrease barriers to women in the business sector, and create a critical mass of gender studies programs around the country.

Yet activism along these lines has been virtually silent and barely resonates with most government officials and the Russian public. In the specific case of sexual harassment, Khotkina notes that discussing the issue is even a terminological problem in Russian translation: there is no satisfactory Russian term for "sexual harassment." She states that "it is probably symptomatic that the problem itself is clear, but a developed, accepted name does not exist, since the problem is practically not talked or written about; it's not appropriate to discuss it as a social problem rather than simply someone's 'personal' problem or gossip behind someone's back, and in such instances the question of terminology isn't so important" (Khotkina, 1996a, p. 8).

As indicated by the projects cited above, the activities of women's NGOs on issues of labor discrimination and sexual harassment have typically taken the form of seminars and analytic discussions of the problem among women activists and government officials. But rarely has the broader public outside these venues heard anything about the problem of discrimination, and few realize that, officially, laws exist that prohibit it.

Why has activism on sexual harassment and employment discrimination taken the forms of seminars and analysis of legislation, rather than street demonstrations or the development of hotlines and legal clinics, which would connect with the public in significant ways? Part of the answer is that the activists for whom these issues are salient tend to be feminist intellectuals, such as in the Moscow Center for Gender Studies, whose natural tendency is to turn to analysis rather than protest or public outreach in dealing with societal problems. Feminists in Russia do tend to be intellectuals rather than activists, and they realize that the wider public has a hostile orientation toward feminism. Foreign donors have preferred to support these intellectuals, who espouse a gender perspective similar to the Western feminist ideals of many donors themselves, rather than supporting women's initiatives that are more oriented toward outreach but less feminist in their approach to discrimination against women in the labor sector.

Russian women did create numerous organizations in the early 1990s, when massive layoffs first began to take place, specifically to tackle women's employment issues. However, as several authors note, most of these have pragmatically aimed to retrain women or create opportunities for new jobs (Bridger, Kay, and Pinnick, 1996; Sperling, 1999, p. 163). In this sense, they have worked *around* the issue of discrimination rather than tackling it head-on. The creation of organizations aimed at retraining women for other professions or building networks of businesswomen has been a far more popular and widespread phenomenon than mobilization around issues of discrimination and harassment. Many organizations have worked on retraining women for types of work that most Western feminists would view as dangerously gender stereotyping and even exploitative—such as hairdressing, dressmaking, cosmetology, and piecework from home—encouraged by organizations such as the Union of Russian Women and the Alternativa center in

St. Petersburg. Indeed, transnational actors have not typically supported these kinds of practical job retraining endeavors, unless they have been programs to assist women in forming their own businesses.[53]

All available evidence indicates that discrimination against women in hiring and firing processes and instances of sexual harassment have become more blatant and widespread than they ever were in the Soviet period. According to the standard social movement theory notion of relative deprivation, this should lead women to resent the loss of status and rights that they once possessed; yet women's mobilization on these issues has been conspicuously absent. The failure of women's NGOs and the foreign donors working with them to inspire any significant public reaction to the problems of employment discrimination and sexual harassment is in large part due to Russian citizens' general rejection of the norms of feminism and gender equality.

Normative Barriers to Mobilization

Only a handful of the thousands of women's NGOs in Russia openly claim to espouse a feminist philosophy. Abubikirova et al. found that only 3 percent of the women's organizations included in their directory proclaimed themselves to be feminist in orientation, although these authors argued that many more organizations may be classified as "latent feminist" groups, since their goals inherently stemmed from "feminist values" (1998, p. 15). My observations supported this contention; discussions with women activists in Russia frequently developed into fiery diatribes against the forms of discrimination that women face and their unequal status in Russian society. Yet most activists steadfastly refused to label themselves feminists.

Why is this the case? Russian women's antipathy to feminism stems mostly from dynamics of the Soviet era, which de facto continued pre-Soviet societal patterns of gender discrimination and inequality, even though Soviet laws, on paper, were some of the world's most progressive in terms of gender equality. Soviet women's right to vote, the principle of equal pay for equal work, and generous leave and daycare benefits were legislated early on.

Yet feminism as a mobilizing concept was never accepted by many Russians. Beginning with the Bolshevik revolutionaries, and even more so as industrialization picked up in the late 1920s, Soviet authorities placed feminism firmly on their list of non-class-based, and therefore bourgeois, ideologies. Official sources described feminism as a radical and ridiculous hobby of Western bourgeois women, completely unsuited to the realities of the Soviet Union, where men and women were in all respects already "equal." Russian scholar Olga Khasbulatova has pointed out that even the Russian Bolshevik women revolutionaries—recognizable in all respects as Marxist feminists—

did not call themselves feminists: "They avoided the word, and applied it only to the Western [women's] movement. But that division, that there were feminists 'over there,' but that we're not feminists, was a purely ideological one."[54]

The ideologues of the Bolshevik women's movement, such as Aleksandra Kollontai and Inessa Armand, who espoused fairly radical ideas of social reorganization and sexual liberation, inspired early Soviet policies aimed at dismantling traditional gender inequalities. They were key in establishing the *Zhenotdel*, or "women's division" of the CPSU. The *Zhenotdel* did work intensively on improving women's equality with men in the Soviet Union. However, the influence of the Bolshevik women revolutionaries was short-lived. Soon, Soviet authorities abandoned not only feminism as a word but also the previous official commitment to pursuing equality between men and women. In 1930, Stalin closed the *Zhenotdel*, declaring that Soviet women had attained freedom and equality with men and that there was no need for special women's organizations. From that point on, until the late Soviet period, official discussion of eroding gender inequality was virtually nonexistent.

Feminist ideas have not inspired significant women's activism since the short-lived mobilization of the Bolshevik women's movement. Instead, two general tendencies in Russian public opinion have resulted from Soviet antifeminist propaganda and the failure to bring about actual equality, in spite of the prominence of "equality" as an ideal in official declarations. First, to a considerable extent, Russian men and women believed Soviet official descriptions of Western feminism and the argument that it was entirely unsuited to Russian conditions. But second, women also saw with abundant clarity that in fact they were not equal to men, despite Soviet declarations of equality and the defeminization of the Soviet ideal woman, with images of male and female tractor drivers toiling side by side, for example. Yet the official *zhensovet* women's organizations worked vigorously to ensure that women more effectively fulfilled their "double burden" of duties at home and at work in order to support state goals, instead of focusing on developing more equitable domestic and professional roles for men and women. Understandably, because of this lack of attention to women's actual quality of life, most Soviet women related to the *zhensovety* with considerable skepticism.

The end result is that, in the post-Soviet context, Russian women tend to view feminist organizations as espousing an alien Western ideology unsuited to their conditions. Russians tend instinctively to perceive feminist organizations negatively, as being composed of radical, lonely, and probably lesbian women. They view feminism as advocating equality as "sameness" with men, in fact wiping out the appealing differences between the sexes just as Soviet ideology did. At the same time, they view nonfeminist women's organizations that stem from the old *zhensovet* organizations as being state-dominated organizations that have no interest in resolving women's real problems. As a result, as Irina Jurna has described it, Soviet women's experience with gender issues consisted of "legally consolidated but unrealized equality," which "drove the women's movement into a blind alley" (1995, p. 482).

Some exceptions are gradually developing to this general dismissal of women's organizations. Crisis centers that work on preventing and dealing with violence against women are gaining considerable respect in both society and state structures. This exception is due to the fact that concern over violence against women stems from a nearly universally shared norm against bodily harm to innocent people and violation of basic human dignity. Certain other areas, such as women's business organizations, have also begun to gain respect in some regions—but very slowly, and only in those cases where they have demonstrated over time that their members generate significant economic activity. In contrast, other NGO efforts that are often supported by foreign donors—to promote such goals as expanding gender studies in higher education, improving portrayal of women in the mass media, and battling sexual harassment against women in the workplace— have been largely unsuccessful and poorly received by the wider public. This, I argue, is because it is difficult to frame these issues without using language resembling feminism or demands for equality. Valerie Sperling has also pointed out this distaste among Russian women for framing issues in terms of feminism or equality (1999, p. 90).

Most Russians reject the concept of "gender"—that is, the socially constructed aspects of male and female roles—and instead "essentialism regarding men and women is widely accepted in Russian political discourse" (Vannoy et al., 1999, p. 5; see also Baskakova, 2000, p. 63; MCGS, 1998; Zdravomyslova and Temkina, 1997). Essentialist views of men's and women's roles include the idea that men are destined to be breadwinners and women's primary place is in the home; therefore, women are ancillary members of the paid labor force. Such ideas contribute to toleration of various forms of workplace discrimination, including sexual harassment, as acceptable phenomena.

Surveys confirm the prevalence of this view of traditional roles. In 1996, Vannoy et al. conducted a survey of Muscovites in which less than 20 percent of the married women respondents and even fewer married men thought that income-earning should be a shared responsibility rather than the sole responsibility of the husband (1999, pp. 52–53). By comparison, when the same question was asked of Midwestern Americans thirteen years earlier, 47 percent of wives and 31 percent of husbands believed that the responsibility should be shared (Vannoy et al., 1999, p. 53). The 1990–93 World Values Survey, which studied people's values in forty countries around the world, found that 40 percent of Russians agreed with the statement that "When jobs are scarce, men have more right to a job than women" (Inglehart, Basanez, and Moreno, 1998, p. V128). In contrast, 24 percent of Americans, 19 percent of Canadians, and 8 percent of Swedes agreed with the statement.

At the end of the Soviet period, in 1990, a survey of workplace managers found that 79 percent would select a woman for a job only if the position "was not suitable for a man" (cited in Bridger, Kay, and Pinnick, 1996, p. 81; see also Ayvazova, 1998, pp. 110–11). Along similar lines, in the World Values Survey, 91 percent of Russian respondents "strongly agreed" or "agreed" with the statement that "A job is alright, but what most women really want is a home and children" (Inglehart, Basanez, and Moreno, 1998, p. V220). This compared with 59 percent of Irish, 56 percent of American, and 43 percent of Canadian respondents.[55]

From the perspective of many Russian women, the Soviet state granted them legal equality with men and promoted uniform images of men and women, particularly in the labor market—yet this "equality" did not improve women's lives. Observers of Russian gender issues widely acknowledge that the Soviet treatment of female roles created a backlash against the idea of "equality" between the sexes. As Irina Jurna states, "the hardship that women endured under the Soviet system of 'equality' has left a legacy that defines equality with men as an undesirable goal for many Russian women" (1995, p. 477). Feminist Olga Voronina explains that "for the average Soviet woman, emancipation is what she already has, that is, a lot of work, under the guise of equality with men" (1993, p. 223). Women were comrades along with men in every occupation, or so official texts proclaimed, despite extreme occupational segregation in reality.

This rejection of equality as "sameness" and uniformity between the sexes extends to the issue of sexual harassment. In an atmosphere of hardship and few consumer goods under the Communist regime, women were discouraged from engaging in frivolous pleasures of female fashion or cosmetics; and in reaction to this, many Russian women are now struggling to reclaim signs of their femininity (Drakulic, 1993, pp. 21–30; Sperling, 1999, p. 68). As a result, most Russian women today do not respond positively to feminist criticisms of media representations of women as sexual objects. Jurna states that "their striving, through the clothes they wear and their behavior, to underline their sexuality, often shocks representatives of Western women's movements" (1995, p. 481). In this context, a sizable proportion of Russians believe that treating women as sexual objects is perfectly acceptable or at least should be tolerated, even in the workplace, as a "natural" consequence of women's femininity. Elena Ershova remarks that the biggest challenge to the women's movement is the general "patriarchal character" of Russian society: "Even my friends and colleagues are hostile. Everyone knows that violence, harassment, and discrimination exist, but no one is willing to discuss it."[56]

DOMESTIC VIOLENCE

According to the Russian President's Special Advisor on Women's Issues, over 14,000 Russian women are killed by their partners every year. A comparative analysis of spousal murder based on 1991 data showed that Russian women are 2.5 times more likely than American women to be murdered by their partners—and American women are already twice as likely to be murdered by their partners as West European women (UNICEF, 1999, p. 82). In October 1997, the Russian Department of Internal Affairs under the Internal Affairs Ministry acknowledged that a woman is beaten in Russia every two seconds (Sinelnikov, 1998).

Traditionally there have been serious problems with how Russian law enforcement and judicial organs treat the problem of domestic violence. The view that domestic abuse is not a crime, but a private matter, is widespread within the Russian police force (Human Rights Watch 1997).[57] Police often refuse to respond to calls from women who are being beaten unless they promise to press charges. Russia has no state-enforced civil protection order mechanism, and thus the state has no legal way to keep batterers away from their partners unless the abused victim lays criminal charges.

Relative Success in Mobilizing

In the area of domestic violence, women's organizations' have had very little success in their efforts to adapt the criminal code to prevent and prosecute instances of domestic abuse. Several dozen versions of a proposed law on prevention of domestic violence have failed to make substantial progress through the State Duma.

However, women's NGOs and the foreign donors who work with them have experienced some success in recent years in changing the attitudes of police, prosecutors, and lawyers who deal with domestic violence cases. Whereas prosecutors, for instance, have traditionally treated domestic violence as a private matter outside their scope of responsibility, the project manager for one major foreign donor working in this area, the American Bar Association, claimed to have seen a complete change in the actions and views of some prosecutors with whom she has worked. The deputy director of the General Prosecutor's office in St. Petersburg, for example, shifted from denying that domestic violence lay within her responsibilities to vowing among her peers that the prosecutor's office must work to stop it.[58] The Moscow organization Syostry, a center for assisting victims of sexual violence, reported that some rape victims are now being referred to them by the police; while just a few years earlier, the police would dismiss crisis center activists entirely.[59] Women's NGOs gradually have managed to encourage some domestic violence victims to launch civil damages suits against their abusers and have begun to train lawyers to prosecute in the area of domestic violence.[60] Since 1997, they have experienced success in winning such cases, although the number of Russian women willing to bring court cases against their abusers is still small, due to a shortage of legal representatives expert in this area and the common Russian belief that appearing in court is shameful (Human Rights Watch, 1997).

Foreign donors have devoted considerable resources to combating violence against women in Russia in recent years. The U.S. government in particular, since 1996, has committed millions of dollars to tackling the problem, particularly through training programs for Russian law enforcement officers, lawyers, and healthcare providers (Human Rights Watch, 1997). In addition, USAID and other nongovernmental foreign donors such as the International Research and Exchanges Board (IREX), an American NGO, have heavily supported Russian crisis centers for women.

Due in part to this foreign assistance, a network of Russian crisis centers that offer services such as telephone hotlines, counseling, and legal and medical assistance has grown rapidly over the past decade. The first crisis centers appeared in Moscow in 1993 and have since grown across Russia to number more than forty. These centers work actively in providing much-demanded services to victims of violence.

For the most part, they have enthusiastically adopted methods that Western NGOs and shelters use for dealing with gender-based violence. Training sessions with police, lawyers, and medical professionals have been largely based on Western techniques, even though Russian experts often conduct the sessions. Public awareness campaigns have used similar techniques as are used in the West, such as role-playing games for children and adolescents, bumper stickers stating "There is no excuse for domestic violence," and graphic posters showing a woman's bruised face. A senior staff member at the Syostry Crisis Center in Moscow responded as follows to a question about the adaptability of Western experience in Russia: "Of course we have our own conditions, our own laws, which are not usually so bad—you just need to use some experience and information and analyze them. Once you have that, you can already use [Western techniques] in our conditions. Personally, I have no problems with getting experience from someone else."[61]

In some cases, understandably, Russian activists feel that certain Western methods, especially legal and financial mechanisms, are simply not possible in the near future. For example, during a 1995 roundtable on violence in Moscow, activists from the United States mentioned procedures such as removing an abusive spouse from the home, requiring him to pay damages, and even the idea of funding shelters by devoting state marriage license fees directly to them. While the Russian activists in attendance seemed to view these ideas as excellent, they responded that such developments would only occur "in the distant future" (Khotkina, 1996c, pp. 84–89). Thus, the typical point of view of domestic violence activists in Russia is probably more like that of Anna Shunkova, a staff member of the Aleksandra center in St. Petersburg. She stated:

A woman from the European Women's Police Network affected me a lot. But you can't take everything straight from there to here. It's also wrong to say that nothing is transferable; many people who are new to involvement with Westerners reject all advice as impossible to implement here. Both extremes are wrong, and there needs to be a mixture. We need to have training in pairs, with one foreigner and one local specialist.

Despite the problems of adaptability, Russian resistance to Western methods in the area of domestic violence is generally much less than resistance that Russian activists express in certain other areas of foreign assistance, such as NGO management techniques or promoting women in politics.

In nearly every city I visited in Russia, members of women's NGOs expressed concern about domestic violence, and many, in both traditional and feminist organizations, were seeking resources to develop crisis centers in their communities. As mentioned in Chapter Two, the Russian Association of Crisis Centers for Women, formed in 1994, is a highly mobilized and effective organization. There is no question that the crisis centers' work is in high demand: at the time of the study, centers in Moscow and St. Petersburg each received over 70 calls per month, and a crisis center in Izhevsk that established a hotline in 2000 received 600 calls in the first two months of operation.[62]

Until very recently, domestic violence, like sexual harassment, was a "silent problem" in Russia—it simply was not considered to be a problem by law enforcement agencies and most of society (Buckley, 1989, p. 204; Vannoy et al., 1999, pp. 142–43). The Soviet Union collected no statistics on incidents of domestic abuse. Although Russian legal treatment of the problem is appalling and certain ideas about domestic violence that are unacceptable now in the West remain widespread, most Russians do believe that physical violence in the home is wrong. The problem continues to be plagued with silence, but in the post-Soviet period, women's NGOs have begun to work aggressively and successfully in providing assistance to victims of violence and changing public and official views on the issue.

Bodily Harm as a Frame for Mobilization

Why has there been progress in the campaign by women's NGOs against domestic violence, when other women's issues have failed to bring about successful mobilization? As with soldiers' rights issues, the answer is that domestic violence is a clear case of bodily harm to individuals.

In Russia specifically, survey data on attitudes toward domestic violence are limited. However, one large recent survey provides some substantiation of the norm against bodily harm as opposed to nonphysical forms of violence. Ninety-three percent of female and 87 percent of male respondents recognized physical beatings as a form of violence, while only 76 percent of women and 41 percent of men considered verbal threats to be a form of violence (Zabelina, 2002, 42–43).

Of course, the domestic violence issue is not completely divorced from beliefs about gender roles, and as a result, discriminatory attitudes toward women emerge in public views on domestic violence. For example, Andrei Sinelnikov of the Moscow organization ANNA (Association No to Violence), which assists victims of domestic violence, reports from a survey that "80.5 percent of Russian women and 63.6 percent of men identify violence in the family as a crime," but that "at the same time, around half of those surveyed believe in the myth that it is women who provoke such violence against themselves" (Sinelnikov, 1998). Even among NGO activists who wish to become involved in preventing domestic violence, one can encounter the attitude that women "provoke" their partners to beat them. One NGO leader in St. Petersburg, who lamented the frequent occurrence of domestic violence and had submitted a project proposal to a foreign donor for creating a volunteer violence prevention program, stated that "women sometimes provoke these incidents," and planned to focus on training women in less aggressive ways of speaking to their husbands.[63] The widespread view that women provoke domestic violence clearly impedes immediate success in building public concern about the problem; however, the fact that the overwhelming majority of Russians seem to consider domestic violence a crime bodes well for the eventual success of women's NGOs in combating the problem at both legal and societal levels.

While most foreign donors and the leading Moscow organizations (ANNA and Syostry) that deal with domestic violence approach the issue from a feminist perspective that sees domestic violence as part of a larger problem of women's inequality, many other crisis centers and women's organizations wish to stop domestic violence but view it mainly as a problem of protecting women from bodily harm, without perceiving it as a symptom of systemic degradation of women (Johnson, 2004, pp. 224–25). As James Richter has argued, the movement has "helped to build bridges between different types of women's organizations," despite their differing perspectives, because "there is no monolithic definition of their mission binding on all centers" (Richter, 2002, p. 35). They merely concur that any physical abuse of women is wrong.

The relative success of transnational mobilization on the issue of domestic violence and the ability of women's organizations to build broad coalitions to fight domestic violence are not peculiar to the Russian case. Generally, internationally, mobilization of women's organizations to protest and prevent violence against women have been extraordinarily successful, growing into "the most important international women's issue, and the most dynamic new international human rights concern" by the mid-1990s (Keck and Sikkink, 1998, p. 166). Scholars and activists alike have argued that framing the issue of violence against women as one of basic human rights has brought greater unity to transnational women's networks (Clark, Friedman, and Hochstetler, 1998, pp. 24–25; Bunch, 1990). Indeed, then, there seems to be a fairly universal quality to the norm against physical harm, which makes transnational assistance efforts in the area of violence against women particularly successful.

AN ALTERNATE ROUTE FOR TRANSNATIONAL INFLUENCE: THE BEIJING WORLD CONFERENCE ON WOMEN

Although foreign donors are typically unsuccessful in creating domestic-level change where domestic ideas contradict international norms, there does appear to be an indirect mechanism by which transnational actors can increase the legitimacy of NGOs and catalyze changes in domestic public policies, even in such contested areas as women's rights. By developing new international conventions, organizing prominent international conferences, and thereby pressuring national governments to commit to new legal norms on paper, international organizations—in Russia's case, particularly the UN and the European Union—can bring about noticeable changes in the conduct of political and bureaucratic elites, even in areas such as labor policy, where domestic resistance to feminist arguments generally hinders the removal of gender-discriminatory policies. Such international conventions can even induce more immediate change, in terms of concrete policies and the political legitimacy of domestic NGOs, than foreign funding for projects that individual NGOs carry out.

A good example of this kind of influence is how the 1995 Fourth World

Conference on Women in Beijing prompted policy developments and discussions in Russia. Irene Tinker and Jane Jaquette point out the tremendous, if intangible, psychological influence that the UN conferences on women have had on women's mobilization around the world. They state, in reference to the UN Decade for Women, that "[t]he psychological dimensions of this mobilization process should not be underestimated: the Decade provided the opportunity for women to recognize that a women's agenda is legitimate and feasible, and that such an agenda commands agreement and support across national boundaries and international conflicts" (1987, p. 426).

Numerous interview subjects in the study noted that the 1995 Beijing Conference and simultaneous NGO Forum brought about significant changes in the attitudes of Russian government officials. Suddenly, advocates of women's rights both within and outside government were understood as advocating norms that were not extremist, but rather were part of mainstream expectations in the international community. Sperling notes that "by making reference to such documents, activists lend a certain amount of legitimacy to their demands in the eyes of the Russian government" and that "activists have benefited from increased respect by government officials since the [Beijing] conference" (1998, pp. 2–3). Olga Samarina of the Department for Family, Women, and Children within the Russian Ministry of Labor and Social Development noted particularly vividly how the Beijing Conference and NGO Forum boosted the legitimacy of women's NGOs and her own department:

[The conference allowed us to] have all of this passed as government policy, and in general to prove to the male majority located in all areas of power that it's not nonsense coming from some separate department or a handful of women. It showed that this is definitely the direction in which the whole world is going . . . The conduct of the conference, I would say, facilitated things for us because then it wasn't necessary for us to prove anything further.[64]

Although the formal creation of new legislation and policies often does not lead to effective implementation of those policies, it does provide a focal point to which NGOs can refer in order to shame their governments into practicing what they preach. In the case of the Russian government and the Beijing Conference, the lead-up period to the conference led to the creation of a National Action Plan for improving women's status and the formation of national machinery dedicated to gender equality. Samarina's department within the Ministry of Labor and Social Development was created expressly to prepare for the Beijing Conference and then was transformed into a permanent department. A governmental Commission on Improving the Status of Women was created in 1996 to monitor implementation of the National

Action Plan. Of course, as numerous NGO activists, an alternative NGO report to the UN, and even sympathetic bureaucrats have remarked, there has been no money dedicated to implementing the National Action Plan.[65] In fact, the national machinery offices only hold consultative status and, so far at least, have not exerted a major impact on legislation and especially its implementation (*National Report*, 1999).

In addition to the problem of actual implementation, another problem with these kinds of transnationally induced changes at the political level is that they only immediately affect that level. Public policy changes may occur, but there is no guarantee that they will affect the norms that citizens espouse. Campaigns that NGOs conduct at local levels to raise public concern about problems are thus crucial to the process of changing societal norms.

Differential Effects of Foreign Assistance

Because of the historically developed norms discussed, generally positive toward the goals of soldiers' rights organizations and negative toward women's rights organizations, the efforts of foreign donors to support the development of each of these NGO subsectors have had varying results. In the case of soldiers' rights NGOs, the strength of the norm against bodily harm has shaped the impact of foreign assistance on NGO mobilization concerning soldiers' rights to humane and lawful treatment. Assistance to build the infrastructural capacity of organizations, support monitoring of rights violations, and train activists in using international human rights conventions has had mainly positive effects. It has made these organizations stronger, more resistant to being coopted by the state, and more persuasive in their arguments to the state regarding military reform and human rights observance, without forcing them to change their fundamental goals.

In contrast, among most women's organizations, with the exception of crisis centers, foreign assistance has in fact tended to increase the detachment of women's NGOs from the wider Russian population. Women's NGOs tend to have very small memberships, they rarely conduct outreach activities with the public, and they are not well understood in public opinion or the mass media. The lack of connection between transnationally active women's NGOs and ordinary Russians is, to a large extent, a result of the fact that foreign donors, rather than emphasizing funding to work on problems that large constituencies of Russians consider important, have focused on funding organizations that espouse (or are willing to adopt) the specific strategies that they bring from Western experience. As mentioned earlier, foreign donors have preferred to support feminist intellectuals and professionalized NGO

leaders who speak in terms familiar to Western actors, rather than traditionally minded activists who often work more closely with average citizens.
Compatibility of recipients' concerns and value orientations with donors'
ideals has been more important to donors than the degree to which activists
try to mobilize public consciousness-raising and support. Rebecca Kay
points out that "an ability to grasp and reflect the language, theoretical perspective and statements of principal of the donor" has been important in
determining which NGOs obtain transnational support. Arguably, she states,
this ability to "speak the language" has become "more important than the
actual content or target group of the programmes delivered" (2000, pp.
193–94).

Even worse, donors' own programmatic focus on internal NGO development and professionalization rather than external mobilization has widened
the gulf between recipients of Western assistance and potential constituencies
in society in cases where donors' normative concerns are at odds with
Russian societal norms. Some activists have argued that the techniques that
foreign donors have taught for internal NGO professionalization are themselves at odds with Russian realities. For example, Olga Lipovskaia of the
transnationally active Petersburg Center for Gender Issues stated that "many
Western, especially American, organizations organize programs that don't
apply well to our conditions. This includes programs of public management,
PR, and fundraising—they're not generally well oriented to our problems."[66]
In the event that foreign funding should cease, it is unclear how such NGOs
would sustain themselves in an inhospitable domestic environment.

The principle of gender equality is one example of this lack of fit
between foreign donors' approaches and dominant Russian norms. In the
United States, for instance, women's organizations have tackled the problem
of sexual harassment by arguing that women are entitled to equal treatment
in the workplace, and the Equal Employment Opportunity Commission is
the government body responsible for collecting and pursuing complaints of
sexual harassment. A similar approach might work well in Russia if the concept of "equality" between men and women resonated well with Russian citizens. But, given the history of women's negative experiences with what was
called "equality" under the Soviet regime, strategies that women's NGOs
used in the West to raise public concern about the issue are not likely to succeed in Russia. Sexual harassment and employment discrimination are just a
few examples of issues in which these patterns have been visible. Other
examples include media images of women and political leadership training.
In contrast, when the issue involves a question of physical violence to innocent individuals, similar approaches advocated by transnational actors are

likely to work in a broader spectrum of locations, since the norm against bodily harm is practically universal.

The diverging impact of foreign assistance on the two subsectors of NGOs is also related to the different stages of NGOs' development at the point when donors began to support them. Women's NGOs typically have received foreign funding at an earlier stage in their organizational histories than have soldiers' rights NGOs. Large amounts of foreign funding began to enter the Russian women's movement at a stage when very few NGOs existed that were acceptable to foreign donors (that is, not successor organizations to Soviet official women's organizations). As several activists complained, a flood of money entered organizations to conduct projects that transnational actors specifically requested. This relatively generous source of money, in an atmosphere of suddenly declining employment prospects for women in the early 1990s, even led to the establishment of new women's NGOs oriented specifically toward conducting foreign grant projects. To some extent, as Natalia Abubikirova and Marina Regentova of FALTA pointed out, this meant that Russian women's NGOs "didn't have time to develop their own priorities."[67]

This is certainly not true of all women's NGOs, and it is not possible to say of most longtime feminist activists in Russia that their views were inspired by the lure of foreign grants. For example, activists from Feminist Alternative (FALTA), the Feminist Orientation Center, and MCGS in Moscow, as well as the Petersburg Center for Gender Issues—all espousing openly feminist views—were active in the late 1980s, long before foreign grants became available. Their views developed largely by noticing the dramatic inequalities in Russian women's lives and later adopting a coherent approach to these personal observations through exposure to Western feminist literature.[68] Yet, as the tables in this chapter show and other authors have confirmed (Henderson, 2003; Sperling, 1999), large numbers of women's organizations have been receiving most or all of their resources from foreign grants, and foreign grant programs generally have emphasized particular kinds of objectives and themes, defined by donors themselves rather than by the needs that NGOs observe on the ground in Russia. Foreign donors have also concentrated their resources on Russian NGOs that advocate their particular viewpoints rather than on those that do not—such as NGOs that counsel unemployed women or train women for rather traditional female occupations.

In contrast, the bulk of soldiers' rights NGOs were founded earlier than independent women's NGOs, and initially, foreign donors were somewhat afraid of working with them, since the issues they dealt with concerned the Russian military and in the beginning often involved a confrontational relationship with the state. Later, foreign donors decided to direct significant support to soldiers' rights NGOs, and because they were already well established as organizations by that time, soldiers' rights NGOs managed to develop their own strategies more clearly, based on domestic rather than foreign priorities, before foreign funding became a possibility.

By no means is the intended implication of this discussion that foreign assistance should not support feminist NGOs in Russia. Foreign donors would be more successful in creating change in domestic contexts if they funded a far broader variety of NGOs in Russia, including those that do not specifically embrace a Western feminist philosophy. In order to succeed in encouraging citizen involvement in public affairs, donors should support NGOs that conduct work on problems that Russian citizens view as important. In addition, they should continue to fund NGOs that have identified problems such as sexual harassment and employment discrimination of other sorts, which are undeniably huge but relatively silent in the Russian public space. Foreign assistance in the area of domestic violence is an example of the positive influence that transnational actors can have when they support local activists in amplifying previously silent problems.

It is possible that certain undeniably severe problems that Russian women experience, such as sexual harassment, could be issues for successful NGO mobilization if they were framed not in terms of women's rights to equal (read "identical" or "same") treatment with men, but in terms of violations of a basic human right to bodily integrity. Framing discussions in terms of the rights of women to be treated as human beings, and to be free of bodily harm, is likely to be a more successful strategy than asking for them to be treated in the same way as men. The enormous general success of this normative frame—"women's human rights"—in strengthening international networks of women activists from around the world suggests that it appeals to people in a variety of cultural contexts.

Over time, as norms change in Russia with incremental NGO campaign successes, it may be possible to introduce concepts of equality and feminism. Indeed, more and more young women in Russia are learning that feminism can include a quite reasonable set of concepts with which they agree. Likewise with soldiers' rights NGOs; over time, antimilitarist ideas may become more accepted if activists blend them skillfully with opposition to instances of bodily harm. The success of the SMSP in attracting allies and volunteers, even while espousing an antimilitarist philosophy, shows that it may indeed be possible to attract supporters initially through opposition to bodily harm, and then persuade them that the root problem is excessive militarization of Russian society.

CHAPTER 4

Regional Realities: The Influence
of Local Political Environments
on Foreign Assistance Outcomes

DURING THE FIELD research for this book, interview subjects often offered their opinions on how the NGO environment in their region compared with those of other regions. Typically, they emphasized one or both of two factors: how hospitable the local levels of government were toward NGOs, and the extent of foreign assistance to NGOs in the area. As time went on and I compared locations, I began to see clearly not only that the presence of foreign donors plays a crucial role in shaping NGO development in a region, but that regional and city governments in Russia also have a fundamental impact on the success of local NGOs and the foreign donors interacting with them.

A tremendous degree of regional variation exists among local governments in Russia in all aspects of politics, and the area of NGO development proves to be no exception.[1] Some local administrations appear to perceive NGOs as helpful to them and society, and some of these are even wealthy enough to offer grants, office space, and social service contracts to NGOs. Many other governments, though, view NGOs as at least an annoyance if not an outright threat to the stability of current political leaders' careers in office.

Thus, foreign donors do not always affect NGO sectors in the same way. Their involvement in NGO development in any given region is affected dramatically by the nature of the local government. Each of the four archetypal combinations of high or low levels of foreign assistance with high or low political support for NGOs produces a local NGO sector with a particular set of characteristics. Where foreign donors are heavily involved and local government is supportive, NGOs tend to be large in number, active, and independent and to enjoy a strong sense of community. Where donors maintain a strong presence but the local government is discouraging, NGOs may be large in number, but they lack strength. Decoupling of formal statements and policies from day-to-day behavior frequently results, as organizations are forced to speak and act in one style to foreign audiences but in a different style to their inhospitable political leaders and local population.[2] Where local governments are supportive of NGOs but foreign donors are largely absent, the NGO community tends to be very small yet active, strongly networked, and effective in resolving social problems of concern in the area. Finally, where local governments are discouraging and foreign donors are also weakly involved, we can expect that the NGO community would be small, weak, and dependent on the local administration, although none of the cities of the study fell into this category.

It is important to note that the term "supportive local political environment" is intended to be a relative term that compares local governments with one another across Russia's regions. Overall, it is doubtful that one could find any level or locality of government in Russia that could be called "supportive" relative to the more positive environment for civil society that is found in many liberal, long-standing Western democracies. Even in regions that are relatively supportive, such as Moscow, Novgorod, or Izhevsk, the government is typically unwilling to allow NGOs that openly challenge the government to exist without barriers or attempts to quiet them. These hindrances to NGO development often happen in the form of "random" tax inspection visits, pressure on media sources not to cover NGO activities, or restrictive regulations on public assembly. In the most friendly cases, NGOs that are critical of the government are simply excluded from any institutionalized dialogue, if not actively punished. For example, Novgorod, classified here as the most supportive environment for NGOs among the seven cities examined, is widely known for the extent to which the regional Social Chamber for NGOs is a functioning, influential body. Yet that chamber is still chaired by the governor, and in order to become members NGOs must be officially registered—thus disliked or unregistered NGOs can be easily marginalized (Lankina, 2004, p. 158).

Of course, this regional political environment is not the sole factor influencing NGO development. As the previous chapter argued, societal norms regarding particular NGO issues also affect the impact of foreign assistance on NGO development. I do not take this interaction explicitly into account in this chapter, yet these two factors do influence the development paths of individual NGOs, either by working together to multiply positive or negative effects or by counteracting each other. Two perhaps obvious examples are that (1) an NGO pursuing societally rejected norms in a region where the political environment is negative will mobilize even less successfully than one in a relatively positive political environment, and (2) an NGO pursuing universally accepted norms will mobilize more successfully in a positive or negative political environment than one that pursues specifically Western norms in the same environment. I suspect that NGOs that pursue specifically Western norms would be even more decoupled in their behavior and discourse than those pursuing universal norms, because they are even greater misfits in their environment than are politically threatened but universal norm–promoting NGOs. But this is a question that demands more systematic future research.

Potential Determinants of Regional NGO Development

This section begins with two important socioeconomic factors that are not relatively constant across the cities: urbanization and militarization, although variations on these factors did not ultimately seem to affect NGO development. Regional political factors and foreign assistance were far more consequential in shaping local NGO communities.

We now turn to each of the studied cities in succession for a detailed picture of the background characteristics, nature of the local political environment, involvement of foreign donors, and the size and characteristics of the local NGO sector.

MOSCOW

Background Socioeconomic Factors

With a population of over ten million, Moscow is by far the largest city in Russia and the capital of government.[3] It is also the capital in most other major aspects of life. Relative to the other regions in the study, Moscow is a fairly open city for visitors and residents to enter and leave, having never been a major center of militarily sensitive production.[4] According to Soviet state figures, in 1985, just 5.7 percent of the overall Moscow labor force was employed in defense-related production.[5] This is a much lower figure than in nearly all of the other cities studied. Moscow's economic diversity also far exceeds that of other Russian cities and offers residents a multitude of employment options. The vast majority of money for the entire country flows through the capital. Moscow is also the most highly educated city in the study, although, as mentioned in Chapter One, the small variation in levels of education across the Russian cities included here is not a factor affecting NGO mobilization levels. All of these socioeconomic factors suggest that Moscow should be fertile ground for collective organization and social movements. Large city populations generally offer residents more chances to find like-minded individuals with whom to organize, and they often provide a greater sense of political freedom through anonymity. The low level of military production in Moscow also suggests fewer historical restrictions on citizen mobility.

Political Opportunity Environment

The stance of the local government toward NGOs in Moscow was relatively encouraging. Barriers confronting NGOs in their efforts to create a supportive operating environment certainly existed, and activists frequently encountered much less understanding or appreciation from the Moscow administration than they would prefer. Nonetheless, relative to most other regions in Russia, Moscow NGOs existed in a supportive political environment.

One peculiar aspect of Moscow, which it shared only with St. Petersburg, is that it is a region unto itself. Unlike all other regions, neither Moscow nor St. Petersburg has separate administrative structures for region and city. Other regions, being larger in territory, have an overall government (*krai,* oblast, republic, or autonomous oblast or *okrug*) headed by a governor or president and seated in the regional capital. In addition, they have municipal governments for each city and town, headed by mayors. Since all of my research took place in regional capitals, in most cities I was conducting research in locations where two levels of government were jockeying with each other for administrative territory. The concept of autonomous municipal government was a new one in Russia since its inception in the post-Soviet period, thus in many regional capitals considerable tension centering around turf battles existed between the city mayor and the regional head.[6] The root problem causing these conflicts in most regions was that, although municipal governments in Russia were mandated by law, the financial provisions for municipal functions were not clearly specified. The existing laws delegated many responsibilities to municipal governments—especially as concerned public services—but did not grant them sufficient budgetary powers to fulfill those responsibilities.[7] Most municipal funds came from the federal and regional budgets. Because of a lack of legislative clarity, city and regional governments were often at odds with one another concerning questions of jurisdiction and finance in various areas of public policy. This was a common outcome wherever regional capital mayors and regional governors were ambitious politicians and independent of each other. Typically, only in regions where mayors were politically dependent allies of governors (such as in Khabarovsk) did these conflicts fail to exist.

In Moscow, however, this particular tension was nonexistent, since Mayor

Yuri Luzhkov acted also as the region's de facto governor. Moscow NGO leaders often complained to me that Luzhkov's administration had its "favorite" NGOs and did not treat all organizations equally; in this way, the fused municipal and regional levels potentially played to some NGOs' disadvantage, since they could not turn to a second level of government for assistance. Yet, at least Moscow NGOs did not have to deal with the need to choose sides between two warring administrative levels, as NGOs in many other regions did.

According to social movement theory on Western political opportunity structures, this unified line of authority should be less advantageous to social activists than would a system of divided authority and multiple, independent administrative levels (Gelb, 1990, pp. 137–39).[8] However, in most cities of this study, the opposite circumstance existed. That is, where authority was divided, political activists were caught between two battling levels of government and forced to ally with one or the other. At the very least they were unable to switch back and forth freely in their appeals or to "play off" one side against another in trying to gain resources or assistance from their regional and municipal governments.

The Moscow government offered a comparatively high level of material support for local NGOs. Most notably, the regional government's Committee for Public and Interregional Relations had held an annual grants competition for NGOs since 1996. Grants were awarded for NGO projects that the judging committee deemed to be "socially meaningful" (mainly defined as projects that provide social assistance to the population, particularly "vulnerable groups"). In 1998, grants were awarded in amounts ranging roughly from 30,000 to 100,000 rubles (approximately US$4,800 to $16,100 at that time).[9] The program was growing steadily in its total budget and volume of grants awarded. In 1996, just 12 grants were awarded for NGO projects; in 1997, 38; in 1998, 55; and in 1999, over 80 (Committee on Public and Interregional Relations, 1999, p. 34).[10]

Several NGOs among those I interviewed had received grants from the city government under this formal grant competition. In line with the emphasis on social assistance projects, the grants were awarded to NGOs that provided social services and basic charity, rather than to rights-advocacy organizations. One NGO, Order of Mercy, had even received three grants to support its centers for teenagers and the unemployed.[11] Several others, however, complained that the basis upon which grant recipients were chosen was unclear to them, and some even insinuated that political loyalty to the mayor of Moscow was an implicit condition for receiving a grant.[12]

It is likely that these complaints had some basis in reality, since multiple respondents made such claims, and a bias did seem to exist in that one organization had received grants three times between 1996 and 1999, while apparently equally well-established organizations with worthwhile projects were rejected repeatedly. Nonetheless, in contrast with other regions' grant programs (in the few regions where they existed), the Moscow program was at least set up with written, formal criteria for evaluating projects and assembling the judging committee. While its decisions might not have been made entirely objectively, a wide range of organizations received grants on the basis of an openly publicized competition with prior established guidelines and without a huge amount of duplication of results from year to year.

Another material benefit that the Moscow government often provided was affordable office space for NGOs. Approximately one-quarter of the Moscow NGOs interviewed had office space that the city government (or its neighborhood divisions) had assisted them in locating, where rent was either subsidized or entirely paid for by the city. Several NGO activists from other cities, especially St. Petersburg, commented on this benefit to Moscow NGOs and stated that the Moscow mayor was much more generous in granting office space than their own city government was. For example, the leader of a St. Petersburg organization for disabled women stated that "the St. Petersburg administration is much less encouraging of disabled people's organizations than [Mayor] Luzhkov in Moscow—we have no chance to get free or subsidized office space, while in Moscow this is very common."[13]

Moreover, the conditions for awarding subsidized office space, while not set out in formal city policies, did not seem to be based on political allegiances or ties with the old Soviet *nomenklatura*, as they were in many other cities. New organizations headed by people who were completely neutral politically (such as the women's crisis centers ANNA and Syostry) as well as figures politically close to the mayor (such as Evgeniia Poplavskaia of Order of Mercy) had received such benefits. Nevertheless, the city government's procedures for granting office space and other benefits, such as assistance with publications or events, could be improved. As Eleonora Luchnikova of the city government's Committee on Public and Interregional Relations described the process in 1999, it was extremely informal and decided on the basis of each individual request, without any officially specified guidelines.[14]

The programs of the Moscow government for working with NGOs were much more sophisticated and formalized than those in many other regions. However, despite the presence of such resources, it is worth noting that several NGO leaders, in both Moscow and St. Petersburg, complained that the very size of their cities caused problems for engaging in dialogue and obtaining a response from their regional governments. Since the two cities are so large compared to other Russian cities, government officials were more distanced from ordinary constituents and often did not respond to organizations' queries. Several activists claimed that the situation for NGO-government relations in more remote provinces might, as a result, be better. For example, Irina Chernenkaia of Syostry complained that, while in Moscow there was no shelter for battered women, in several smaller cities such shelters did exist and were assisted by local governments.[15] In Novgorod, the director of a women's NGO remarked that "in Moscow they have a lot more problems with the administration—they are basically totally ignored—than we do here. It's such a huge city, so things are much worse there."[16] Olga Lipovskaia of the Petersburg Center for Gender Issues (PCGI) stated that the situation for women's activism was better in several regions than in Moscow, partly "because it's easier to make contact with regional government—power is simply closer there. In Leningrad Oblast, for example, several women's organizations have managed to get support, office space, et cetera, which is almost impossible in the huge cities."[17] Tatiana Matveeva of the League of Women Voters in St. Petersburg similarly noted that "[w]e have a huge city of course; the city is like a country, and in order to reach the leaders in such a city, you need to use tough measures."[18]

Exposure to Foreign Assistance

Moscow is unquestionably the city in which domestic NGOs have the greatest amount of contact with and access to transnational actors, in terms of both foreign donors who are directly involved in NGO development and transnational actors who are merely present as indirect potential influences on Russian activists. Most foreign businesses and diplomatic representatives, in addition to foreign donor organizations, are based in Moscow. Moscow is also the best physically situated city in the sample for transnational contact. With a large international airport served by many foreign airlines, travel to and from Moscow from overseas is relatively easy.

Statistics from the study sample confirmed this overall impression of high levels of foreign assistance. For example, 64 percent of the NGOs I interviewed received the majority of their funding from foreign grants, higher than in any other city in the study (see Table 4.1). Moscow NGOs also experienced high levels of nongrant types of transnational interactions, such as overseas travel, participation in seminars hosted by donors, and membership in international organizations (see Table 4.2).[19] However, it is important to note that Moscow did not consistently measure highest on these nonmonetary forms of interaction.

Appendix 4 lists the foreign granting organizations, nongranting technical assistance organizations, and foreign NGOs with which interview subjects had interacted directly in each city. This list shows how much richer the foreign assistance environment was for Moscow NGOs in terms of funding

TABLE 4.1. NGO funding sources, by region.

NUMBER OF NGOS IN REGION

City	Exclusively foreign	Frequently foreign	Primarily foreign	Exclusively domestic	No funding	Occasionally or infrequently foreign	Little or no foreign	Total
Moscow	8	10	18	3	1	6	10	28
St. Petersburg	4	5	9	5	4	4	13	22
Ekaterinburg	1	3	4	5	0	2	7	11
Izhevsk	0	1	1	7	1	2	10	11
Vladivostok	1	1	2	3	0	2	5	7
Khabarovsk	1	0	1	1	0	4	5	6
Novgorod	1	2	3	1	0	2	3	6
TOTAL			38				53	91

PERCENTAGE OF NGOS IN REGION

City	Exclusively foreign	Frequently foreign	Primarily foreign	Exclusively domestic	No funding	Occasionally or infrequently foreign	Little or no foreign	Total
Moscow	29%	36%	64%	11%	4%	21%	36%	100%
St. Petersburg	18%	23%	41%	23%	18%	18%	59%	100%
Ekaterinburg	9%	27%	36%	45%	0%	18%	64%	100%
Izhevsk	0%	9%	9%	64%	9%	18%	91%	100%
Vladivostok	14%	14%	29%	43%	0%	29%	71%	100%
Khabarovsk	17%	0%	17%	17%	0%	67%	83%	100%
Novgorod	17%	33%	50%	17%	0%	33%	50%	100%
TOTAL	15%	20%	35%	31%	4%	29%	65%	100%

TABLE 4.2. Nongrant transnational interactions, by region.

	N of location	Foreign donor–sponsored training seminars		Visits and information exchanges with transnational organizations		Membership in transnational organizations		Submission of cases or reports to transnational organizations	
Moscow	28	16	57%	6	21%	3	11%	1	4%
St. Petersburg	22	9	41%	11	50%	0	0%	1	5%
Ekaterinburg	11	4	36%	2	18%	1	9%	1	9%
Izhevsk	11	3	27%	3	27%	1	9%	0	0%
Vladivostok	7	5	71%	0	0%	1	14%	0	0%
Khabarovsk	6	4	67%	3	50%	0	0%	1	17%
Novgorod	6	4	67%	3	50%	0	0%	1	17%
Total NGOs in column/ overall percentage	91	45	49%	28	31%	6	7%	5	5%

opportunities. Moscow NGOs in the sample had received funding from a far more diverse set of foreign donors than NGOs in any other city. A further advantage that the Moscow NGOs possessed was that a large number of the donors with which they had interacted had offices located directly in Moscow; for NGOs in other cities, this convenience of having donor offices within their own cities was far less common. The closest competitor to Moscow along these lines was St. Petersburg.

ST. PETERSBURG

Background Socioeconomic Factors

St. Petersburg is just under half the size of Moscow, with a population of 4.7 million, and has an economic history of being much poorer. Some activists even attribute the political activism of Petersburgers, traditionally more liberal and radical than Muscovites, to the physical resource deprivation experienced in St. Petersburg relative to Moscow. Back in 1981, in their *samizdat* journal, members of the dissident women's organization Maria (whose efforts were quickly quashed by Soviet authorities) considered why a women's dissident movement began in Leningrad and not elsewhere. One reason they noted was that "in Leningrad, the life of dissident families differs dramatically from Moscow life. This is a city of poverty and unsettled life. Women have a double burden placed on them—the burden of the fight for freedom and the everyday, exhausting worry over our daily bread" (*Maria*, 1981, p. 24). More recently, in 1999, Olga Lipovskaia of PCGI stated similarly that, in addition to other reasons, the Petersburg women's movement is more politically active than the Moscow women's movement because "the situation in Moscow economically is better, so there is no political demand for activism—people are not agitated enough."[20]

It is difficult to say for certain how much of this explanation is credible and how much is simply a defensive reflex that Petersburgers habitually express in comparing themselves with Muscovites. Nonetheless, it is worth keeping in mind that the relative poverty of St. Petersburg compared to Moscow, and people's awareness of that difference, may have contributed historically to more active political agitation on the part of St. Petersburg residents.

While these factors may encourage civic activism on the part of Petersburgers, we should expect the extent of secret military production in the city to discourage citizens from independent activism, relative to Moscow citizens. The concentration of workforce employment in the defense industry in St. Petersburg was approximately double that of the Moscow workforce: 11.9 percent of the labor force in the mid-1980s, according to Soviet sources. However, as we shall see, the extent of military production in St. Petersburg appears not to have affected its residents' activism in the least.

Political Opportunity Environment

Despite St. Petersburg's status as the second-largest city in Russia and the "European" and artistic capital of the country, a comparison between its regional government's treatment of NGOs and the situations in other regions did not reveal a particularly supportive political opportunity environment. The comments of NGO activists in St. Petersburg concerning regional politics and government confirmed this assessment.

In contrast to the Moscow city government, the St. Petersburg administration did not offer any financial resources to NGOs. There was no grant program for NGOs, and although for some years there was a budget allocation of funds for NGO participation in city events (such as festivals and holidays), those funds were removed from the city budget in 1999.[21]

Moreover, the St. Petersburg administration was far less generous than the Moscow administration or many other local governments in terms of granting office space to NGOs. In St. Petersburg, by all accounts, free or subsidized office space was a rare and extremely selective benefit from the regional government. Olga Lipovskaia of PCGI argued that the basis for receiving free office space in the city was membership in the old "club" of Soviet *nomenklatura* organizations, such as *zhensovety* or other organizations headed by former Communist officials.[22] Administration officials maintained that the City Property Committee always considered NGOs' requests for rent reductions or allocation of free office space.[23] In practice, however, very few of the organizations I encountered had received any help from the administration, and several had been rejected when they requested assistance. One interview subject, Natalia Khodyreva of the St. Petersburg Psychological Crisis Center, stated that she had to locate commercial-rate office space for her organization, although the administration stated that regulations for city property required that NGOs be charged lower rental rates than commercial organizations.[24]

According to the director of the city's Committee on Press and Public Relations, which was the chief administrative body responsible for relations with NGOs, the role of the committee was mainly to coordinate with NGOs that participated in large, organized, citywide events. The committee also worked with the region's substantive committees and territorial administrations (of each city *okrug*), most of which had some form of regular roundtable or council that included local NGOs.[25] For example, the region's Committee on Social Protection and Committee on Family and Youth were the main committees that worked with women's NGOs.

According to the city administration, in 1998 the Committee on Press and Public Relations founded the Petersburg Citizen Forum and Citizen Council. Under the auspices of this body, two hundred NGO representatives

held a one-day meeting with Governor Yakovlev and other regional officials
at which they discussed potential forms of cooperation between the administration and NGOs. Beyond that, the city had not organized regular forums
for including NGOs in dialogue at an administrationwide level.[26] None of
the NGO activists I encountered mentioned having attended this forum;
indeed, only three of the NGOs whose representatives I interviewed appeared on the committee's list of NGOs with which the administration
maintained contact. Two of these were organizations headed by individuals
that several interview subjects identified as prominent *nomenklatura* officials
from the Soviet regime.[27]

Exposure to Foreign Assistance

Among the cities studied, St. Petersburg had the second-highest number
of foreign donor offices. It also ranked second in the number of transnational
actors that NGOs had received funding or training from, held memberships
in, or shared information with. In terms of the proportion of NGOs that had
received foreign assistance, St. Petersburg also scored highly. It took second
place in the proportion of NGOs that received the majority of their funding from foreign donors and in the number of activists who had traveled
overseas; but it scored lower than several smaller cities in the sample with
regard to the frequency of training sessions with transnational actors (see
Tables 4.1, 4.2, and 4.3).

St. Petersburg is also easily entered and exited via direct international
flights, although not to the same degree as Moscow. The city is geographi-
cally very close to Northern European countries and thus hosts consulates of
Finland, the Netherlands, Denmark, Sweden, and other countries. Nonetheless, I was surprised to discover that Scandinavian and other European organizations were less active in St. Petersburg than I had expected. Where they
might have claimed the northwestern region of Russia as a region of especially strong interest for NGO development efforts, in fact the U.S. government was just as dominant within the foreign donor community in St.
Petersburg as it was in Moscow (see Appendix 4).

EKATERINBURG

Background Socioeconomic Factors

Ekaterinburg is the fifth-largest city in Russia, with a population of 1.3
million. Like many other cities located in the Urals area of Russia, it was a site
of heavy military production during the Soviet era. According to 1985 statistics, 15.4 percent of the labor force in the Sverdlovsk Oblast region in
which Ekaterinburg sits was employed in military production.[28] This makes
it the region with the second-highest concentration of military industrial

TABLE 4.3. NGO travel and grants combinations, by region.

City	N of location	No grants, no travel		Grant recipients, no travel		Grant recipients plus travel		Travel, no grants	
Moscow	28	0	0%	1	4%	23	82%	4	14%
St. Petersburg	22	4	18%	0	0%	13	59%	5	23%
Ekaterinburg	11	2	18%	1	9%	5	45%	3	27%
Izhevsk	11	4	36%	0	0%	3	27%	4	36%
Vladivostok	7	1	14%	1	14%	3	43%	2	29%
Khabarovsk	6	0	0%	0	0%	5	83%	1	17%
Novgorod	6	1	17%	1	17%	4	67%	0	0%
Total number of NGOs in column / overall percentage	91	12	13%	4	4%	56	62%	19	21%

workers, next to Izhevsk, which is also located near the Urals. Unlike Moscow and St. Petersburg, the city was closed to entry by foreigners until 1991. In theory, the high number of people employed in sensitive military production should suppress the activism of Ekaterinburg residents. As we shall see later in the discussion on NGO development levels, this did not seem to be the case.

Political Opportunity Environment

The overall level of support for the NGO community from local government in Ekaterinburg can be described as approaching that of Moscow. It was the only city aside from Moscow in this study that had a municipal NGO grants competition. Founded in 2000, the competition was quite new at the time of the field study, and its future funding was uncertain. Nevertheless, the program structure was developed with the input of local NGOs, including the organization Good Will (*Dobraia volia*), which was well known as a provider of a great deal of training and funding information to local NGOs. The annual grant competition was designed to have thirteen judges, including representatives of NGOs, and to focus on two or three different issue areas each year.

Occasionally, the city administration also contracted out programs to local NGOs. However, the process of granting these contracts was less formal and transparent than the grant competitions. In addition, according to the head of the city's Division for Relations with NGOs and Religious Organizations, Maia Mikhailova, social contracting was plagued by two problems: a lack of city finances and a lack of NGOs that had the expertise and capacity to manage municipal programs.[29]

The city rarely granted office space directly to NGOs. According to Mikhailova, the administration had only one small room in city hall, which fifteen NGOs shared by dividing up their work periods. Two of the NGOs whose representatives I interviewed, the local Committee of Soldiers' Mothers and the Association of Victims of Political Repression, were among those sharing the small room. In addition, other institutions that were financed and managed by the city administration sometimes granted free office space to local NGOs. For example, the head of the city library granted office space to the Ekaterina Crisis Center for Women in three of its branches in different neighborhoods of the city.[30]

With Ekaterinburg, we see a structure of levels of government that is more typical for Russia than that in Moscow and St. Petersburg. Ekaterinburg NGOs deal with two separate levels of local government: regional and municipal. As in many other regions, relations between the municipal and regional levels of government in Ekaterinburg were tense. Most NGOs and government officials at both city and regional levels noted that there was a high degree of conflict between the two levels of government.

Sometimes this conflict led to considerable pressure on NGOs to side with and support either the oblast governor, Eduard Rossel, or the city mayor, Arkadii Chernetskii. Occasionally, NGOs were encouraged to support either the governor or the mayor publicly, with the promise of favors such as office space or funding in return.[31] In a situation where most NGOs were nascent and weak, the political battles were difficult to avoid. Nadezhda Golubkova of the Ekaterina Women's Center stated that "the women's movement is just getting on its feet, [and] the problem is that, thus far, these organizations have not been able to stand on their feet independently, in order to conduct themselves as an independent political force."[32] Those who refused to be drawn into political battles felt that they were excluded from dialogue with government as a result, and those who cooperated with one level of government were effectively precluded from any consideration by the other level.

I found only one NGO leader who had managed to work well with both the city and oblast administrations. This was Vera Samsonova of the Regional Foundation for Support of Women in Business. As she described it, her success in forging cooperation with both levels of government was a surprise to many other NGO leaders: "People often say to me: 'How can it be? You work with one and you also work with the other?' But in our founding documents, it's written that we don't engage in politics; we engage in concrete actions . . . And now we have achieved this . . . Maybe this isn't modest, but what we have done as a foundation is to unite representatives of the oblast and city."[33]

The Sverdlovsk oblast administration, according to my own criteria and the assessments of most local NGOs, was less supportive of the Ekaterinburg NGO community than the city administration. According to Marina Chashchina of the Sverdlovsk Oblast Department for Public Relations, the oblast provided no financial assistance to NGOs and no office space. Instead, the role of the oblast department, in her words, was to "coordinate" the work of NGOs: helping them to organize events, providing them with information, and attracting media attention to the work of NGOs.[34] Despite this less proactive role of the oblast administration with NGOs, there were some NGO leaders who praised members of the administration for taking NGOs fairly seriously.[35]

The oblast administration did sometimes contract out social programs to NGOs. The first contract to be publicly announced was awarded to the Urals Association of Women (UAW), the most prominent and politically influential women's organization in Ekaterinburg since its founding in late 1993. With great fanfare in 1996, the president of the UAW, Galina Karelova, concluded an agreement with Governor Rossel concerning "social partnership" between

the UAW and the oblast.[36] This provided a mechanism for the UAW to receive government contracts to carry out government-funded social programs
and set a precedent for a number of other NGOs in the oblast to conclude
such agreements. The UAW had carried out a number of government contracts, such as children's summer camps, on the basis of that agreement.[37]

While this was a good development for the local NGO community on
the face of things, the process of granting social contracts and concluding
social partnership agreements was a selective one. Many of the UAW leaders
were extraordinarily close to the oblast government; in fact, a leading member of the UAW Council worked as a top official in the oblast Public Relations Department, and the vice-president of the UAW also worked in the
oblast administration.[38] Social contracting was rare because many officials in
the city and regional governments were still suspicious of NGOs, and funding for the social programs that might potentially be contracted out for the
social programs was sparse. As a result, social contracts tended to be granted
on a very selective basis, without any transparent decision process.

A positive aspect of the NGO environment in Ekaterinburg was the presence of some government officials who supported the idea of NGO development. Especially in the city administration, Maia Mikhailova tried to forge
constructive relations with a variety of local NGOs and to find ways for the
government to encourage NGO development. She initiated the city's grant
program for NGOs and solicited the input of prominent local organizations
in planning the program. Several interview subjects praised the city administration for acting honestly to improve the working environment of
Ekaterinburg NGOs. Nadezhda Golubkova of the Ekaterina Women's Center stated that "[w]e are lucky with the city administration," and that, with
regard to the idea of forming a crisis center for women, the city "supported
the idea from the very beginning."[39] Even a leader of the Ekaterinburg division of Memorial, which focuses mainly on human rights issues, stated in
1998 that she had recently begun to cooperate with the city administration;
such positive relations with government are not often found in Memorial's
human rights divisions.[40] The head of a local NGO that specialized in third-
sector development and NGO training stated that she is in contact with the
city administration practically every day on questions of improving the local
working environment for NGOs.[41] Indeed, as shown in Table 4.4, NGOs in
Ekaterinburg expressed relatively positive assessments of their relationships
with local and regional levels of government, compared to NGOs in other
regions. Only Izhevsk (and, stragnely, Vladivostok) NGOs felt more positive
about their relations with local levels of government.

The statements that Mikhailova made concerning the roles of NGOs suggested that the city administration viewed them as partners of government

TABLE 4.4. NGO evaluations of overall relations with regional and local governments, by region.

City	Negative		Positive		Mixed		Total*
Moscow	5	36%	2	14%	7	50%	14
St. Petersburg	5	36%	3	21%	6	43%	14
Ekaterinburg	1	14%	4	57%	2	29%	7
Izhevsk	2	25%	5	63%	1	13%	8
Vladivostok	1	20%	3	60%	1	20%	5
Khabarovsk	1	17%	3	50%	2	33%	6
Novgorod	0	0%	2	33%	4	67%	6
Total number of NGOs with this impression	15		22		23		60
Overall percentage of NGOs with this impression	25%		37%		38%		

*Totals include only those 60 NGOs from the study whose members commented on this topic.

rather than subordinates, and she admitted that "activists (*obshchestvenniki*) often know a lot more about their issue than state officials do." Nonetheless, her view of the ultimate necessity of NGOs seemed to be limited to the idea that their role is to carry out social functions in areas where the state does not manage to fulfill them; in other words, NGOs were seen as supplemental social service providers rather than as organizations that might fulfill other kinds of valuable civic or political roles.[42]

Exposure to Foreign Assistance

Although a number of foreign technical assistance organizations and foreign consulates were located in Ekaterinburg, the city had experienced relatively low contact with foreign donors working on NGO development, given the size of the city. Ekaterinburg was also once a greater center of attention for foreign donors than it was by the late 1990s. Several foreign donors, such as the Eurasia Foundation and NDI, focused considerable attention on Ekaterinburg in granting and training programs in the early to mid-1990s. However, toward the end of the decade, some organizations began to withdraw from Ekaterinburg, with the feeling that the city's NGO community had already been "saturated" with assistance.[43] The Eurasia Foundation ceased maintaining a representative there in 1998.

Ekaterinburg fell fourth in the list of cities, below Novgorod, in the level of foreign funding among NGOs (see Table 4.1). Just over one-third of Ekaterinburg NGOs in the sample had received the majority of their funding from foreign donors. The same proportion had attended foreign donors' seminars at some point. Only small minorities of NGOs had experienced other forms of transnational interactions, including travel overseas. NGOs in Ekaterinburg had also interacted with fewer transnational actors than had NGOs in the much smaller city of Khabarovsk (see Appendix 4). International travel to Ekaterinburg was much more limited, expensive, and inconvenient than travel to Moscow or St. Petersburg. In short, the Ekaterinburg NGO community had experienced relatively low levels of exposure to foreign assistance and travel overseas, especially considering the size of the city, compared to NGOs in several much smaller cities in the study, namely, Vladivostok, Khabarovsk, and Novgorod.

IZHEVSK

Background Socioeconomic Factors

With Izhevsk, we leave the country's larger cities and enter the truly provincial cities of Russia. Izhevsk, situated in the autonomous republic of Udmurtia, has a population of approximately 632,000 residents, which makes it similar in size to the far eastern cities of Khabarovsk and Vladivostok.

Izhevsk had the honor of being the most closed city among the locations in the study. A home to arms production since the eighteenth century, Izhevsk is also the birthplace of the Kalashnikov automatic rifle and a center for various forms of military production, including telemetry systems, rockets, and small arms. At the beginning of the 1990s, the military industry, which made up a quarter of Udmurtia's industrial complex, produced about 80 percent of the republic's GDP (EastWest Institute, 2000a). Official statistics from 1995 claimed that 24.9 percent of the labor force in Udmurtia was employed in defense-related industry; this is significantly higher than the figure for the next-highest military production region in the study, Sverdlovsk Oblast (Ekaterinburg). The city was not opened to foreigners until 1992, which was earlier than Vladivostok's opening; however, restrictions on entry and exit to and from the city remained stricter in Izhevsk than in the other cities of the study. During various periods over the ensuing years, foreigners have been required to obtain special permission from the regional government to enter the republic (in addition to a regular Russian visa).

We should expect, given what we know about these socioeconomic factors, that the level of closedness in Izhevsk would suppress levels of nongovernmental activism in the region. However, there was little evidence that NGO activities were threatened or suppressed by military enterprise managers or the regional administration. Instead, the main impact of Izhevsk's historic closed status to the outside world was that its NGO community had experienced very little transnational exposure. Because of the difficulties for foreigners to travel in Udmurtia, as well as Izhevsk's small size, Izhevsk

NGOs had the lowest levels of interaction with foreign donors among the seven cities of the study.

Political Opportunity Environment

In Izhevsk, as in Ekaterinburg, a serious rivalry prevailed between the city mayor and the head of the region concerning powers and budgetary allocations.[44] The conflict was long-standing, and the president of the republic, Aleksandr Volkov, was one of the first Russian regional leaders to challenge the authority of local governments in court. Volkov lost that battle in a 1997 Constitutional Court decision, but a standoff remained between the municipal and regional governments over division of powers and budgetary resources.

As in Ekaterinburg, this conflict between the two levels of subnational government in the region contributed to some problems in the NGO community. Two of the major local women's organizations did not get along well with one another. The leader of the republic-level *zhensovet,* Zoia Stepnova, was dependent on Volkov, while the leaders of the Regional Division of the Women of Russia Movement were somewhat more sympathetic to the mayor, Anatolii Saltykov. The two organizations refused to work with one another on local projects, despite efforts by the city's Committee on Family, Women's, and Children's Affairs to bring about cooperation among women's NGOs.[45] Yet this friction between the two organizations was not completely a result of the conflict between the municipal and regional governments. It was also rooted in personal political rivalries between NGO leaders and the rift that occurred between Alevtina Fedulova's Union of Russian Women—the national umbrella organization of Russia's *zhensovet* structure—and Ekaterina Lakhova's Women of Russia Movement at the federal level. A consequence of this conflict in Moscow was poor relations between the regional divisions of these organizations.[46]

Despite the conflict between the municipal and regional administrations, and the fact that the local government did not offer any grants and rarely offered social contracts to NGOs, NGO leaders I interviewed in Izhevsk were relatively satisfied with how they were treated by local government structures—particularly the city, more than the republic-level administration (see Table 4.4). Women's organizations felt an especially close alliance with the Izhevsk city administration's Committee on Family, Women's, and Children's Affairs.[47] The committee, headed by Galina Shamshurina, had played a key role in founding a municipal crisis center for women and children together with local activists and devoted a considerable amount of funding to its maintenance. It had also organized a number of conferences and seminars together with Izhevsk NGOs over the years on topics such as women in business, family violence, and drug abuse.[48] One sign of the committee's openness to dialogue with NGOs was that it subscribed to informational materials from several women's NGOs in Moscow, including the ICIWF and the "East-West" Women's Innovation Fund, an NGO that publishes a journal on women's activism (*Zhenshchina-Plus*) and feminist thought as well as maintaining an extensive website for the women's movement.

The office space situation for NGOs in Izhevsk compared favorably to the situations in other cities of the study. A majority of the NGOs interviewed had been allocated office space by the city or oblast administration, while several others had obtained space from local factories, institutes, or businesspeople. Only two organizations had no office space, and none paid with its own funds for office rent.

In Izhevsk, even the local Committee of Soldiers' Mothers (CSM) had relatively amicable relations with the city and republic governments, compared to many soldiers' rights organizations elsewhere, including Moscow, St. Petersburg, and Khabarovsk. While the Izhevsk CSM was not one of the most radical antimilitary CSMs in Russia, it also was not a state-formed "twin committee" (see Chapter Three). It was a member of the Russia-wide Committee of Soldiers' Mothers of Russia and worked to assist draftees with legal means of avoiding conscription. Yet the Izhevsk CSM reported that it had constructive relations with both the city and republic governments and that it had members sitting on the military draft committees of each *raion* in the city.

On the whole, interview subjects tended to be less enthusiastic about and more suspicious of the republic administration than they were of the city administration. A recent development that concerned many local NGO activists was the regional administration's attempt to organize a social chamber *(obshchestvennaia palata)* of Udmurt NGOs. The reaction of several activists—including the appointed press secretary of the Congress!—was that this was an initiative from above, designed to rally public support for Volkov prior to elections in 2000, which was destined to fail since serious activists recognized its flaws.[49] Others were also suspicious but thought that NGOs should take part in the project anyway, since this was an opportunity to create a constructive dialogue with the administration.[50]

Exposure to Foreign Assistance

Izhevsk was the least transnationally linked of all of the cities in the study. Since it was closed as a militarily sensitive city in Soviet times, and still maintained entry restrictions on foreigners, it experienced late and weak exposure to transnational actors, compared to the other regions.

Only one foreign donor had a representative stationed in Izhevsk. In 1997, the Open Society Institute (OSI) appointed a local resident as a regional coordinator to represent OSI's grant programs as well as to manage a

Soros-funded Internet center at the local university. Other than this, a few organizations that had access to communications with foreign donors and other NGOs around Russia had learned about grant programs offered by other foreign donors, such as IREX and TACIS, and received grants from such organizations. Occasionally, Western organizations had rotated through Izhevsk, offering short training programs. For example, the U.S. organization CEDPA (Center for Development and Population Activities) had conducted training programs for women's NGOs that were interested in reproductive health.[51] Eurasia and NDI jointly funded a seminar program run by the National Peace Foundation for women leaders in 1995.[52] Some academic women leaders maintained contacts with universities in Europe and North America.[53] Yet compared with the other cities in the study, most of the NGO community had rare contacts with foreign donors and other transnational actors, if any at all.

The overall statistics on the Izhevsk NGO interview subjects speak for themselves. Only one NGO was primarily foreign funded, while 73 percent had no experience with foreign funding. Moreover, over one-third of the interview subjects in Izhevsk had neither traveled overseas nor received foreign funding (see Table 4.4). This was the largest proportion of transnationally isolated NGO leaders among all of the cities in the study.

VLADIVOSTOK

Background Socioeconomic Factors

Vladivostok is roughly the same size as Izhevsk, with a population of 592,000. It is a major port city and headquarters to the Russian Pacific Naval Fleet. Despite its historic importance as a port, the city's infrastructure and economy are suffering heavily from declining military budgets, corruption, and strong economic competition from neighboring China.

The city was closed to foreign visitors until 1994, due to its strategic importance as naval fleet headquarters and the nearby location of a large contingent of nuclear submarines. Vladivostok was the last city to open among all of those included in the study; however, after it opened, foreign donors entered the city in force.

Political Opportunity Environment

With Vladivostok, as well as Khabarovsk, we see cases of poor political opportunity environments for NGOs. But one advantage for NGOs in Vladivostok, compared to Khabarovsk, was the presence of some institutions in the regional government that were potential avenues of NGO-government dialogue.

First, there was in fact a government division responsible for working with NGOs: the Division for Relations with Public Organizations within the *krai* administration. The head of this division, like many counterparts in other regional administrations, perceived her role as one of "coordinating" NGOs. The division did organize seminars and conferences for discussions on various topics with regional NGOs, and these sometimes included foreign assistance organizations such as Initiative for Social Action and Renewal (ISAR).

The division head, Tatiana Filonova, was particularly involved in communicating with women's organizations, partly because of the interest of a federal Duma deputy from Vladivostok, Svetlana Goriacheva, who was also the head of the Duma Committee on Women, Family, and Youth. Goriacheva had been active in trying to encourage women's organizations to work on many of the social problems that affected women and children in the region, and according to Filonova, wanted Primorskii Krai to be a "pilot region" in terms of grassroots initiatives by women's organizations for improving women's social status.[54] The *krai* administration also organized a Coordinating Council of women's organizations, aimed at increasing cooperation among women's NGOs on various social issues in the region.

Yet Filonova's division possessed very minimal material resources for NGOs. Only occasionally did the *krai* administration grant office space for NGOs. The only two NGOs that I encountered with government-provided office space in Vladivostok were the *krai* and city *zhensovety*—two former Soviet monopoly organizations that nearly everywhere in Russia occupy government-furnished office space, since they have always possessed this privilege. The rest of the NGOs I interviewed in Vladivostok either had no office space or had located it on their own and paid for it themselves.

Several NGOs complained that the regional administration favored certain politically loyal organizations, such as the *krai zhensovet*, and refused to listen to those NGOs that sought to work as autonomous actors in society. They also complained that the *krai* administration had no idea how to treat NGOs as partners in a democratic society. Instead, some activists argued, the government tended to treat them as subordinate service providers.[55] According to one activist in a women's NGO, officials in the *krai* administration still followed a Soviet-style approach to NGOs:

> They treat us as in the old days. Although we want different relations with them already as NGOs, their perspective hasn't changed . . . The mechanism for working with the people is that they work with those they already know and don't seek further contacts . . . They are used to the past environment, when only one organization existed. The administration wants NGOs to work only on social problems— providing services to the needy—not on politicized questions.[56]

Certainly, the general political context in Primorskii Krai was not conducive to a transparent and constructive working environment for NGOs.

Since 1994, the region had been plagued with bitter political battles, involving four changes of the city's mayor, due to an ongoing conflict between the longtime regional governor, Evgenii Nazdratenko, and an intermittent mayor, Viktor Cherepkov. Multiple lawsuits, invalid mayoral elections, and political maneuverings resulted in Cherepkov being removed by the governor in 1994, being reappointed by President Yeltsin in 1996, and resigning in 1998. Between these interludes and afterwards, other mayors presided over the city. In February 2001, as allegations of corruption and widespread anger grew over yet another sharp energy crisis during the previous winter, Governor Nazdratenko resigned, responding to the federal government's "carrot" of a powerful and lucrative government post in Moscow. Throughout the 1990s, the government was so transient and unstable that several NGO activists commented that they had difficulty maintaining contacts in government to whom they could turn for discussions on various issues.[57] Each time the mayor changed, they stated, almost the entire slate of officials occupying posts in the city also changed.

Exposure to Foreign Assistance

Vladivostok had a somewhat different experience with transnational actors than the other cities. In the Soviet and initial post-Soviet periods, it experienced very little contact with foreigners, since it was a closed city until 1994. Yet when Vladivostok opened up to foreigners, Pacific Rim countries expressed great interest in doing business in the Russian Far East (RFE). Large numbers of Asian visitors began to enter the city, and businesspeople from the west coast of North America also became interested in the region. In addition to pursuing commercial interests, the U.S. government expressed a willingness to channel a considerable amount of foreign assistance into the RFE. Vladivostok, as the largest city and major port, received the largest portion of assistance, including that targeted for NGO development.

As a result, several USAID-funded donors set up programs based in Vladivostok. They include IREX, ISAR, and the Eurasia Foundation—all of which provided grants and/or exchange opportunities for Russian NGOs. The American NGO Project Harmony, which provided training for Russian NGOs, also had a representative in Vladivostok, as did OSI. In reality, the domestic NGO community in Vladivostok, and in the RFE in general, was relatively small.[58] Because of this, the amount of foreign assistance funneled into the area was comparatively large. The presence of several foreign granting organizations in Vladivostok meant that even brand-new NGOs with unclear goals initially were able to obtain grant funds fairly easily, as long as they were not Soviet successor organizations such as *zhensovety*.

The NGO communities in Vladivostok and Khabarovsk had experienced similar levels of foreign funding and training interactions with donors. In both cities, although foreign funding levels were quite low—less than 30 percent of the local NGOs received most of their funding from foreign donors— nongrant forms of contact with donors were relatively high. For example, over two-thirds of the interviewed NGOs from Vladivostok and Khabarovsk had attended foreign donor–sponsored training seminars (see Table 4.2). Only Novgorod matched this high figure, and training with foreign donors in the remaining four cities' NGO communities was considerably less widespread.

KHABAROVSK

Background Socioeconomic Factors

Khabarovsk is slightly smaller than Vladivostok, a medium-sized Russian city with a population of 583,000. Unlike Vladivostok or Izhevsk, it has not traditionally been a region with heavy military production or installations, thus it has never been especially closed to outsiders, relative to other regions. While the small size of Khabarovsk relative to St. Petersburg and Moscow should lead us to expect lower levels of NGO activism in the city, low levels of military production should also provide a more positive environment for independent citizen activism. As it turned out, the lack of formal closure of the city to outsiders was not sufficient to foster a climate of citizen activism, due to a highly repressive political environment in the region.

Political Opportunity Environment

The local political opportunity environment for NGOs in Khabarovsk was one of the poorest among the cities of the study. Occasionally, the Khabarovsk Krai administration offered some material assistance to NGOs, such as office space for the local CSM and the local *Narodnyi Dom* [People's House]. In addition, it sometimes delegated social service contracts and granted contributions-in-kind to local NGOs. The Lebedushka Women's Club, for example, received a grant from the Krai Ecology Committee to organize an environmental summer camp for teenagers.[59] The CSM received significant assistance from the regional administration in terms of hotel space and a meeting venue for a conference of the Russia-wide organization Women for Life without Wars and Violence that it hosted in Khabarovsk in September 1999.[60] However, no official systematic policies were in place for granting material assistance or subcontracting social programs to NGOs in the region.

Aside from these examples of occasional material assistance, there were considerable negative aspects to the political environment for NGOs in Khabarovsk. The regional administration was well known for governing with a heavy hand that was intolerant of oppositional forces (EastWest Institute,

2001; McFaul and Petrov, 1998, p. 413). This attitude extended to NGOs, so that organizations that seriously criticized the regional governor, Viktor Ishaev, sometimes came under intense government pressure. For example, Aleksandr Bekhtold, head of the local division of For Human Rights, a Russian organization that was part of the Moscow Helsinki Group network, reported that he had suffered significant personal harm as a result of his public criticism of the governor.[61] Bekhtold stated that he was fired from his private-sector job when the governor applied pressure to the company's board of directors after a critical article by Bekhtold appeared in a local newspaper.[62] During the 1999 federal Duma election campaign, Bekhtold was working as the local representative of a nonpartisan nationwide network of NGOs monitoring the campaign, called Civil Society and Elections. He stated that he received a threatening telephone call during the campaign period from a regional government official, warning him that *krai* administration organs were closely investigating the past work of his former company with the hope of prosecuting him unless he ceased his criticism of the governor's administration.

Bekhtold's story was the most severe one I directly encountered during my research around Russia. Leaders of another well-known NGO in Khabarovsk also complained to other sources that they had come under strong pressure from the regional government to be politically loyal to the governor. *Krai* officials had apparently threatened to evict the organization from its office space during a disagreement over the alliances that would be fostered by a conference organized by the NGO.[63] For the resource-poor NGO, which could not afford to pay office rent, this was a fundamental threat. A staff member of a local NGO resource center also claimed that the regional government doled out office space and other resources based purely on personal ties and political loyalty.[64]

In terms of formal institutional mechanisms for fostering dialogue between NGOs and government, Khabarovsk was also one of the least developed among all of the regions studied. Although the regional administration had a formal committee responsible for working with NGOs, representatives of the two NGO resource centers in Khabarovsk attested to the fact that the committee in no way viewed its role as extending beyond merely registering NGOs to supporting their development and involving them in government.[65] None of the NGOs in the sample mentioned ever having received any assistance or communications from the committee.

One small, positive aspect of the political environment in Khabarovsk was that at least it was stable.[66] The mayor of the city of Khabarovsk was dependent on Governor Ishaev. The mayor at the time of the study, Pavel Filippov, was originally appointed by the governor in 1994 and was elected by popular vote only several years later.[67] The city in fact made very few independent, consequential decisions. Thus, in contrast to Izhevsk, Ekaterinburg, and much of Vladivostok's recent history, there was a virtual absence of political conflict in the city. While NGOs lacked political freedom, they existed in a fairly predictable political environment.

Strangely enough, despite the negative aspects of the political opportunity environment in both Vladivostok and Khabarovsk, half of the NGOs I interviewed in the two cities had generally positive impressions of their relationship with the state, while only two had overall negative impressions (see Table 4.4). This compared quite positively against other regions; in cities such as Moscow and St. Petersburg, NGOs were less satisfied with the political environment. I return to this puzzle of NGO satisfaction later in the chapter.

Exposure to Foreign Assistance

Even more than Ekaterinburg, Khabarovsk was a city in which foreign donors had alternated between involvement and absence. Khabarovsk was originally intended to be the main headquarters city for the U.S. government Regional Initiative (RI) program in the RFE.[68] The RI program concentrates U.S. technical assistance programs in particular locations. After a few years of focus on Khabarovsk, some U.S.-funded programs and foreign organizations vacated the city, and most Western staff of remaining foreign technical assistance organizations departed, as the U.S. government decided to shift its focus from Khabarovsk to Yuzhno-Sakhalinsk and, to some extent, Vladivostok.[69]

Because of the existence of an RI region in the RFE, U.S.-sourced assistance was much more prevalent in Khabarovsk and Vladivostok than assistance from other countries. European assistance was virtually nonexistent due to a lack of European interest in the far eastern reaches of Russia. I had anticipated that assistance from Asian countries such as Japan would likely be prominent in the region. Indeed, some cultural exchanges occurred between Russian NGOs and Asian NGOs as well as occasional humanitarian donations from Asian organizations to charity organizations in the RFE.[70] Nonetheless, the Asian contacts were far less pronounced, and overall assistance was more dominated by connections with the United States than I had expected.

While attention to Khabarovsk had been erratic, given the number of NGOs in the city and the small population of the region, foreign attention to Khabarovsk was actually relatively high in comparison with the remaining cities of the study.[71] Like NGOs in Vladivostok, Khabarovsk NGOs had been more saturated with training through seminars and overseas exchanges than with grant funds (see Tables 4.1, 4.2, and 4.3).

Yet we should keep in mind that in both Khabarovsk and Vladivostok, interactions with transnational actors have indeed been sporadic. Foreign donors tended to support short-term programs with temporary foreign representatives, and the number of transnational actors that were active in the region was far smaller than those in several western Russian cities such as Moscow, St. Petersburg, and Novgorod. One NGO resource center staff member in Khabarovsk noted that "with 30 percent of the territory and only 7 percent of the population of Russia in the Russian Far East, in reality, we don't matter [to foreign donors]."[72] The population is simply too thinly spread for donors to exert a great deal of effort in the region. But relative to the large city of Ekaterinburg and the comparably sized city of Izhevsk, levels of foreign assistance in the two eastern cities were high.

NOVGOROD

Background Socioeconomic Factors

Novgorod (known officially as Velikii Novgorod) is by far the smallest city in the study, with a population of only 240,000. It also falls in the top half of cities in the study with regard to military production levels. Novgorod exceeded St. Petersburg and fell just below Ekaterinburg in this category, with 13.8 percent of its labor force officially counted as employed in defense-related production in the 1980s.

Based on these socioeconomic factors, we might expect Novgorod to have a low potential for independent activism in civil society. Yet, surprisingly, Novgorod is renowned among Westerners and in the Russian NGO community for having an especially active NGO sector. The city is a "success story" in foreign donors' accounts of Russian NGO development. Novgorod is a showcase model for the great influence that foreign donors can exercise on NGO development if they concentrate resources intensively in a community where the local political opportunity structure is relatively encouraging.

Political Opportunity Environment

Among foreign donors involved in assistance to Russia, Novgorod oblast is known as somewhat of an oasis of progressive, market-oriented government, led by a young and popular governor, Mikhail Prusak.[73] It has a proud early history of democratic institutions often alluded to by politicians and citizens alike. Founded in 859, long before Moscow, the city was governed during its early period by a sovereign assembly of citizens, called a *veche,* rather than a king. Today, although the Prusak administration has been extremely welcoming to foreign investors and has made great progress in improving the oblast economy, the government's pro-reform approach has not extended as far to questions of democratization and civil society development.

The feeling among some observers was that the benevolent political and economic environment in Novgorod was largely due to the personality of the powerful Governor Prusak himself, and not an institutional characteristic of the region. Prusak governed with a fairly centralized hand in the region. Some feared that when a new governor came to power, the positive environment could disappear. For example, the politically active director of a women's organization in Novgorod, Nadezhda Lisitsina, lamented that "our governor is a real politician and has wanted to bring about more beneficial conditions for cooperation with the third sector, but this is purely a personal characteristic [of the governor]. It's not a system. I, for one, have real fears that as soon as the governor leaves . . . the new person who comes to power may not adopt [these practices] as a system."[74]

In terms of material support to NGOs, the regional and city governments provided little more than occasional office space. Most prominently among women's NGOs, the administration granted a very large office with several rooms to the Novgorod Women's Parliament. The city and oblast *zhensovety* have also had a one-room office directly in the oblast administration building since 1987. Just as often, though, NGOs located office space on their own, either paying rent or relying on the charity of other institutions.[75]

The administration did not give any social contracts to local NGOs, nor did it have a grant program for the local NGO sector. Dmitrii Zavedovskii, head of the administration's Division for Public Relations, which was responsible for working with NGOs, explained this as a consequence of both a lack of government funds in the difficult economic environment and a perception that most NGOs in the city were not yet organizationally ready to take on important public programs. But, he added, "no one can say we're against it—we're for [social contracting] under the condition that the majority of organizations in the social sphere have become professional enough."[76]

In fact, Zavedovskii seemed to be well educated concerning the NGO sphere in Novgorod and earnestly interested in its development, despite the fact that he had very few material resources to assist NGOs. He had a good relationship with the local nongovernmental NGO resource center and often attended its events. Several NGO activists spoke favorably about the regional administration's general attitude toward them. Roman Zolin, director of the Novgorod NGO Support Center, stated that "our relations with the regional administration are much better than in neighboring regions, and they're getting better over time."[77] Yet Zolin pointed out that the governor had only a partial love of NGOs, limited to the fact that he loved foreign investment in the region, and funding for NGO development is a constant part of Western donors' investments.

One bright spot in NGO-government relations in the region was the existence of a definite institutionalized channel for NGO input into public policy. There is a regional Social Chamber (*obshchestvennaia palata*) for NGOs in Novgorod that, unlike in many regions, actually works to include the voices of active NGOs in public policy. In fact, regional law requires that before legislation can be considered by the regional Duma, it must first be reviewed by the Social Chamber. According to Nicolai Petro, who has written extensively on Novgorod politics, chamber meetings are well attended by a wide variety of NGOs, the agenda is easily modified by attendees, and chamber rules require documentation of minority opinions (2004, p. 46). A number of activists who could not in any way be classified as loyalists to the regional government commented that the Social Chamber is an active and effective means of dialogue with government.[78] Irina Urtaeva, head of the Novgorod Women's Parliament, stated that one victory of the Social Chamber was that the regional government adopted wholesale its proposed program on entrepreneurship as a statement of government principle. The program proposed by the Social Chamber included a section on assisting women in business.[79] As mentioned earlier, however, NGOs must be officially registered with the state in order to participate in the Social Chamber.

Generally, local activists' assessments of the regional and city governments' treatment of NGOs were either positive or that "at least they don't bother us."[80] In the smaller city of Staraia Russa within the oblast, a two-hour bus ride away from Novgorod, women's NGOs expressed largely similar sentiments: the local municipal administration and regional government gave them positive moral encouragement, but no material assistance.[81] No one mentioned any instances of government harassment or pressure.

Exposure to Foreign Assistance

Novgorod, despite being a small city and region, had been the target of extremely intensive involvement by transnational actors, particularly from the United States. In 1997, the U.S. government, under the auspices of the Gore-Chernomyrdin Commission, announced that it had chosen Novgorod oblast to be the first region for the Regional Investment Initiative (RII, now simply RI). Along with the initial announcement of the Novgorod RII, the U.S. government–funded Eurasia Foundation was given the mandate of issuing grants to 30–39 regional NGOs within a period of eighteen months. For a capital city of only 230,000 people with few NGOs (and a total oblast population of only 738,000), this was a heavy inflow of resources.

Other transnational actors with representatives in Novgorod include OSI and IREX. OSI makes grants to NGOs, and IREX sometimes issues grants, such as in a program several years ago on domestic violence. Mostly, though, IREX's interactions with domestic NGOs involve training seminars and overseas exchanges.

These investments of foreign assistance resources were certainly confirmed in the profiles of Novgorod NGOs. Half of all interview subjects in Novgorod received their funding primarily from foreign donors, while two-thirds had attended donor-sponsored training seminars. This ranked Novgorod's NGO community near the top among the seven cities in terms of exposure to foreign assistance.

A WORD ON PERSPECTIVE

Having assessed the ways in which different local governments interacted with NGOs and the resources they offered local organizations, as well as the statements local NGO leaders made regarding their relationships with local governments, I was amazed to discover that activists in Moscow and St. Petersburg were the most frequent interview subjects to characterize their overall relations with the state as negative, or mixed and leaning toward negative, rather than positive (see Table 4.4). After all, in Moscow the local government had clearly developed the most advanced resources for NGOs among all the regions; St. Petersburg, moreover, while not as positive in its treatment of NGOs, was certainly not the least supportive of the remaining cities.

When I looked more closely at the content of statements that NGO members in different locations made, a clear tendency seemed to emerge. NGO activists in Moscow and St. Petersburg who believed that the state treated NGOs unsatisfactorily usually justified this opinion with examples in which the government had not implemented the NGOs' policy recommendations. In spite of opportunities for NGO members to discuss public policy with state bureaucrats and politicians at roundtables and conferences, NGO members had been left dissatisfied by the government's lack of follow-up. While several of these comments were directed at the federal government rather than regional governments, they point to an important pattern. For example, longtime domestic violence activists in St. Petersburg stated, "We were at the unsuccessful [federal] government hearings for a law on domestic violence. We considered and commented on every single article, and then it was killed."[82] Another crisis center leader said of the St. Petersburg administration that "Bureaucrats in the government nod their heads and say it's an important problem, but then do nothing."[83]

The coordinator of the Consortium of Women's Nongovernmental Organizations in Moscow also complained about the formalism of the state's inclusion of women's organizations:

Representatives of women's organizations are either on the Advisory Council of the Duma Committee, or are members of the governmental or presidential commissions. At the Ministry of Labor, there is a regular bimonthly roundtable, to which a large number of women's NGOs are invited. *But* not one of those organs has the power to make decisions; it is all consultative and coordinative functions. That's the first thing. The second thing is that there is not a single kopeck in the budget dedicated to improving women's status. That means that everything looks well resolved on paper, but in reality, there are practically no concrete solutions.[84]

In contrast, members of NGOs in the smaller cities seemed to be satisfied in most cases merely by the opportunity to meet and discuss policy proposals with the regional administration. They also were aware in many cases that the administration had failed to implement any of those proposals; however, they were more prone to view their overall relationship with the state as either "positive" or "mixed" rather than "negative" as a result of these interactions. One typical example is a member of the Urals Association of Women in Ekaterinburg, who assessed the organization's interactions with the regional government as very positive, on the basis of the tone of their meetings rather than policy results: "The governor relates very well to the Urals Association of Women and supports all of our initiatives. Whenever we hold some sort of hearing, we always invite the representatives of the governor, and someone always attends."[85] The *krai zhensovet* leader in Vladivostok, Zinaida Iovkova, stated similarly: "The *krai* administration supports us. The governor met personally with our *zhensovet* during the election campaign."[86]

Part of the reason for this difference in expectations indeed seems related to transnational exposure. Far more NGO activists in Moscow and St. Petersburg had been exposed to information regarding the influential role that NGOs in Western countries often play in public policy processes. Far more of them had traveled and observed this role during training excursions to the United States or Europe. Thus, their expectations were greater, and the feeling of "relative deprivation" that they experienced when officials ignored their advice was greater than that experienced by the more provincial NGO activists, many of whom had never left Russia for overseas training. Their reference point was therefore often the past; that is, the subordinate way in which Soviet and early post-Soviet regional officials typically treated citizens. For them, dialogue alone was a significant improvement.

DEVELOPING ROUGH RANKINGS

Having described each of the seven cities in turn, it is now worthwhile to see how the *independent variables* of political environment and foreign assistance related to the *dependent variable* of NGO development. On a scale from "most positive" to "most negative" political opportunity environment, how do the cities rank? And on another scale of highest to lowest levels of transnational involvement, how do they rank?

Political Opportunity Environments

In Table 4.5, I have attempted to develop a reasonably objective ranking of the seven cities' political environments. Clearly, the task of trying to judge political environments as "positive" or "negative" is fraught with dangers of bias, due to both my own biases and inadequate information as an observer, and the biases or misinformation that NGO activists in the various cities may have communicated to me during interviews. It is also important to note that, had I chosen to study other kinds of NGOs, the results concerning regional political environment could well have turned out differently. Had I targeted environmental NGOs or other human rights groups, for example, I might have found most local governments to be more negative than they were toward women's NGOs. There has been a growing trend in recent years of the central government punishing environmentalists who document nuclear contamination and human rights activists who criticize the Russian military campaign in Chechnya.[87] Increasingly, NGOs or indeed individuals that pose a direct political challenge to governments in Russia are punished in various ways (see Evans, 2005b), while NGOs that provide services without openly opposing the government are tolerated or even appreciated. Since many women's NGOs and some soldiers' rights NGOs provide services more than expressing political dissent, or lobby for change on issues like domestic violence that are not political hot-button topics, the situation I found in each region uniformly may have appeared rosier than it would from the perspective of some other types of NGOs. Indeed, the human rights groups and antimilitarist soldiers' rights groups interviewed in the study advocated a much more adversarial approach as the appropriate relationship between NGOs and the state, while the vast majority of women's NGOs expressed the proper NGO-state relationship as being one of constructive give-and-take between partners (Sundstrom, 2001, p. 245).

Although the overall appearance of local political environments might have appeared more negative had I studied more politically contentious NGOs, the rank order of regions is unlikely to have changed substantially. The point of Table 4.5 is to determine which regions were more positive relative to the others, and not to claim that a city such as Novgorod, which ranked better than all others in the study, was thoroughly supportive of NGOs in an absolute sense. The table represents a best attempt at trying to separate subjective impressions from concrete evidence of the substance of NGO-government relations in the seven cities. Although this simplifies the earlier, more nuanced narrative discussion of each region's political environment, it seemed necessary to develop indicators of political opportunity structure that could be compared across regions, given the limits of the information that could be gathered in all regions and the inevitable subjectivity of interviewees' statements.

Table 4.5 includes forms of NGO interaction with the local government, on the basis of which each city had points added to or subtracted from its score. The criteria include, first, forms of material support for NGOs. Cities were awarded points for providing office space, contributions-in-kind, social contracts, and grants to NGOs. Each of these merited one point if it existed. Next is the category of institutionalized forms of dialogue with NGOs. Of each city, I asked whether there was: (a) a "social chamber" or "council" of NGOs in the city; (b) a municipal resource center for assistance to NGOs; and (c) a formal department in the administration for working with NGOs. Each of these merited one point. Although these kinds of government-created bodies were often impotent or served only the chosen "friends" of the regional/city administration, in some cases they worked to the benefit of NGOs (for example, the Novgorod Social Chamber and the Ekaterinburg city government's Committee on Social Communications), and they certainly carried the potential to be transformed into effective mechanisms for dialogue. Moreover, in cases where there was evidence that these bodies were used to favor certain NGOs and exclude others, points awarded in this area were offset by deduction of points in the "negative" category described below.

Another category that stands alone is whether or not a number of NGOs referred to particular people as allies within the regional or city government. "Allies" did not mean personal contacts for obtaining favors according to *blat* (the Russian term for the power of personal connections), but instead people in the administration who believed in the importance of NGOs as a general principle. If yes, this asset merited three points, since conversations with NGOs indicated that having a specific influential person or persons as allies in government was a major asset in Russia. Moreover, social movement theorists of political opportunity structure have specifically mentioned allies as an important component (McAdam, 1996, p. 27). Of course, allies in Russian governmental and state structures are often temporary due to the instability of political coalitions and institutions in the current regime (Sperling, 1999, p. 115). Nonetheless, when they do exist they can assist NGOs tremendously in obtaining resources or promoting their status in governing institutions. In the cities that received points for this (Ekaterinburg, Izhevsk, and Novgorod), the allies that NGOs mentioned had held their institutional positions for several years.

Finally, we move to three "minuses"—areas of government conduct toward NGOs that were unquestionably damaging for NGO development. First, as discussed at several points earlier: Was there an open conflict between the city and regional administrations? If so, I subtracted one point from that city's

TABLE 4.5. Overview of political environments, by region.

	Definition of Measure	Moscow
Material support for NGOs? (max. points 4)	1 = office provision (1 pt.) 2 = contributions-in-kind (1 pt.) 3 = social contracting (1 pt.) 4 = grants (1 pt.)	1,2,3,4 → 4 pts.
Institutional dialogue with NGOs? (max. points 6)	1 = existence of "Social Chamber" of NGOs (1 pt.) 2 = municipal resource center for NGOs (1 pt.) 3 = formal department for NGOs (1 pt.)	1,2,3 → 3 pts.
Known existence of NGO allies in administration? (3 or 0 points)	Yes or no, expressed by NGOs interviewed	
Open conflict between city and regional administrations? (−1 or 0 points)	As stated by NGOs, media, and administrations. Not applicable in Moscow and St. Petersburg due to unique status as cities that are themselves regions.	N/A
Concrete examples of NGOs being "punished" by administrations for holding wrong positions? (−3 or 0 points)	Yes or no	
Clear that administration plays "favorites" with a few select NGOs? (−2 or 0 points)	Yes or no	Yes → −2 pts.
Total points for city		5

total. It seemed inaccurate to instead add points to those regions where there was an absence of conflict, since in Moscow and St. Petersburg this positive aspect was merely a by-product of having a unified city and regional government, rather than anything specifically laudable about the manner in which the local government conducted itself. Next: Was there evidence that NGO activists were punished by the administration for opposing government policies? If so, three points were subtracted from the city's record, since punish-

St. Petersburg	Ekaterinburg	Izhevsk	Vladivostok	Khabarovsk	Novgorod
1,3 → 2 pts.	1,2,3,4 → 4 pts.	1,2,3→ 3 pts.	1,2 → 2 pts.	1,2,3 → 3 pts.	1,2 → 2 pts.
1,3 → 2 pts.	3 → 1 pt.	1 → 1 pt.	1,3 → 2 pts.	3 → 1 pt.	1, 3 → 2 pts.
	Yes → 3 pts.	Yes → 3 pts.			Yes → 3 pts.
N/A	Yes → −1 pt.	Yes → −1 pt.	Yes → −1 pt.	No	No
			Yes → −3 pts.	Yes → −3 pts.	
Yes → −2 pts.	Yes → −2 pts.				
2	5	6	0	1	7

ment creates fears among activists that quash NGO freedom of speech and action; this has roughly the equivalent impact of having an ally in government, but in the opposite direction. Last, I asked: Were there clear instances of the administration playing favorites with a few politically loyal NGOs, while refusing to help others? If so, I subtracted two points, since favoritism for some along with a lack of rewards for others is a less oppressive, more permissive environment than one in which dissenters are actively punished.

What results is the following rank order, with 10 being the maximum potential number of points per city:

1. Novgorod (7)
2. Izhevsk (6)
3. Moscow (5)
4. Ekaterinburg (5)
5. St. Petersburg (2)
6. Khabarovsk (1)
7. Vladivostok (0)

The first feature worth noting about these scores is that none of the cities came close to scoring all 10 possible points, demonstrating that even within the range of institutional features and alliances that local political environments display in Russia, none of the cities was ideal. Moreover, Russia generally exhibits a hostile and discouraging political institutional context for NGOs, when compared with institutionalized democratic regimes. The legal barriers to NGOs, in terms of registration requirements and the absence of tax benefits for nonprofit organizations, are formal Russia-wide legislative obstacles to NGO development.[88] In addition, informal problems such as rampant government corruption, demands for loyalty as a prerequisite for NGOs to receive government assistance, and harassment of dissenting voices are aspects hampering NGOs' cooperation with government in many locations.[89]

In order to simplify the task of categorizing cities to combine the factor of political environment with foreign assistance, I divided the cities into two groups, making political opportunity environment, at its very simplest, a binary variable of "positive" or "negative." Since the cities' total points ranged from 0 to 7, I placed cities with scores of three or below in the negative category. As a result, Novgorod, Izhevsk, Moscow, and Ekaterinburg were classified as relatively positive environments for NGOs; and St. Petersburg, Khabarovsk, and Vladivostok as basically negative environments. Note that I experimented with a number of different points schemes (both in terms of points awarded for various features and institutional features included in the count) and always ended up with the same groups of cities in the positive and negative categories, although sometimes with slightly different rank orders.

Exposure to Foreign Assistance

Fortunately, it is less difficult to find uniform indicators to gauge exposure to foreign assistance. Here, I refer to several measures gleaned from the collection of interviews, such as the extent of foreign funding and training, and

TABLE 4.6. Foreign assistance exposure rankings, by region.

Percentage of NGOs with a majority of foreign funding	Percentage of NGOs that have attended foreign donor–sponsored seminars	Number of foreign assistance providers (with whom NGOs had contact), per NGOs interviewed
Moscow (64%)	Vladivostok (71%)	St. Petersburg (2.1)
Novgorod (50%)	Khabarovsk (67%)	Khabarovsk (1.9)
St. Petersburg (41%)	Novgorod (67%)	Novgorod (1.9)
Ekaterinburg (36%)	Moscow (57%)	Moscow (1.6)
Average across cities (35%)	*Average across cities* (52%)	*Average across cities* (1.5)
Vladivostok (29%)	St. Petersburg (41%)	Vladivostok (1.2)
Khabarovsk (17%)	Ekaterinburg (36%)	Izhevsk (0.85)
Izhevsk (9%)	Izhevsk (27%)	Ekaterinburg (0.76)

the diversity of foreign donors that the NGOs encountered in each of the cities. While the NGO samples in the seven cities varied somewhat in their ranks on these different indicators, a general picture did develop. At the very least, we can roughly divide the locations into two categories: NGO communities with "high" and "low" levels of foreign assistance, in order to find some patterns in types of local political environment matched with different levels of foreign assistance. The picture was in fact more complex, with a few of the cities exhibiting mid-range levels of foreign assistance. These differences are not brought out in the simple classification of high versus low exposure combined with negative versus positive political opportunity environments. I highlight the subtler differences among the regions later in the chapter in the section that explains regional NGO development patterns.

The percentages of NGOs in each city that received the majority of their funding from foreign donors (taken from Table 4.1) are shown in the first column of Table 4.6. In the second column, the cities are ranked in terms of the proportion of NGOs whose members had attended foreign donor-sponsored training seminars (shown in Table 4.2). These seminars often were led by Russian citizens—but they were paid for by foreign donors, and the seminar leaders had been trained by Western staff of foreign donor organizations. Finally, in the third column, cities are ranked according to the ratio of the total number of transnational actors who had assisted NGO interviewees to the total number of NGOs interviewed (full details on the foreign assistance providers for each region are given in Appendix 4).[90]

Why did I choose these particular measures of foreign assistance? The first two columns provide a clear indication of the sheer proportion of interviewed NGOs in each city that had interacted with foreign donors. It was easy to look at these regional proportions and use a visible natural gap to distinguish between NGO communities with high or low levels of funding and training. For the funding measure, I used as the cutoff point the average proportion of NGOs interviewed that had received the bulk of their funding from foreign donors among all of the cities. Similarly, I used the average proportion of NGOs that had attended foreign donor-sponsored training seminars in all of the cities as the cutoff point between high and low levels of foreign assistance on that measure. This seemed to be a good method of distinguishing among cities, because the proportions of transnational contact on these measures varied widely.

The third column is perhaps a less obvious measure of regional exposure to foreign assistance. Yet it is an important one, in that it gave the best available approximation of the size of the foreign assistance community involved and the diversity of transnational contacts that NGOs from each region possessed. One might ask why I did not try to count the overall number of foreign assistance providers located in a region, or to measure the ratio of all foreign assistance providers to all of the region's existing NGOs. The latter ratio would be an excellent measure to use; however, as stated in Chapter One, it was impossible to obtain accurate comparable NGO counts for each city. Moreover, it would be impossible to obtain an accurate count of all assistance providers involved in each city without interviewing all of the NGOs in the entire city. Some donors have offices in the cities; others work with Russian NGOs exclusively through their overseas offices (Appendix 4 includes these distinctions among the foreign donors encountered). Therefore, one must speak directly with Russian NGO leaders in order to obtain an accurate picture. For these reasons, it was necessary to settle for comparing the ratios of foreign assistance providers that the interviewees had encountered to the total number of NGOs interviewed. Here again, I used the average ratio among all of the cities as the cutoff point between "high" and "low" exposure to foreign assistance.

Some inconsistencies in the rankings are apparent in Table 4.6. We can say with some certainty, though, that Moscow and Novgorod had high levels of exposure to foreign assistance, since they rank in the upper tier on all three measures. Izhevsk definitely ranks low on all measures of foreign assistance. Ekaterinburg ranks low on training seminars and very low on foreign donor diversity, while it barely edges into the "high" category on funding; because of this, I rank it as having low exposure to foreign assistance overall.

Other cases are more mixed. While Khabarovsk ranks low in terms of the proportion of organizations receiving funding primarily from foreign grant programs, it ranks very high in training and diversity of foreign assistance

TABLE 4.7. Combinations of foreign assistance and local
political environment.

Local political environment	*Exposure to foreign assistance*	
	High	*Low*
Positive	Novgorod Moscow	Ekaterinburg Izhevsk
Negative	Vladivostok St. Petersburg Khabarovsk	

providers. St. Petersburg also ranks high on two of the measures—funding
and diversity of assistance—while ranking slightly low on the measure of
donor-sponsored training. Vladivostok ranks low on funding levels and
donor diversity, but it ranks extremely high on the training measure. I have
decided that if a city ranks extremely high on any ranking, as Vladivostok, St.
Petersburg, and Moscow do, it should qualify as having high levels of foreign
assistance. We are thus left with just two definite cases of low exposure to foreign assistance: Izhevsk and Ekaterinburg.

The Resulting Categories of Cities

What results from this simplified classification of cities are four basic
potential combinations of local political environment and exposure to foreign assistance. The cities here fall into only three of the four categories,
however. The category of low foreign assistance exposure and negative political opportunity environment is unrepresented among the seven cities of the
study. The next step is to see how NGO development has proceeded in each
of these combinations (see Table 4.7).

Regional NGO Development

How, then, did the cities compare with one another on the dependent variable of NGO development? Chapter One provided a list of characteristics
that I argued should be included in a measure of democracy-promoting
NGO development. These included characteristics of both individual organizations and the NGO community as a whole. Among individual NGOs, I
included the elements of well-defined goals; autonomy from state manipulation; knowledge of and communication with other NGOs; outreach to relevant public constituencies; turning to state and government institutions to

advocate improved public policy (when appropriate); and finally, material sustainability. In the NGO community overall, I included the size of the NGO community; the degree of NGO voice in public affairs and politics; and the existence of actually working NGO associations or networks. In this section, I examine each city in turn to describe the relative condition of NGO development.

The question of material sustainability of NGOs is not discussed in comparing across cities. This is because it is widely admitted in Russian NGO and donor circles that a lack of financial sustainability is rampant among NGOs throughout the country. There were some exceptions among interviewees, such as ARA in Moscow, which received a minimally sufficient stream of income from the Transnational Radical Party headquarters in Italy, based on international party member dues. ARA was receiving enough funds from that source to maintain its organizational operations, although not sufficient funds to carry out projects that require any material resources, so it sought additional grants for project work. A few NGOs had patrons in the Russian business sector that were, thus far, steady supporters. But on the whole, NGOs with steady incomes in Russia are reliant on foreign grants. The problem with this is that many donors plan to scale down their operations in Russia over the next several years (or at least claim such an intention), while the domestic granting foundation sphere is still in its infancy and focuses mostly on apolitical charity causes rather than the explicit goal of strengthening civil society. The practice of gathering membership dues or donations is extremely rare; only a handful of NGOs in the study had attempted this, and none had been successful in any significant way.

The only regional pattern that pertained to material sustainability was that in Moscow, and to a lesser extent St. Petersburg, NGOs had access to a wider variety of foreign donors, domestic foundations, and business philanthropists, and this diversified funding base potentially reduces their reliance on any single source and increases sustainability. But in Moscow, where NGOs were the most reliant on foreign funding, the mounting panic about what to do upon foreign donors' departure was the most pronounced. Thus, the sustainability situation throughout the cities was bleak.

MOSCOW

In NGO development characteristics, Moscow was once again one of the leading regions. Individual organizations in Moscow tended to be specialized and focused in their activities, and there was less of a tendency to drift from project to project on widely varying topics than in some other, smaller cities, including Khabarovsk, Vladivostok, and Novgorod. Specialized women's associations were established—of rural women, doctors, businesswomen, journalists, and lawyers, for instance—that worked almost exclusively on issues that concerned those particular constituencies. Other organizations were dedicated to a broad spectrum of issues, such as the Order of Mercy, Women of Russia Movement, the Moscow Center for Gender Studies (MCGS), Women for Life Without Wars and Violence, and Feminist Alternative (FALTA). In comparison with most other cities, the NGOs found in Moscow were focused and specialized, yet well networked within the NGO community.

The vast majority of Moscow NGOs were also clearly autonomous from the state and did not depend on the government for favors or approval. A few organizations—particularly the Union of Russian Women—were very friendly with government and largely dependent on state resources, but such organizations were exceptions to the prevailing pattern. One indicator of this was that only 11 percent of NGOs in Moscow received most of their funding from domestic sources (many of which were nongovernmental). While 39 percent stated that they had received some funding at some point from a state source, usually the amounts were very small, and many NGOs expressed considerable caution about accepting money from the government for fear of losing their autonomy. The Information Center of the Independent Women's Forum (ICIWF), for example, received the equivalent of US$1,500 from the Russian Ministry of Labor to print conference materials. Yet its leader, Elizaveta Bozhkova, harbored a skepticism about the transparency of government funding that was typical of most Moscow activists: "At the level of Moscow city, a grant program has been passed into law, but all the same, there isn't a normal, open mechanism for providing grants."[91]

The one aspect in which NGO development was somewhat lacking in Moscow was outreach to public constituencies. As Table 4.8 shows, Moscow NGOs were heavily engaged in internal organizational development activities and communications within the NGO community through conferences, trainings, and information distribution. Yet very few NGOs in the city interacted significantly with average Russian citizens. Some exceptions to this were the crisis centers, soldiers' rights groups, and the Goluba organization for assistance to adolescent women, which went into schools to conduct sex education classes in order to raise awareness about teen pregnancy and sexual assault. Moscow NGOs were relatively highly developed in coalition building and advocacy in political circles, but they did not often work with the wider public. This is likely to be a common characteristic of NGOs in capital cities around the world: they work heavily on advocacy at elite levels but have little to do with grassroots citizens. This is highlighted in this book's preface, which discusses scholars' concerns regarding trends in American civil society, and if we think of typical NGOs in cities such as Washington, D.C., or Ottawa, we see similar characteristics.

TABLE 4.8. NGO activities, by region.

City	N from location	NGO Management training		Monitoring of rights violations		Training in substantive issues		Information distribution		Conferences		Education and collaboration with outside groups		Increasing public participation	
Moscow	24	2	8%	3	13%	10	42%	15	63%	12	50%	5	21%	1	4%
St. Petersburg	22	3	14%	3	14%	9	41%	8	36%	8	36%	4	18%	2	9%
Ekaterinburg	7	1	14%	0	0%	4	57%	3	43%	1	14%	1	14%	0	0%
Izhevsk	8	0	0%	0	0%	3	38%	1	13%	3	38%	3	38%	3	38%
Vladivostok	7	0	0%	0	0%	4	57%	2	29%	3	43%	1	14%	0	0%
Khabarovsk	6	0	0%	1	17%	1	17%	2	33%	3	50%	0	0%	0	0%
Novgorod	6	1	17%	0	0%	4	67%	2	33%	1	17%	1	17%	3	50%
Total number and percentage of NGOs conducting such activity	80	7	9%	7	9%	35	44%	33	41%	31	39%	15	19%	9	11%

(continued)

TABLE 4.8. (*continued*)

City	N from location	Women's business support or microfinance		Self-help to members		Charity		Exhibitions and festivals		Legal consultation		Psychological consultation		Social service receptions	
Moscow	24	1	4%	1	4%	6	25%	4	17%	7	29%	2	8%	2	8%
St. Petersburg	22	2	9%	5	23%	3	14%	1	5%	7	32%	7	32%	3	14%
Ekaterinburg	7	1	14%	1	14%	2	29%	1	14%	3	43%	2	29%	3	43%
Izhevsk	8	1	13%	3	38%	1	13%	3	38%	2	25%	2	25%	1	13%
Vladivostok	7	2	29%	1	14%	2	29%	0	0%	2	29%	3	43%	2	29%
Khabarovsk	6	1	17%	1	17%	2	33%	0	0%	1	17%	2	33%	1	17%
Novgorod	6	4	67%	3	50%	3	50%	2	33%	1	17%	2	33%	2	33%
Total number and percentage of NGOs conducting such activity	80	12	15%	15	19%	19	24%	11	14%	23	29%	20	25%	14	18%

Moscow had one of the largest NGO sectors in terms of absolute numbers, with approximately 24,000 organizations registered officially by 1999. If we take into account the size of Moscow's population in order to develop a measure of NGO density, we come up with a figure of somewhere between 1.5 and 2.4 NGOs per thousand Muscovites. This is at the higher end of NGO density among the seven cities, although not the highest. See Appendix 5 for a display of various calculations of NGO numbers and densities for each city, as well as an account of the reasons for difficulty in obtaining a precise and reliable measure of NGOs in any location.

Moscow NGOs also tended to network with other NGOs around the city and around the country. Among women's NGOs, several large communication networks were based in Moscow, such as the ICIWF, Consortium of Women's Nongovernmental Organizations, and the Union of Women of Russia. As reported in Chapter Two, communication in these networks tended to flow from Moscow rather than among regional members.

There were also frequent events at which members of Moscow's NGO community saw one another and discussed issues. Foreign donors funded many of these events, such as conferences and seminars, and in this manner facilitated the development of more frequent communications among NGO activists in the city. Locations such as Sakharov House, MCGS, and the offices of the American Bar Association's CEELI program in Moscow were frequent venues for gatherings of women's and human rights NGOs. Some events occurred annually and involved collaboration among several organizations. An example of this was the annual March 8 (International Women's Day) demonstration, called "Let's stop violence against women" (*Ostanovim nasilie protiv zhenshchin*), which was organized by the three crisis centers for women—Syostry, ANNA, and Iaroslavna—with participation by several other local women's NGOs. Soldiers' rights NGOs such as the Antimilitarist Radical Association (ARA) and the Union of Committees of Soldiers' Mothers of Russia (UCSMR) had collaborated in demonstrations against conscription and the war in Chechnya. During interviews, nearly all subjects could name a wide range of local NGOs with whom they communicated regularly.

NGOs based in Moscow were able to build broad coalitions on policy issues that concerned the entire NGO community. Some examples were the failed campaign to have the government's NGO reregistration deadline extended from July 1999 to July 2000, and the partially successful, ongoing campaign to have NGO activities and grant funds remain tax exempt under the new federal tax code. The latter campaign was initiated in 1998 by the Center for Development of Democracy and Human Rights in Moscow and has continued to lobby the Russian government, with incremental success, since then (ASI, 2004a; 2004b). These coalitions included NGOs of many types, such as women's, human rights, environmental, and ethnic organizations, as well as individual organizations that did not always agree with one another. The anti-taxation campaign has included NGOs from over 50 Russian regions, according to the director of the Charities Aid Foundation in Moscow (ASI, 2004a). However, most of the active participants have been located in Moscow.

Another important example of an active communication network in the Moscow NGO community was discussion surrounding attendance of a government-organized forum for NGOs. To indicate that it considered NGOs to have some clout in society and in order to forge a dialogue, the federal government organized a national Civic Forum, which took place in Moscow in November 2001 and was attended by President Putin. NGOs from around Russia were invited, and a heated discussion ensued in the NGO community—with heavy participation by Moscow NGOs—over whether or not to attend.[92]

ST. PETERSBURG

St. Petersburg was similar to Moscow in its characteristics, and in fact its NGOs were more highly developed in one aspect: outreach to communities of ordinary Russian citizens. Table 4.8 testifies to the somewhat higher degree of public outreach that St. Petersburg NGOs in the sample conducted. More NGOs in St. Petersburg than in Moscow were involved in efforts to increase public participation, psychological and social service consultations, and women's business support. Meanwhile, fewer were involved than in Moscow in the internal NGO sector development activities of conferences and information distribution among NGOs. As was typical in all cities and discussed in Chapter Three, the crisis centers for women (Aleksandra and the St. Petersburg Psychological Crisis Center) and soldiers' mothers' organizations conducted a great deal of public outreach. Many other women's NGOs were also involved in activities working directly with the wider public. For instance, my interview sample included a counseling organization for women with breast cancer (Nadezhda), an organization to retrain women for new forms of employment (Alternativa), a Business and Professional Women's Club, and a League of Women Voters that held citizen consultation sessions. Even the Petersburg Center for Gender Issues (PCGI), a feminist gender studies center of the sort that is typically alienated from the wider population, held public events, employed a full-time staff member for public relations, and had an open-door policy for its library, videos, and even yoga classes. Olga Lipovskaia of PCGI stated that "Our activities have moved toward more work with the social women's movement, and more and more toward operating directly through education about pragmatics—'direct serv-

TABLE 4.9. Frequency of communication among NGOs, by region.

City	N from location*	Frequent Russia-wide within organization		Frequent Russia-wide within issue area		Infrequent Russia-wide within issue area**		Frequent local within issue area		Frequent local outside issue area		Infrequent local		Member of formal network or association	
Moscow	24	6	25%	11	46%	0	0%	14	58%	2	8%	1	4%	6	25%
St. Petersburg	22	1	5%	8	36%	3	14%	14	64%	6	27%	2	9%	6	27%
Ekaterinburg	7	2	29%	3	43%	0	0%	5	71%	0	0%	1	14%	2	29%
Izhevsk	8	4	50%	2	25%	1	13%	4	50%	3	38%	1	13%	1	13%
Vladivostok	7	2	29%	3	43%	3	43%	4	57%	2	29%	1	14%	2	29%
Khabarovsk	6	3	50%	2	33%	2	33%	2	33%	4	67%	1	17%	2	33%
Novgorod	6	1	17%	2	33%	2	33%	5	83%	1	17%	1	17%	1	17%
Total number of NGOs in this category	80	19	24%	31	39%	11	14%	48	60%	18	23%	8	10%	20	25%

*Actual row totals for locations may exceed the number of NGOs in category, as organizations often measure in more than one category of relations.

**Answers of "no relations" are not included in the chart

Totals include only those 80 NGOs from the study (1999–2000) whose members commented on this topic.

ices,' such as consultations with a lawyer and a psychologist, yoga lessons, courses on computers, and courses in English language."[93]

Approximately 9,600 NGOs were officially registered in St. Petersburg in 2000. Depending on whether we use this official count or experts' estimates of the number of functioning NGOs, the density of NGOs in the city worked out to be between 1.7 and 2.6 NGOs per thousand city residents, which was similar to NGO density in Moscow.

NGOs in St. Petersburg had slightly less frequent communications with NGOs outside the city than Moscow NGOs did, largely because Moscow is headquarters to many nationwide organizations and networks. Yet note that in Table 4.9, significantly more St. Petersburg NGOs reported communicating frequently with local NGOs outside their particular issue area. For example, relations between the SMSP and women's NGOs in St. Petersburg appeared much closer than relations between the UCSMR and women's NGOs in Moscow. One women's NGO in Moscow even reported hostility directed at them by the soldiers' mothers, who argued that rape was a far less important issue than brutality against soldiers.[94] St. Petersburg organizations such as Mothers Against Narcotics and Alternativa reported maintaining contact with a variety of NGOs; the former worked with both women's and human rights NGOs, and the latter worked with veterans' and disabled people's organizations in addition to women's NGOs.

As concerns NGOs' likelihood to turn toward the state for dialogue and assistance, the situation in St. Petersburg was noticeably worse than that in Moscow. While few NGOs in Moscow reported having little or no contact with the regional or federal government, nearly half of the NGOs in St. Petersburg that commented on their relations with government reported such a state of relations. Several, such as Lipovskaia of PCGI, Natalia Khodyreva of the Psychological Crisis Center for Women, and the leaders of the Aleksandra crisis center, who said they had tried at one time to pursue dialogue with the administration, had subsequently given up due to a complete lack of response.[95] Larisa Korneva of Aleksandra stated with resignation that "it's probably better to get hold of students early and train them and encourage them into [state] structures, rather than to try to change the old ways of veteran workers."[96]

To sum up the situation in the St. Petersburg NGO community, we can say that the community was highly developed, as in Moscow, with some features that constituted improvements over the Moscow NGO sector. NGOs were more involved in public outreach and more connected with other organizations outside their narrow issue areas. Yet they were also less willing to engage in dialogue with government; this is not surprising, given the generally poor political opportunity environment for NGOs that existed in the region.

EKATERINBURG

Organizations encountered in Ekaterinburg were fairly evenly divided between those that were focused on well-defined aims and those that took on a very amorphous and unstructured set of activities. For the most part, newer NGOs, such as the Ekaterina Crisis Center, the Regional Foundation for Support of Women in Business, the Ekaterinburg Movement Against Violence, and Good Will tended to be clearly focused in their activities—choosing two or three related issues on which to concentrate their efforts. Other, mostly older organizations or those headed by leaders from the Soviet era, often have extremely vague mandates. Examples of this were found in the oblast *zhensovet* and in the Ekaterina Women's Center. The head of the Ekaterina Women's Center, Nadezhda Golubkova, described the organization's major activities as including work on violence against women, work with military wives, an association of women in productive enterprises, an association for preschool education, and a youth club.[97] NGO communities with a mixture of well-focused organizations and vaguely defined ones were typical of many of the cities. Ekaterinburg thus seemed to fall in the middle range of cities in terms of the degree of focus in organizations' profiles. While NGOs there tend to be less specialized than those in St. Petersburg, Moscow, and Izhevsk, they were more focused than those in Vladivostok and Novgorod.

Compared to NGOs in the other cities, Ekaterinburg organizations were strong in both public outreach and internal development work (see Table 4.8). A great deal of NGO work involved outreach to ordinary citizens, through activities such as charity, legal consultation, and social services. Yet the city also had an active contingent of NGOs that worked on training specialists in NGO management and professional skills, such as counseling techniques and business management.

NGOs in Ekaterinburg tended to maintain frequent communications with other organizations in their issue area, both locally and around Russia, as shown in Table 4.9. Relations were not always friendly, and sharp conflicts occurred both within and between organizations. At least one major conflict concerned regional politics and foreign grant money.

The Urals Association of Women (UAW) split apart over the questions of whether to become involved in politics and whether to ally itself with the mayor or regional governor. The UAW was founded in part by Galina Karelova, a local politician who later went to Moscow as a federal Duma deputy and became deputy minister of Labor and Social Development. The UAW had maintained an official policy of nonpartisanship; nonetheless, its membership included numerous high-level regional bureaucrats and political activists, and the organization managed to exert a significant influence in the regional administration's policy deliberations. It had also successfully supported the electoral campaigns of many women candidates in the region. But in the spring of 1998, a crisis developed over whether the UAW should allow itself to have partisan alignments with either the mayor's or governor's political blocs or whether it should remain nonpartisan. Members of the organization's leadership took opposing positions on these issues.

Foreign funding also played a role in the development of this crisis. Just as divisions within the organization were beginning to heat up, the European Union and the U.S. government jointly awarded the organization a prestigious prize in recognition of its contribution to the development and formation of civil society.[98] The monetary award was US$20,000, to be used for a project of the UAW's choosing. In addition to the pressure of political disagreements between Karelova and other leaders of the organization, a battle ensued over who would decide how to spend the award money. The tensions led to the resignation of one prominent member and a deepening lack of direction because of an absence of clear leadership. In the end, with a sense that her vision of the organization had been rejected, one of the founding members of the UAW and a prominent democratic activist in Ekaterinburg, Tamara Alaiba, resigned. When asked which was worse for the organization—involvement in political battles or the influx of money—Alaiba explained the crisis as follows: "Everything. The thing is that money did not drown the organization. It just appeared at a crisis moment, during an internal fight for leadership and the line of development of the organization . . . Those twenty thousand dollars appeared at exactly the moment when there was a crisis in the organization."[99]

Other, milder disputes occurred between organizations, such as disagreements between the oblast *zhensovet* and the UAW and among soldiers' rights organizations in the city. These disputes were generally rooted in disagreements over basic ideology and tactical approaches to the substantive sociopolitical issues they worked on, rather than disputes over how to react to battling levels of government or foreign funding. Despite these disputes, NGOs generally were aware of one another's existence and engaged in communications when there were issues of mutual concern.

Organizations in Ekaterinburg, through their own efforts, had attained some constructive dialogue and cooperation with the regional and city administrations. The UAW lobbied successfully to obtain from the oblast government what it claimed to be the first social partnership agreement in Russia (regarding contracting out state social services to the UAW). Following that victory, the UAW hosted seminars funded by a Eurasia Foundation grant to train other NGOs how to secure and manage social partnership contracts (it was not clear that NGO "trainees" had then succeeded in actually securing

TABLE 4.10. NGO attitudes toward relations with the state, by region.

City	N from location*	Very little to none	Some, but little effect	Adversarial but engaged	Active and cooperative	Frequent but reluctant, dependent	Enmity and avoidance	Close partnership	Support the state
Moscow	14	1 7%	4 29%	4 29%	3 21%	0 0%	1 7%	1 7%	0 0%
St. Petersburg	14	6 43%	1 7%	2 14%	3 21%	1 7%	0 0%	1 7%	0 0%
Ekaterinburg	7	0 0%	1 14%	1 14%	4 57%	0 0%	1 14%	0 0%	0 0%
Izhevsk	8	2 25%	1 13%	1 13%	1 13%	0 0%	0 0%	3 38%	0 0%
Vladivostok	5	0 0%	1 20%	0 0%	1 20%	0 0%	0 0%	1 20%	2 40%
Khabarovsk	6	2 33%	1 17%	0 0%	1 17%	1 17%	1 17%	0 0%	0 0%
Novgorod	6	0 0%	2 33%	2 33%	1 17%	0 0%	0 0%	0 0%	1 17%
Total number and percentage of NGOs in this category	60	11 18%	11 18%	10 17%	14 23%	2 3%	3 5%	6 10%	3 5%

*Totals include only those 60 NGOs from the study whose members commented on this topic.

such contracts).[100] The city's NGO grants program developed through prodding from organizations such as Good Will.[101] The majority of NGOs in Ekaterinburg reported that they approach their relations with the state in a positive manner—some with an adversarial tone, some viewing the relationship as a partnership, and others completely cooperative—but as Table 4.10 shows, nearly all who commented on their relationship stated that they sought some form of constructive dialogue with the state on issues. This table cannot be interpreted as a perfect reflection of NGO relations with local and regional administrations, since only sixty NGOs in the study were asked about their relations with the state, and of those, only seven were in Ekaterinburg.

The NGO community was rather small in Ekaterinburg, compared to Moscow and St. Petersburg and even when compared to some smaller cities such as Novgorod and perhaps Vladivostok. Ekaterinburg's density of NGOs was lower than that of St. Petersburg and Moscow, although how much lower depends on whether one uses the count of officially registered NGOs or the somewhat lower estimate of active NGOs at the time of the study. NGO density reached only 1.2 to 1.5 NGOs per thousand residents. The general condition of NGO development in Ekaterinburg, then, was that of a relatively small community of organizations that were well aware of one another, with significant numbers actively seeking dialogue with the state and strongly involved in outreach to the local population.

IZHEVSK

The NGOs from Izhevsk did not appear to harbor a subordinate attitude toward the state, even though a sizable proportion of them (45 percent) had received state funding at some point. As Table 4.10 shows, there was considerable variety in the attitudes of NGO activists toward local government in Izhevsk. Some avoided contact with the administration, some actively cooperated with it, and others adopted an adversarial but engaged relationship; but none implied that they either were dependent upon the state or viewed their role as supporting the state. Even the republican *zhensovet* (called the Union of Women of the Udmurt Republic), which conducted activities that were generally friendly toward the state's aims, nonetheless asserted its concerns to a reluctant administration. For example, its leader stated: "We have some victories in areas where we raised problems two or three years ago, and now in this year we are seeing results on them. For example, for the first time this year the spending on social needs exceeds that of last year's budget—and we are sure it is our achievement. Without our authority and persuasion of leaders, it wouldn't have happened."[102] The *zhensovet*'s role in this budget modification may or may not have been crucial; the important point here is that the organization actively pushed in budget negotiations, while many *zhensovety* in Russia would not become so involved in policy discussions. The city *zhensovet* had even taken to the streets to protest reductions in state social benefits.[103] The independent-mindedness of the *zhensovety* in Izhevsk should not be overestimated. Generally, they supported the aims and desires of the regional government, yet they were more autonomous in Izhevsk than in several other regional cities, such as Novgorod and Khabarovsk.

As Table 4.8 indicates, the most common activities in which Izhevsk NGOs participated involved education and collaboration with outside groups (such as sessions in schools concerning date rape), training in substantive issues (for example, training women in new job skills), projects to increase public participation, and public exhibitions. Thus, their activities involved a considerable amount of public outreach, compared to other cities in the study. Nearly all of the NGOs in Izhevsk—with the exceptions of the International Women's Club, the Club for Breast Cancer Patients, and the Women of Science Association, which were narrower interest and self-help groups— spent significant amounts of time working with average citizens in Izhevsk. For example, the Warm Home (*Teplyi dom*) Crisis Center for Women ran a 24-hour telephone hotline, consultations with specialists for women experiencing abuse, support groups for abused women, and antiviolence educational programs for schoolchildren, teachers, and parents. The Rifeia-Art Women Artists' Association had organized an art gallery and held nine public exhibitions of women's art over the course of a year. The Udmurt Division of the Confederation of Businesswomen of the Russian Federation had founded a center that offered courses to retrain unemployed women for competitiveness in the new labor market. As typical for their organizations around Russia, the city and republic *zhensovety* and the Committee of Soldiers' Mothers held regular consultation sessions for those who needed their services.

Some weak aspects of the Izhevsk NGO community were definitely apparent. Chief among them was its tiny size. Unfortunately, I was unable to obtain an alternative estimate of the number of NGOs existing in Izhevsk other than the official state count, since there was no NGO resource center in the region—such centers are typically good sources for alternative estimates of NGO populations. The official count of registered NGOs indicated a density of less than one NGO per thousand residents. Given the very small number of women's and soldiers' rights NGOs that I was able to locate through inquiries with city and regional officials, NGOs, and the Open Society Institute representative in Izhevsk, it was apparent that the number was relatively low compared to some other regional cities of similar or smaller size, like Vladivostok and Novgorod.

Communications within the local NGO community were not exceptionally well developed, although local NGOs seemed to be aware of one another and NGOs across issue areas often knew a considerable amount about one another's activities. Table 4.9 indicates this. NGOs in certain issue areas gathered together occasionally. For example, prior to the 1999 Duma elections, women's organizations that were forwarding electoral candidates met to decide on a unified approach to the campaign in order to avoid running competing candidates within the same constituency. Yet communications with NGOs outside Izhevsk were much less frequent, likely because most organizations in the city did not have access to e-mail. In addition, there were no regular meetings among local NGOs, nor was there an NGO association to promote third-sector interests in Izhevsk. As noted above, the regional government was attempting to build such a forum, but this plan met with definite skepticism from many NGOs.

In sum, we can say that the Izhevsk NGO community was small and poorly networked but that the existing NGOs were generally well integrated into their communities. They did not tend to be heavily involved in agitating against the government, as several organizations were in Moscow and St. Petersburg in particular. Nonetheless, many NGOs were active in pressing for public policy change, and they resisted becoming dependent on the state and subservient to its wishes.

VLADIVOSTOK

Many NGOs in Vladivostok lacked meaningful autonomy from the state. They were well aware of this, and many resented it. Numerous interview subjects commented that the administration expected political loyalty from them and refused to provide any assistance to NGOs that did not openly support their policies. For example, the *krai zhensovet* leader, Zinaida Iovkova, reported that in the late 1990s, the *krai* administration annulled its provision of reduced rent and free utilities to the *zhensovet* office for a year when the organization refused to support a political candidate that the administration was backing. While this insulted Iovkova, she generally accepted her role as one of supporting state policies and stated that she only remained in her leadership position because the *krai* governor demanded it of her.[104] Other NGO activists did not accept this role so readily, complaining that the administration was wrong to expect such loyalty and submissiveness from NGOs. Yet they perceived no realistic way to escape this position.[105] A leader of one occasionally foreign-funded women's organization in Vladivostok complained: "The [regional government's] Committee for Public Relations tells me that there are certain organizations they are 'friendly' with, and others with which they are not, and that we must stick to their list of 'friends' as partners to work with . . . The administration often tells us we 'must' do things. But we're a free NGO—they don't accept such freedoms yet."[106]

The soldiers' rights subsector was sorely underdeveloped in Vladivostok.

The only organization I located that worked on the problems of soldiers was a local Committee for Servicemen's Parents (*Komitet roditelei voennosluzhash-chikh*). The *krai zhensovet* played a key role in forming this committee, and in Iovkova's words, "Our role there is to lift soldiers' spirits (*podniat' nastroenie*)" through activities such as collecting clothing and food for soldiers in Chechnya.[107] This is exactly the kind of "twin committee" role, supporting the Russian military, that the soldiers' rights organizations opposed. There was no NGO oriented toward soldiers' rights in Vladivostok.

Nor was there any unifying association of NGOs in Vladivostok. To some extent, the local office of the U.S. organization ISAR played a coordinating role for the independent NGO community by creating a database of NGOs, publishing a monthly periodical on NGO activities in the RFE, and providing training sessions. There was a roundtable of women's NGOs that was organized by the *krai* administration to discuss social issues involving women, but this was engineered from above and the administration did not extend invitations to all of the local women's NGOs. According to NGO activists' self-reported communications with other organizations (see Table 4.9), they communicated frequently with some other local NGOs, but during interviews activists rarely mentioned a wide range or large number of organizations with whom they cooperated. Indeed, a staff member at the local ISAR office, who had also once led a women's organization, argued that women's NGOs in the city were largely isolated from one another and unaware of one another's existence: "There are entirely no lines of communication among these organizations . . . I know that we have several women's organizations who believe that only they have a crisis center, and no one else is doing it; that they have a hotline, but no one else has one. I mean right in this city! They don't know about one another, although they should."[108]

Although few lines of communication existed among NGOs and organizations were fairly dependent on the approval of the local government, the city had a relatively large population of organizations. The true overall NGO population was difficult to gauge, since there was a wide disparity between official and alternative counts, leading to a calculated density of NGOs between 0.3 and 3.4 organizations per thousand residents. This means that Vladivostok had either one of the lowest or one of the highest NGO densities among all of the cities (see Appendix 5)! Nonetheless, I found significantly more women's NGOs in Vladivostok than I did in Khabarovsk or Izhevsk, which are cities of similar size.

Some, like the former Bluebird and the Women's Business Club, experienced a decline in activities after having carried out foreign grant projects immediately following their formation. In the case of Bluebird, this was mainly because a division developed within the organization among members who were interested in working on completely different kinds of issues (some on women's issues, some on ecological education, and others on early childhood education); this eventually caused the organization to die.[109] The Women's Business Club was still operating in 1999, but in fits and starts of different activities, depending on the availability of funding. Others, such as the International Women's Club and Women of Primorie, went through spurts of activity sponsored by state funding sources or political figures, followed by periods of dormancy. Very few had remained steadily active, and those who had—the Far-Eastern Confederation of Businesswomen, the city and *krai zhensovety*, and the Amazonka athletic club—tended to engage in service provision activities with average citizens, such as basic charity, job retraining, and self-defense classes. They cooperated with local government and did not engage in any adversarial or controversial advocacy activities. Those who came and went were more often involved in policy advocacy directed at the *krai's* political elite, training seminars for NGOs on organizational management techniques, or educational programs on topics such as gender issues or ecology.

In some small discussion forums, Vladivostok NGO leaders who had interacted with foreign donors professed allegiance to the principles of NGOs behaving as autonomous actors or of women being equal to men. Yet most of the activities and more public statements of these leaders expressed a lack of autonomy from the state and more traditional views of gender roles.

For example, while the city *zhensovet* leader, Natalia Shcherbakova, was clearly dependent on the regional administration for financing and office space for her organization and on the Union of Russian Women for program guidance, she had also attended several trainings by foreign donors and frequently used the Internet to read about NGOs.[110] Shcherbakova was a rarity among *zhensovet* leaders in that she engaged in enthusiastic dialogue with transnational actors. She did not espouse a completely subordinate view of her organization's proper relationship with the state, as do many *zhensovety*. She instead argued that her organization and NGOs more generally should rightfully engage with the state as equally legitimate representatives of society. During an interview, Shcherbakova complained about the regional administration: "They don't understand that we are also representing society. People also come to us! Certain people go to the state, and others come to us. We also express the opinions of a certain class of society. You can't ignore that class. You have to take it into account. You can't build society for certain people and forget about the existence of others."[111]

In another instance, Shcherbakova clearly articulated that her view of partnership with the state stood in contrast to both subordination and opposition: "We consider ourselves to have partnership relations with the administration—we don't go and beg from them or get into confrontations, which don't solve anything."[112]

In another instance, an appearance on a local television program, Shcherbakova explained how she viewed the ideal role of NGOs: "NGOs' role is to activate public opinion and the population so that the public itself can unite and try for itself to solve some of its problems. I saw yesterday on TV how women [from a city factory] picketed and voiced their demands. Good for them! [*Vot—Molodtsy!*] That's also a role of society, and I consider it important—people carrying their problems up to government."[113]

This statement did not at all resemble the views of most *zhensovety*, which typically focused on roles of social services and supporting government; but most *zhensovet* leaders had no access to the Internet and had never attended NGO training seminars led by foreign donors. The foreign donors from whom Shcherbakova received training were thus likely sources contributing to her demands for autonomy and her views on civil society.

Yet the main activities of the city *zhensovet* fell within a more subordinate civil society model, in which NGOs' function is to support the state. Activities consisted mostly of charity programs, such as gathering clothing for the poor or visiting orphanages, and events that were often paid for and sometimes devised by the city administration. For example, Shcherbakova explained that for the holiday "Family Day" in May 2000, the *zhensovet* organized a large, fair-like event and the city administration paid for food and a discotheque. The event included bringing in specialists from all kinds of official agencies that dealt with family-related affairs to consult with citizens on topics such as utilities, state benefits, and housing. Shcherbakova portrayed the event in a positive light, not suggesting that she was "forced" to conduct this kind of support work against her will. The divergence of Shcherbakova's opinions from her everyday activities showed that even if transnational actors had altered her views on relations with the state, the changes were not thorough.

Another example was the Women's Business Club in Vladivostok, which had conducted seminars on women's rights and whose leader, Elena Kurakulova, claimed to espouse a feminist philosophy during an interview with me. Yet in another context, Kurakulova gave an interview to a local newspaper under the auspices of the *krai zhensovet*, in which she was cited as stating, "We are not feminists—we are businesswomen!"[114] This form of decoupling between the statements of activists in some arenas and their statements and daily activities in other contexts also occurred fairly often in Khabarovsk. The explanation I posit for such disjunctures in NGOs is discussed later in this chapter in the section on categorizing regional NGO sectors.

KHABAROVSK

Khabarovsk NGOs, like those in Vladivostok, tended to be quite dependent on remaining in the *krai* administration's favor. Only one NGO in the sample, the *krai zhensovet*, expressed a positive attitude of voluntary engagement with the state (see Table 4.10). Others preferred to avoid interactions with the government but were often forced to behave in a formally supportive way in order to avoid harassment. As noted earlier, both the regional Committee of Soldiers' Mothers and the regional representative of the "For Human Rights" network had been threatened by the regional government as a result of opinions they expressed.

As in Vladivostok, decoupling between statements and everyday behavior was common. For example, the staff members of an NGO resource center, who were very well versed in Western concepts of NGO development, were also working directly on the 1999 Duma election campaign of the pro-presidential party Edinstvo, albeit reluctantly, under the orders of their employer. This direct party campaign work contradicted the image they were trying to promote as a nonpartisan resource for the NGO community as a whole. A similar example was that of the leader of the Union of Businesswomen, Svetlana Zhukova, who had received foreign grants and been on several overseas internships and training seminars on women in business and women's leadership. She professed during an interview that her organization maintained a distance from politics, but somehow she wound up running against Governor Ishaev as a "straw man" weak candidate during the gubernatorial elections in December 2000, after the governor "personally asked her" to run against him so that there would be more than one candidate.[115] In another vein concerning advocacy for women's equality, Tatiana Shepel, leader of the Lebedushka Women's Club, stated that she developed an interest in working on women's rights following her acquaintance with a well-known Russian woman activist during an exchange trip to the United States, funded by IREX. Yet she stated firmly that she was not a feminist and that most female politicians in Russia could use her help with personal appearances: "Just look at them! They clearly need help with their health."[116]

In terms of activity profiles, some organizations—such as the Union of Businesswomen, the Lawyers' Association, and the Committee of Soldiers' Mothers—were quite focused in their aims and engaged in some policy advocacy. About half of the NGOs interviewed, such as the Russian-American Education Center (RAEC), Lebedushka, and the *krai zhensovet*, were much less focused—one might even say scattered—in their profiles. Lebedushka, for example, had engaged in activities ranging from weight-loss programs to ecological education for children and charity drives for orphanages. Some of this lack of focus in Khabarovsk was a result of foreign-funding patterns. A staff member of one NGO resource center in Khabarovsk maintained that, since there were few domestic sources of funding for Russian NGOs, and "writing grant applications is a more reliable and worthwhile method of obtaining income" in terms of time invested versus results, foreign funding was beginning to have dangerous effects on the long-term development of NGOs. Fads come and go in grant programs, and "organizations as a result lose their missions," through adopting the strategy of writing proposals for any and all grant programs, no matter how much they differ from the organization's original goals. In the end, he argued, the organization either dies or becomes unneeded in society. He maintained that since there was not a wide diversity of foreign donors present in the RFE, and NGOs therefore did not have many funders to choose from, this tendency was very pronounced.[117]

The population of NGOs in Khabarovsk was small. There were only 842 NGOs officially registered in the entire *krai* as of mid-2000, which worked out to a density of approximately 1.5 NGOs per thousand residents. Local NGO resource centers estimated the number of active NGOs in the city to total between one hundred and two hundred (see Appendix 5).

Despite this small number, the city was home to two NGO resource centers—the Center for Social Information of the Far Eastern People's Academy of Sciences, and the Russian-American Education Center (RAEC)—and one *krai*-wide association of NGOs. Unfortunately, friction among the leaders of the two resource centers and the NGO association led to a fracturing of the sets of NGOs that interacted with each of the three organizations. Those who were friendly with the Center for Social Information, for example, tended to avoid interacting with RAEC.[118] Thus, communication networks among NGOs in Khabarovsk were not terribly inclusive, although NGOs tended to be aware of one another because of the small size of the city and NGO community.

Overall, then, we can describe Khabarovsk's NGO community as being small and fractured, with NGOs lacking in both organizational focus and autonomy from the regional government.

NOVGOROD

As indicated in Appendix 5, Novgorod had a remarkably high density of NGOs, compared to the other cities. Despite the fact that Novgorod was the smallest city in the study, its NGO community was the densest of all the locations, having between 2.3 and 4.8 NGOs per thousand residents.

Moreover, Novgorod NGOs tended to be well developed in terms of their clarity of aims and the extent of communications among them and between them and the regional government. In both the capital city of

Novgorod and the smaller city of Staraia Russa (population 60,000, two hours from Novgorod), the majority of interviewed NGOs conducted considerable grassroots work with the public. Examples of well-focused organizations that conducted frequent public outreach work in Novgorod included the Sisters Hotline, the Novgorod Consumers' Society, the Faith, Hope, and Love organization for disabled children in Staraia Russa, and the Success Center for Support of Women in Business, also in Staraia Russa. Some other organizations, such as the city and oblast *zhensovety*, conducted a great deal of grassroots work with women but were less clearly focused in their aims—they worked to assist groups ranging from World War II widows to single parents and disabled children. There were some exceptions: a few organizations interacted very little with the public and had poorly defined aims, such as the Novgorod League of Businesswomen, which gradually deteriorated into a social club for a group of friends after having completed a number of foreign grant projects in women's business development.[119]

Institutions did exist in the NGO community to facilitate communications and collaboration among NGOs. The Novgorod NGO Support Center was one hub through which NGOs met at seminars and could find information about one another. The other major mechanism for networking was the regional Social Chamber. As such, there was a significant amount of dialogue that took place between NGOs and the regional government in Novgorod, yet NGO activists maintained a fairly autonomous existence. Among the Novgorod organizations interviewed, only one, the oblast *zhensovet*, stated that its proper position in relation to the government was a subordinate one. Its leader, Evgenia Ivanova, stated: "We support the administration in all affairs and help them to solve problems."[120] Other than the *zhensovety*, though, most of the NGOs interviewed adopted a position of either cooperation or adversarial dialogue with the administration (see Table 4.10).

One strange aspect of Novgorod, which diverged from the generally well-developed, autonomous character of the NGO sector, was the absence of a strong soldiers' rights organization in the city. As in Vladivostok, only a twin committee type of soldiers' mothers' committee was present. The head of the NGO Support Center in Novgorod said that the center did not have any contact whatsoever with the local soldiers' mothers' committee because of its formalized, dependent character.[121] It is unclear why these two cities in particular lacked strong soldiers' rights NGOs. We could postulate that the high concentration of military personnel in Vladivostok and historically high level of militarized production in Novgorod may have led to a lack of local support for the idea of refusing military service. However, in such a case, why did reasonably strong soldiers' mothers' committees exist in Ekaterinburg and Izhevsk?

Overall, NGOs in Novgorod were well focused, fairly autonomous from the state, and integrated into the local community. The NGO sector as a whole was large and had developed significant networks of communication both among organizations and with government.

Patterns of Interaction Between Foreign Assistance and Local Political Environment

Based on the above descriptions of each city's NGO community, we can now try to distill some features that characterize cities with various combinations of foreign assistance and political environment. Some common features emerge that characterized the NGO communities in each of the three categories from Table 4.7.

As discussed in Chapter One, factors of socioeconomic modernization, such as urbanization and economic wealth, and levels of military importance might have constituted plausible explanations for variations in regional NGO development. We can now say with some confidence that we cannot account for NGO development outcomes in the seven cities by looking primarily at the socioeconomic factors of city size, economic wealth, and militarization. The small influence of urbanization and militarization in these seven cases is partly a result of the fact that the study did not explore the full range of potential values on these variables, since I was not primarily interested in them. That is, all of the cases are sizable cities rather than small villages, and none of the cities remains highly closed for military reasons (as some Russian cities still do). Had I explored such extreme cases, the results undoubtedly would have been different.

Local political environment and transnational interactions played a larger role in determining the character of NGO development. The smallest city, Novgorod, which also had one of the highest measures of military production levels, also had one of the largest and most active NGO communities. NGOs in the most heavily defense-oriented city, Izhevsk, acted no more timidly than NGOs in any other city; in fact, compared to organizations in the less militarized city of Khabarovsk, Izhevsk NGOs were much less fearful of state repression.

Economic development likely provides the strongest evidence of influence on NGO development, since the most flourishing NGO communities, in Moscow and St. Petersburg, existed in some of the country's wealthiest regions. Yet in Novgorod and Ekaterinburg, two cities that also had vibrant NGO communities, per capita income and unemployment levels were worse than average for Russia.[122] Moreover, the declining military-industrial city of Izhevsk had an NGO population that was growing noticeably and becoming more active and independent. This set of outcomes indicates that, while economic wealth may help to facilitate NGO development, active NGO communities can certainly develop without it.

It is true that the largest cities, Moscow and St. Petersburg, had the most diverse NGO communities, due in part to the sheer size, diversity, and relative wealth of their populations. Yet I was still able to separate the influences of high urbanization and wealth from those of foreign assistance by observing the NGO communities in smaller and/or poorer cities that were targets of foreign donors—Novgorod, Khabarovsk, and Vladivostok. There were vast differences among NGO communities in these smaller cities that the socioeconomic factors alone could not explain. City size did appear to affect the strength of the impact that local political environment had upon NGO development. NGO communities in large cities seemed to be less strongly influenced by their local governments—whether positively or negatively—than were NGOs in smaller cities.

HIGH REGIONAL SUPPORT / HIGH FOREIGN ASSISTANCE: MOSCOW AND NOVGOROD

As we might have suspected from the outset, the combination of a positive regional political environment for NGOs and a great deal of foreign donor involvement in the cities of Moscow and Novgorod had resulted in large, active NGO sectors in which many organizations had absorbed donor-promoted ideas in areas such as human rights, gender issues, and democratic citizenship. In both of these locations, the NGO community had developed especially strong networks among organizations and had pursued avenues of dialogue with the regional government. In terms of internal management techniques that are recognizable to Westerners, such as formal decision rules, accounting procedures, and advisory boards, NGOs in these two cities were much more advanced than those in cities where foreign assistance is low. NGOs in these locations also tend to have a considerable amount of autonomy from the state.

One important difference between the NGO communities in Novgorod and Moscow was that Novgorod NGOs were doing more work that interacted with significant numbers of citizens. NGOs in Moscow tended to be far more oriented toward lobbying the government or working with elites such as academic experts and other activists than they were toward interacting with the wider public. As mentioned earlier, this is likely to be a characteristic of NGO communities in other capital cities around the world as well. I also contend that the lack of public outreach among Moscow NGOs was partly a result of the abundance of foreign funding in Moscow. Among all of the regional NGO sectors, NGOs in Moscow had the highest levels of foreign funding. Throughout this book and elsewhere, I and others have argued that foreign grant projects have not typically emphasized public outreach (Sundstrom, 2001, 2002; Carothers, 1999; Henry, 2002; Ottaway and Carothers, 2000). During the 1990s and the time of this study, most foreign donors were not funding certain types of activities that are common among Russian NGOs. These included charity or social services (unless through encouraging "social contracting" of state social services to NGOs), job training in most areas aside from business management, public protest campaigns, and cultural programs (such as sports or arts and crafts). These were not seen as promoting nonpartisan political advocacy, which has been the ideal-type civic activity on the agendas of most donor organizations. Donors also rarely funded public information campaigns aimed at changing large-scale citizen consciousness on issues, since such projects do not produce rapid, measurable results that can be checkmarked as "achieved" at the end of a grant.[123] Sarah Henderson has described this need for donor field offices to obtain easily quantifiable results for their reports (2003, p. 88). These granting preferences on the part of donors were leading many heavily foreign-funded NGOs to stray away from interacting with average citizens.

HIGH REGIONAL SUPPORT/LOW FOREIGN ASSISTANCE: EKATERINBURG AND IZHEVSK

In the two cities where the regional political environment was relatively positive for NGOs and foreign assistance levels were relatively low, the NGO sector was small in size compared to those in the other cities. Yet NGOs tended to be relatively well focused in their aims and conducted a great deal of work with citizens in their communities. NGOs in both Ekaterinburg and Izhevsk were also actively involved in dialogue with the regional and city governments. Although the regional political environment in terms of direct relations with NGOs was positive in the two cities, NGOs were affected somewhat negatively by conflicts between the regional and municipal administrations. In both cities, this led to some conflicts among and within NGOs, rooted in political disagreements, which hindered collaboration in the NGO community.

Some organizations in the two cities that had received foreign grants were highly developed in terms of particular internal management techniques, such as appointing formal advisory boards and adopting budgeting procedures. Examples of this were the UAW in Ekaterinburg, which had appointed a formal board, and the Warm Home crisis center in Izhevsk, which had implemented financial planning procedures. The typical pattern in organizations from these two locations, though, was more fluid governing structures than in organizations from Moscow or Novgorod. In certain cases, a formally elected leader was not the de facto decision maker. For instance, again in the UAW, the formally elected leader, Evgenia Barazgova, was virtually powerless in comparison with the vice-president, Valentina Deryabina, despite the existence of a board of advisors. Another example was the Union of Women of the Udmurt Republic, in which the unelected secretary played a far greater decision-making role than the elected chair. In many other cases, leaders emerged without any formal process of election. Thus, while NGOs tended to be active and well integrated with their communities in these locations, most also lacked the Western-style internal management techniques and formal authority structures that, for others, have typically come from a history of working according to the demands of foreign donors.

LOW REGIONAL POLITICAL SUPPORT / HIGH FOREIGN ASSISTANCE: VLADIVOSTOK, KHABAROVSK, AND ST. PETERSBURG

This is an interesting category, first of all, since it helps us to identify the importance of a positive regional political environment, and second, since one of the three cities did not fit the profile of the other two. The St. Petersburg NGO sector differed considerably from those in Vladivostok and Khabarovsk, and I explain this in terms of both transnational factors and city size.

First, however, I turn to the cities that fit the dominant pattern. The local political and foreign assistance environments in Vladivostok and Khabarovsk had produced a large number of organizations that could be described as "decoupled" (Meyer, 1994; Meyer and Rowan, 1977). As discussed above and also in an earlier work (Sundstrom, 2001, ch. 6), many activists in these cities sporadically used transnationalized terms such as "democracy" and "feminism" and articulated the importance of an autonomous civil society. Yet often their daily activities and statements in other circumstances revealed attitudes and behaviors that diverged from the meanings that transnational actors intended when they trained NGOs in these concepts. A component of this decoupling pattern was that many organizations were erratic in their behavior, exhibiting an extremely unfocused activity profile. Some of them, such as Bluebird or the Women's Business Club in Vladivostok, waned in their activism or ceased to exist after a short lifespan. The unfocused profiles and short lifespans were mainly a result of the fact that, aside from waxing and waning foreign grant programs, few sources of domestic funding or even moral support existed for NGOs in these regions.

Why was this happening particularly in these two regions where the regional political environment was hostile, yet transnational involvement was relatively high? The answer had to do with opposing pressures in NGOs' relationships with foreign donors and local elites. In some cases, such as those of the NGO resource center in Khabarovsk and the Women's Business Club in Vladivostok, it seemed that NGO activists truly did believe in the transnationally promoted concepts of independent civil society and feminism as ideals. However, their need to survive in the local environment (whether to avoid being harassed by the government or simply to blend in with prevailing societal norms) forced them to "wear different hats" when they were dealing with the daily local environment versus when they were dealing with transnational actors. In other organizations, NGO leaders may have been using transnationalized language as a tool for currying favor with foreign donors. In some cases, like that of Natalia Shcherbakova of the Vladivostok City *Zhensovet*, activists' interactions with transnational actors were sporadic compared to the regular pressure they experienced from the local government, so that they only partially adopted transnational concepts. Without steady encouragement from both the local political environment and foreign donors to shift toward focused, autonomous, and democratic behavior, NGOs will remain in such a decoupled state, half adopting transnational ideas and half remaining politically dependent.

In St. Petersburg, though, we saw an entirely different NGO community. Here, the negative regional political environment had not caused NGOs' statements and behavior to become decoupled. Instead, NGOs had wholly adopted many transnational ideas about the role of civil society in democracy and the importance of human rights. The NGO community was nearly as dense and well developed as in Moscow, despite the fairly unfriendly stance of the regional government. There were several likely reasons for this. One was the fact that the regional government, although generally poor in its conduct toward NGOs, was not as sharply negative as the local governments in Vladivostok and Khabarovsk, which were qualitatively more hostile toward NGOs. A close look at Table 4.5 reveals this. Activists in Vladivostok and Khabarovsk reported concrete instances of being specifically punished by the government for their opinions or actions; in contrast, activists in St. Petersburg generally only suffered from silence and neglect.

Another reason was the factor of big cities versus small cities, mentioned earlier. NGOs in large cities felt much more distanced from their local governments than NGOs in smaller cities. While this was a drawback when benefits stood to be gained from government (such as grants, office space, or input into public policy), it could also be an asset when the government was not friendly toward NGOs. In such cases, it was better for NGOs to maintain their distance from government as much as possible. In Khabarovsk and Vladivostok, however, it was difficult for NGOs to avoid interacting with the city and regional governments.

Finally, we should take into account the historical background of St.

TABLE 4.11. NGO development outcomes resulting from combinations of foreign assistance and local political environment.

Local political environment	*Exposure to foreign assistance*	
	High	Low
Positive	Large, Active Sector Novgorod Moscow	Small, Integrated Sector Ekaterinburg Izhevsk
Negative	Decoupled, Weak Sector Vladivostok (St. Petersburg—exception) Khabarovsk	Small, Weak Sector

Petersburg and the city's transnational interactions. St. Petersburg was built in the 1700s to be the "window on the West," a "new Holland," and the "European" city of Russia. St. Petersburgers to some extent have always seen themselves as more integrated with Europe than have Muscovites and people in much of the rest of Russia (see McFaul and Petrov, 1998, pp. 41–42). With its close proximity to Finland and the rest of Scandinavia, St. Petersburg has long been strongly influenced by European news and visitors. To some extent, this may have laid a foundation for stronger and earlier absorption of Western concepts of democracy, citizenship, and human rights. Anthropologist Katherine Verdery has pointed out that in Eastern Europe, the idea of civil society was always closely related to the idea of "Europe." She states that " 'Europe' was a vivid presence in the talk of dissidents . . . To build civil society, then, is to return to Europe" (Verdery, 1996, p. 104). Further study would be needed to thoroughly investigate this question of whether St. Petersburg citizens have historically harbored stronger pro-European, and thus pro–civil society, attitudes than citizens of other western Russian cities such as Moscow.

As a result of the characteristics that prevailed in the NGO sectors in the cities of the study, we can add descriptive labels to the categories from Table 4.7, as illustrated in Table 4.11.

While none of the cities fell into the category of negative local political environment and low foreign assistance, we can postulate that in cities with those characteristics the resulting NGO sector would be small, weak, and politically dependent.

The overall picture indicates that foreign donors will be capable of achieving their intended results in NGO development only in those regions where they invest concentrated resources and where the regional political environment is fairly supportive of the idea that a strong and autonomous NGO sector is beneficial to social and political development. Novgorod and Moscow were the only two cities of the study in which these two conditions existed. In the other locations where foreign donors were heavily involved, they acted in the absence of a positive political opportunity environment, and the results in terms of shaping the character of the local NGO community have been incomplete, with unintended side effects.

Conclusion

This chapter has demonstrated that donors are not as positive an influence upon local NGO sectors as we might have expected, in circumstances where the state is hostile to the development of an autonomous civil society. Examples like Moscow and Novgorod can be held up as relative "success stories" of foreign assistance. In those cities, donors helped to increase the numbers of NGOs, increase their communications reach and management capacity, and make them less dependent on the state and freer to pursue agendas that challenged the state on issues such as human rights or the status of women. The downside to this transformation was that many of these NGOs became heavily dependent on foreign assistance as their source of material support. In contrast to these relatively successful cases, the NGO communities of cities like Khabarovsk and Vladivostok illustrated the power of domestic political institutions to distort or block the impact of foreign assistance. Foreign assistance expended in unfriendly political environments resulted in organizational outcomes that were unintended by donors, with NGOs exhibiting decoupled behavior. NGOs in areas where the level of foreign assistance was low but the regional political environment was fairly supportive were small in number and less professionalized in their operations, but they tended to be more autonomous and involved in their local communities than were NGOs in areas where foreign donors were active but the political environment was hostile.

CHAPTER 5

Implications for Theory and Practice

THIS BOOK HAS TAKEN a detailed look at how transnational actors, especially foreign donors involved in the "democracy industry," have affected the development of an important segment of civil society in a transitional regime. By examining the ways in which transnationalized Russian NGO activists work and think, compared to transnationally isolated activists, the study has revealed a great deal about the capability of foreign donors to exert an impact on civil societies in fragile, semidemocratic regimes. This final chapter assesses the implications of these findings for the scholarly fields of international relations and comparative politics, as well as for the enterprise of practical democracy assistance to transitional states and societies. I also assess what the findings suggest about foreign assistance strategies, given changes that have taken place in the Putin era involving greater centralization and restrictions on civil society mobilization. The field research ended in 2000, just as the Putin era was beginning, and much has changed in the political opportunity environment since then.

Reviewing the Findings

Foreign donors, overwhelmingly from the West, have had important and often unintended effects on the development of Russian NGOs. Foreign donors have influenced the capabilities, activities, and language of Russian NGO activists, but the impact of foreign assistance is not uniform across Russia. Donor influences have varied across regions, depending on the local political environment that NGOs encounter, and across issue areas, depending on how compatible transnationally promoted principles and norms are with widely accepted Russian norms.

Without a doubt, foreign organizations have dramatically shaped the kinds of activities in which Russian NGOs engage by investing considerable resources into certain kinds of activities. These have included projects to train activists in professional management techniques and specific issue-oriented skills such as crisis center counseling and political advocacy. Donors have also strongly supported monitoring and information-distribution activities conducted by NGOs. In addition, they have invested heavily in the development of communication networks among Russian NGOs, although closer observation shows that such networks rarely extend beyond simple information exchange to concrete collaboration among organizations. In activities of this kind, foreign donors have focused immensely on building the internal organizational infrastructure of the Russian NGO sector. They have not focused significantly on projects to increase civic participation in public life, nor have they devoted much attention to organizations that engage in charity and service provision activities.

Foreign donor-sponsored training often affects the language that Russian NGOs use, although acquisition of transnationalized language does not always lead to actual use of the techniques or belief in the methods. Generally, one of the most successful aspects of transnational training has been in increasing the professionalism of Russian NGOs, by demanding clarity and transparency in leadership and financial management. In addition, specific training in certain skills, such as how to counsel victims of domestic violence, when welcomed by NGOs, has significantly improved the effectiveness of activists' work.

Across different NGO issue areas, foreign donors have encountered varying levels of success in encouraging domestic NGO development. In issues where foreign donors promote fairly universal norms, programs initiated by foreign donors to encourage NGO development have displayed rapid success and led to an almost wholesale adoption of transnational approaches by local organizations. The efforts of foreign donors to assist crisis centers for women and soldiers' rights organizations on questions of physical abuse are exemplary in this regard. By contrast, foreign assistance efforts have failed to produce significant NGO mobilization when emphasizing norms that are not universal in nature but instead are specific to Western contexts. Women's issues that are difficult to frame without using feminist principles—such as workplace discrimination and sexual harassment—are examples of areas in which foreign donor efforts have largely failed from the standpoint of developing democratic civil society. Only small pockets of Russian activists espouse principles of Western feminism and a gender-analytic approach to the status of Russian women. Most Russians reject such principles, largely in reaction to the way in which the Soviet regime approached gender issues. As a result, foreign donors' work with women's organizations on issues of gender discrimination has been largely isolated from the broader population. Although Russian women's NGOs have attained some victories at elite policy levels, due to the presence of a few powerful allies in the Russian government, they conduct very little outreach with regular citizens and are largely dismissed in the media. As a result, there is hardly any public awareness of women's issues or the organizations that work on them.

Examination of seven different cities—with positive and negative local political environments for NGOs, as well as high and low levels of foreign assistance—showed that domestic political environments play a tremendous role in shaping the ways that foreign donors affect local NGO development. The particular characteristics of heavily foreign donor-supported NGO sectors varied by region, depending on how hospitable the local political environment was. Where foreign donors were especially active and local governments welcomed or tolerated the development of an autonomous NGO sector, the sector was large, active, and well networked. Yet when heavy transnational involvement coincided with local political environments that were hostile to NGOs, local organizations were forced to "wear different hats," depending on whether they were addressing domestic or foreign audiences—thus their statements were often severely decoupled from their everyday activities. When a region combined low exposure to foreign assistance with a friendly local political environment, the NGO sector was small in size due to a lack of material resources, but reasonably autonomous from the state and involved in a great deal of grassroots public outreach. Consequently, NGOs tended to be strong and well integrated into their communities.

Although the study thoroughly examined only two NGO issue sectors, many of the findings are likely to apply to other kinds of NGOs in Russia. The research included organizations with different levels of interaction with foreign donors, as well as ones that existed during the Soviet period and others that had only recently formed. Studies by other scholars regarding different kinds of NGOs in Russia and in other transitional and developing countries suggest that most of my findings can be generalized to other NGO sectors that have experienced foreign assistance. Examples include the works of Laura Henry (2001) on Russian environmental organizations, Marina Ottaway (2000) on African social movements, Kevin Quigley (2000) on East European civil society, and Sarah Mendelson and John Glenn's (2002) collection of investigations into the effects of democracy assistance across Eastern Europe and Eurasia.

A Closer Look at the Impact of
Transnational Actors on Domestic Civil Society

By examining the transnational interactions of activists at local levels, this book has raised some important challenges to the ways in which scholars of international relations have traditionally thought about such transnational dynamics. Most studies of how transnational forces affect domestic civil society have examined a few cases of transnational activism on select issues (see Keck and Sikkink, 1998; Risse, Ropp, and Sikkink, 1999; Wapner, 1995). Detailed and comparative studies of transnational influences on local circumstances—which examine both nontransnationalized local actors and transnationally integrated ones—are less common. This book has looked at precisely that.

The results present a response to recent literatures on global civil society and world culture. Contrary to those authors who report a growing homogenization of the world and a convergence of principles on ideas such as democracy and human rights, this study shows that serious domestic obstacles exist that hinder any uniform absorption of principles circulating at the global level. Instead of being globalized in a homogeneous manner, concepts that enter domestic contexts from the international arena will be distorted through the prism of domestic factors—both political institutions that block full implementation of these concepts, and societal norms that hinder their adoption by domestic actors. The chapter examining the successes and failures of foreign assistance to women's and soldiers' rights organizations shows particularly clearly that some transnationally promoted norms that are fairly universal can be adopted rapidly and almost completely in domestic environments, while other norms on questions such as women's rights or antimilitarism, which have powerful international backers but are more contested in Russia, will not be accepted in their original imported forms. The chapter comparing the effects of different regional political contexts on domestic NGO mobilization shows that foreign donors' degree of success in promoting their principles is shaped considerably by the nature of the local political environment.

Because of the distortions and modifications of transnational concepts that occur in local contexts, the multiplication of these processes in domestic circumstances around the world suggests that transnational civil society will have only limited cohesion and solidarity. While participants in transnational networks from around the world may use similar terminology in talking about topics such as human rights, women's rights, and the third sector, at deeper levels there are disagreements among those participants. Sometimes

NGO members in domestic civil societies who are recipients of foreign assistance use transnationally fashionable language in order to acquire the attention and resources of foreign donors. In other cases, contradictions and decoupling between transnational language and domestic behavior are the result of domestic actors' incomplete absorption or different understandings of the models that foreign donors promote. Thus, what appears on the surface to be the development of a global civil society through shared transnational mobilization on issues is actually much less cohesive than would be required for the existence of such a society.

Reexamining Civil Society and Democratization

Parallel implications emerge concerning theory on civil society and democratization in comparative politics. Civil societies will vary depending on the domestic needs and constraints of the time. While civil society is important for strengthening democratic institutions everywhere, in that the concept implies a means of citizen input and control over governance, the specific model that many Western donors have promoted in Russia is not appropriate everywhere. In fact, we do not even know whether advocacy NGOs are the key democracy-promoting component of civil society in the West. Scholars such as Robert Putnam and Thomas Carothers have strongly suggested that a broader spectrum of social networks, including many completely nonpolitical kinds of citizen interaction, is essential for promoting social trust in civil society and crucial for institutionalizing democracy (Putnam, 1993, 1996; Carothers, 1999a).

In countries experiencing socioeconomic crises, it may be more appropriate that civil society organizations focus as much on service delivery and other socioeconomic development projects as on political advocacy for interest groups. In fact, scholars who study NGO sectors comparatively have pointed out that in Western and Eastern countries alike the prevailing NGO models have fluctuated depending on the capabilities of government to provide public goods. Dennis Young points out that although a strong adversarial tradition runs through the history of NGOs in the United States, in certain periods, especially the late nineteenth and early twentieth centuries, "private parties took initiative to provide for social needs resulting from industrialization and immigration" (Young, 2000, p. 157). In other countries, as well, during periods of massive socioeconomic change, the NGO sector has assumed such a "supplementary" role of providing public services (Young, 2000, p. 158). When foreign donors try to promote particular issues that they perceive to be tied theoretically to civil society, to the exclusion of other questions that citizens in the recipient country may view as more important, they are unlikely to succeed in mobilizing significant public participation.

For the sake of developing a comparative approach to studying democratic institutions, it is more useful and accurate to define civil society as a space—a realm of citizen-initiated, publicly oriented, not-for-profit activity between the household and the state—than as a strict set of organizational types and issues. Civil societies look different around the world, even among democratic states. The values that undergird strong and democratic civil societies—such as citizen efficacy, networks of trust, and the belief that public participation is inherently good—are the important elements of civil society that contribute to democracy. A definition of civil society that includes only organizations that advocate for political change on behalf of particular interest groups, or requires that organizations have no state involvement, does not capture the democracy-promoting aspects of civil society. Foreign donors who have employed such a definition have only exacerbated the elitist and detached character of much of the Russian NGO sector, suggesting that a definition focusing specifically on advocacy organizations neglects many of the important attributes of the sphere.

For studies of social movements, the book reinforces recent work on the importance of ideational issue frames in determining the success or failure of social movement mobilization. For example, women's organizations have largely failed to mobilize Russian women to join the cause, despite serious societal grievances, significant material resources, and nearly identical political environments to those of more successful movements around them. This is mostly due to strong normative resistance in Russian society to arguments phrased in terms of feminism and gender equality.

In trying to understand external influences on civil society development more generally, it is useful to take a step back and recall the reasons why Russia is an illuminating case. I posited in Chapter One that due to a weak civil society and Russian citizens' lack of exposure during the Soviet period to transnational actors, these latter were likely to be able to exert an especially noticeable impact on post-Soviet Russian civil society. In many other transitional states, such as countries in Eastern Europe, Asia, and Latin America, history has not been so unkind to civil society. With the influx of foreign assistance to post-Soviet Russia during the period of initial international euphoria about the idea of democracy defeating Communism, we might have expected to see some striking results.

The results have been mixed. Foreign donors have had a dramatic influence on the quantity, activities, and professional management techniques of Russian NGOs. Yet their ability to fashion NGOs after their own Western image, in terms of the norms that activists espouse, has thus far been weak. The impact of NGO development assistance on the mobilization of political elites and broader society in Russia has been extremely slight. As Mendelson and Glenn have described democracy assistance in the post-Communist period more generally, Western organizations "have played a large role in helping to build institutions commonly associated with democracies but have done little to help these new institutions function well" (2002, p. 22).

In a sense, this judgment is preliminary and unfair. It has been over fifteen years since the Soviet Union fell apart and foreign donors rushed in. Moreover, as mentioned in Chapter One, much less money overall has been devoted to foreign democracy assistance than to economic development or stabilization of Russia's weapons of mass destruction. On a per capita basis, countries such as Georgia, Serbia, or Ukraine have received more democracy assistance—and, arguably, its impact on actors who were later involved in those states' recent democratic revolutions has been much greater. Given Russia's daunting task of building all kinds of democratic institutions—civil society, government, political parties, rule of law, and a free media—as well as a functioning market economy, it is unsurprising that results so far have been modest. All of these aspects of governance are inextricably connected with one another, thus the challenge of reforming them all will continue for a very long time.

Implications for Foreign Assistance Policies

Typically, foreign donors have entered the Russian NGO community with a missionary-like approach—promoting predefined plans for Russian civil society and assuming that they know best what Russian civil society needs, without always considering the knowledge that local activists possess concerning the needs of their own communities. Western NGO assistance has been based largely on trying to reproduce an idealized form of the NGO sectors in the donors' home countries, despite the fact that even in the West these models rarely exist in reality. Assistance policies could be vastly improved by considering what is feasible and what is not in the current local circumstances.

Donors should realize that their ability to shape civil society will be limited and that even limited goals will require several decades of assistance to achieve. In the case of assistance to Russian civil society, donors have begun to realize that their initial goal of ending assistance to Russian civil society within one decade was vastly unrealistic. For example, USAID has stated that "policymakers should not see the cultivation of NGO sectors in [Central and Eastern Europe and the New Independent States] as a short-term, single-stage, restorative intervention. The process by which the independent sectors in these countries are maturing necessitates a long-term approach and changing forms of assistance tailored to evolving needs" (1999a, p. 59). Nonetheless, a general "donor fatigue" with foreign aid to Russia set in long ago, especially sparked by the scandals of the 1998 financial crisis. Most donors have decreased their budgets for Russian civil society development in recent years, and they have adopted more sober assessments of what is possible to achieve. Moreover, there is no clear consensus on what donors' revised goals should be in Russian civil society nor on the most effective means of defining them. Here, I venture several suggestions of realistic, achievable goals that will lead to more fruitful assistance to Russian NGO development.

I. MORE FOCUS ON OUTREACH

To remedy the problem of foreign assistance leading NGOs away from the concerns of local citizens, a much higher proportion of foreign grant projects should be directed at reaching significant numbers of average citizens. Thus far, only a minimal increase has occurred in citizens' awareness of the existence of NGOs and the role of civil society, and only in select locations where foreign assistance has been intensive. The vast majority of Russians still know nothing, or have misconceptions, about what NGOs do and how they are potentially helpful to society (USAID, 2000a, p. 87). A large 1998 poll of Russian citizens found that, while 80 percent of respondents had heard of trade unions, only 31 percent knew of human rights NGOs and only 27 percent knew of any women's NGOs (VTsIOM, 1998, p. 2). Another more recent poll does suggest, however, that public knowledge and confidence in human rights NGOs may be increasing, although the questions asked in the survey do not match the earlier VTsIOM poll precisely. Mendelson and Gerber (2005, p. 9) found in their large 2002 and 2003 surveys that 56 percent of respondents had "highly positive" or "rather positive" views of human rights NGOs. So it is possible that public opinion and awareness are changing gradually.

2. INCREASING PUBLIC AWARENESS

Sponsoring broad public information campaigns is another way that foreign donors can help increase citizens' awareness of how NGOs work to improve public life in Russia. When a significant number of Russian citizens develop positive associations with NGOs and become interested in the work that they do, the NGO sector in Russia will grow and be a more representative component of civil society. The existing NGO community, which is largely detached from society as a whole and easily dismissed by the state, is not strengthening democratic institutions.

3. DEVELOPING NGO–GOVERNMENT DIALOGUE, WHILE HEEDING NGO FEARS

Donors should continue their work on developing dialogue between NGOs and government. By providing training in lobbying techniques, donors can help local NGOs persuade government officials that policies that facilitate NGO development—such as tax privileges for NGO activities and charitable donations—are actually beneficial to society and can help governments to make their policies more effective. In regions and government departments where anti-Western sentiment is subdued, the presence of foreign donors in discussions to encourage such changes may persuade officials to take NGOs more seriously than they otherwise would. In other, more hostile circumstances, though, donors should remain in the background, merely advising NGOs on strategies and granting them the resources to pursue such improvements in government-NGO relations. Donors should also heed NGOs' complaints in certain regions that attempts to work in partnership with government are futile due to corruption, informal power networks, or an absolute hostility to NGOs. As Chapter Four showed, in regions with particularly negative regional political environments, such as Khabarovsk and Vladivostok, pressure on activists to cooperate with both foreign donors and local government structures may lead to undesired, decoupled outcomes in NGOs. Activists often have good reasons to avoid working with government actors prematurely (see Henry, 2001, pp. 17–18).

4. SUSTAINED TRAINING TO A BROADER RANGE OF ORGANIZATIONS

Training for NGOs concerning management techniques and the rights of individuals and organizations under the law should continue. But training needs to be much more inclusive of all kinds of NGOs than it had been up through the study period. In the community of women's NGOs, for example, donors' general rejection of *zhensovet* organizations as potential partners is a mistake. The same applies to nearly all former Soviet monopoly organizations. While many such organizations have no interest in working actively in their communities or promoting democratic principles, several *zhensovet* leaders are in fact anxious to learn more about how to promote democracy and human rights. If they possessed more arrows in their quivers, such as organizational management and fundraising techniques that would help them to become more autonomous from government, they could become effective forces for improving people's lives in their communities. At present, many *zhensovety* conduct an enormous amount of valuable charity work and problem solving for individual citizens. The entire class of organizations should not be written off as hopeless dinosaurs but instead should be considered as potential partners on a case-by-case basis. Ottaway and Carothers have noted this, stating that "aid providers should continue to expand the range of organizations they seek to assist in civil society programs. When it has occurred, the extension of aid from public interest advocacy NGOs to NGOs concentrating on socioeconomic issues has often been useful" (2000, p. 309).

In order for foreign donor-sponsored training programs to have any noticeable impact on domestic NGOs, they must be concentrated, be ongoing, and pursue clear goals. In many cases today, Western experts are not even necessary for conducting such trainings. By now, especially in larger cities like Moscow and St. Petersburg, experienced Russian NGO leaders have adapted Western advice to local conditions and can conduct most NGO training programs themselves. Such an approach to NGO training has the dual advantages of being intelligible to local activists and of having in-country trainers on a permanent basis. Maximizing the use of local trainers is also cost effective. Many donors have wisely worked to minimize the phenomenon of the fly-in, fly-out Western expert since the mid-1990s, as only ongoing work with trainers who are well-grounded in Russian conditions will have an appreciable impact on domestic NGOs.

5. FOCUS ON NGOS WITH CLEAR GOALS

In funding decisions, donors should focus on organizations with clearly defined goals and grant them the resources needed to pursue those goals more effectively. Such organizations, whose members have thought through carefully what they wish to achieve and how to achieve it, are the sustainable organizations in society—the ones that will not fade away due to constantly drifting goals. Throughout the study period, donors were much too focused on particular goals—that is, they supported organizations with a stated willingness to pursue projects that are attractive in Western donors' eyes—rather than on the basic strength and passion of individual NGOs. As one activist put it, "A lot has been done simply because Americans came with ready projects and asked, 'Okay now, who will do this?'"[1]

The need for clearly defined goals as a funding prerequisite does not imply that new organizations should not receive foreign funding or that a limited network of established NGOs should be granted repeated funding. In contrast, if the clarity of the organizations' goals and plans becomes important to donors, then many new NGOs will be good candidates for grants, and many current donor favorites will suddenly appear unsuitable.

Similar advice applies to support for NGOs in politically hostile regions. If donors support the small number of independent-minded organizations in such regions that have clear plans for what they want to accomplish, they may succeed in fostering small and gradual changes in the civic life of the area. Chapter Four suggested that flooding large amounts of funding into these regions is, unfortunately, not a solution, since it merely multiplies the decoupling phenomenon and causes the creation of organizations that are not strong enough to survive on their own, without improving the local political situation.

6. DEVELOP PRIORITIES FROM LOCALLY GENERATED IDEAS

Finally, the overriding recommendation that emerges from this book is that donors should adopt programs that are designed in a much more "bottom-up" manner than is currently employed—whether in terms of the problems that Russians care about most, or of historically developed norms that suggest which ways of framing issues will succeed and which will fail, or of the regional variations in political opportunity structures. Strategies that are sparked by ideas from local activists—as opposed to external requests for proposals on particular topics—are likely to result in more sustainable NGO development. When priorities are developed elsewhere and introduced from above, mercenary organizations with no real passion for the foreign-funded projects appear to fulfill the orders, and their work has virtually no resonance in society beyond the walls of NGO offices. Donors are concerned, as they should be, about the long-term sustainability of Russian NGOs after donors cease their funding and training. One of the best ways to promote sustainability is to allow Russian activists to work on projects that are feasible and in demand in their local contexts. By doing so, NGOs are more likely to succeed in finding local patrons and partners to sustain their activities.

In spite of this emphasis on local priorities and assistance to a broader range of organizations, I am not suggesting that donors wholly abandon organizations pursuing strategic goals that meet resistance in Russian society. There are pockets of indigenous organizations that have consistently worked on issues such as gender equality and the right to conscientious objection. Occasionally, they secure small victories, and this is how norms can change gradually over time. As Chapter Three argued, donors should pursue a balance between encouraging normative change and solving immediate pressing problems. In doing so, however, they should choose grant recipients based on clarity of goals and dedication to those goals, rather than a willingness to fulfill donors' orders.

Into the Putin Era

Where do these conclusions and recommendations take us in terms of recent political developments in Russia? As many authors have observed, the government of President Vladimir Putin has changed much that is significant for civil society in Russia. As part of an overarching desire to centralize authority in Russia, Putin has taken several steps in consolidating a so-called "power vertical." These steps have included measures that more clearly subordinate local governments under regional authority and, in turn, subordinate regional governments under central government rule (Lankina, 2005), and the creation of institutions that appear to be aimed at establishing state control over civil society. The boldest institutional changes have been made in the wake of the Beslan school massacre of September 2004. Putin announced that he would abolish direct popular elections for regional governors and attempt to change the current half of the State Duma that is elected on a single-member plurality basis into seats that are elected on a party-list proportional basis, as half of Duma members currently are. These moves will dislodge the degree of responsibility felt by elected members of government toward constituents in their local regions by making politicians more accountable to Moscow officials for their posts. In addition, the president brought in a new law, effective 2006, that places local mayors much more clearly under the authority of regional governments and removes many local government powers and sources of revenue (Lankina, 2005).

In addition, the Kremlin has worked steadily to restrict the mass media spectrum, particularly in television, but also in national print media. All nationwide broadcasting networks are now owned and managed by the state, and all nationally circulated newspapers produce a consistent pro-Kremlin editorial perspective (Lipman, 2005). Some radio stations, such as Ekho Moskvy, and local newspapers still present a critical perspective, as does the Internet. Yet the Kremlin has been extraordinarily successful in limiting the spectrum of media to which most of Russia's citizens have access.

Finally, there is the "new" Putin project of shaping civil society. Masha Lipman put it this way: "Elites have been subdued, politics are kept under control, and the overall atmosphere of loyalty is undisturbed by the remaining independent media. Yet, the Kremlin is far from relaxed. The next Kremlin objective is to control civil society groups" (Lipman, 2005).

Since the beginning of Putin's rule, critical voices in civil society have come under increasing scrutiny and sometimes criminal prosecution. Such instances have gained momentum in Putin's second term as president, in the government's more systematic attempts to shape civil society activities to its own agenda. There was widespread civil society reaction to Putin's "state of the nation" speech to the Duma in May 2004, in which he complained that many NGOs were following the agendas of foreign donors. Putin stated that some organizations were focused on "obtaining funding from influential foreign or domestic foundations" and thereby acting against the national interest. Several other advisers close to Putin made similar, more expansive statements against foreign-funded and dissident NGOs in the months following that speech (see Lipman, 2005; Evans, 2005b).

The most recent institutional initiative, announced in the post-Beslan period, has been to create a "Public Chamber" (*obshchestvennaia palata*) of NGO leaders to represent citizens' views to the government. The bill passed through the Duma and was signed into law by President Putin on April 4, 2005. NGOs that are independent of the state have heavily criticized the chamber as being designed to control civil society rather than to seek diverse input into policies (Abdullaev, 2005; Bransten, 2005; Evans, 2005b). The chamber setup involves the president choosing one-third of the NGO leaders directly, with those members choosing another third, and then all of those selecting a final third from among regional NGOs. This certainly sets the stage for a heavily controlled mechanism of civil society dialogue with government, in which nonmembers of the chambers—presumably including all critical voices—will be completely isolated from access to government structures.[2]

Reforms to regional and local government structures are likely to affect the outcomes of foreign assistance by making regions more homogeneous in their political opportunity environments—that is, if the central government truly manages to control regional governments. Increased central government vigilance in limiting the ability of civil society to question the state suggests that this more homogeneous environment will also be less supportive of democratic civil society development.

What does this mean in terms of appropriate strategies for foreign donors to pursue in a new, less free context for NGOs? Essentially, it means that they would be wise to pursue the strategy suggested above regarding regions with hostile political opportunity environments, in order to avoid forming decoupled organizations with no real contribution to societal change. Rather than launching enormous initiatives to support NGOs that combat antidemocratic tendencies, donors must work intensively on the ground, with detailed knowledge about which NGOs have clear goals and well-thought-out strategies for their activities. Donors must focus on those NGOs that yearn for independence and have clear mandates. They cannot provide scattered funding to unstable organizations with vague goals, which have sometimes attracted donors when they have mounted an appearance of liberal democratic values. Good candidates for funding may be advocacy groups like human rights organizations that work in opposition to many government policies. They may also be service provision organizations that provide clearly needed resources for their communities, yet are wary of becoming absorbed by the state.

The future of democracy in Russia is unclear in the hybrid regime that prevails today. However, transnational actors have a huge role to play, both through international NGOs pressuring Western governments to make democracy a priority in their diplomatic relations with the Russian government, and through the use of concrete financial support to NGOs within Russia. Many problems and pathologies plague the execution of foreign democracy assistance. Yet the recent cases of mass movements to defend democracy in Serbia, Georgia, and Ukraine, with foreign-funded NGOs providing organizational backbone to those movements, indicate that foreign assistance can emerge as a crucial element protecting democratic values at crucial junctures when that assistance has been sustained. The resources devoted to NGO development in Russia might well play a crucial role in preventing a total backslide away from democracy, even if the role of assistance in strengthening Russian civil society has been incremental and uneven over the past fifteen years.

Reference Matter

This appendix lists all interviews conducted during the course of field research, except those that were conducted on a confidential basis. Interviews from the summer of 1998 are listed separately from those of 1999–2000, as the methods used during the 1998 research differed from those used in the later period. In 1998, the list of discussion questions varied slightly, and none of the interviews was audiotaped. In 1999–2000, nearly all of the interviews were audiotaped; exceptions are noted with an asterisk (*) below.

March 1999–August 2000

MOSCOW

Russian Women's Organizations

1. All-Russia Public Movement of Rural Women (*Obshcherossiiskoe obshchestvennoe dvizhenie sel'skikh zhenshchin*). Rosa Klement'eva, chair, 6 April 1999.

2. Association of Women Doctors (*Assotsiatsiia zhenshchin-vrachei*). Larisa Skuratovskaia, director, 22 March 1999.

3. Crisis Center ANNA (*Krizisnyi tsentr dlia zhenshchin "ANNA," Assotsiatsiia "Net nasiliu," regional'naia obshchestvennaia organizatsiia*). Elena Potapova, hotline director, 12 May and 20 May 1999.

4. East-West Women's Innovation Fund (*Zhenskii innovatsionnyi fond "Vostok-Zapad"*). Galina Grishina, general director; Iulia Kachalova, editor of *Zhenshchina Plus* (journal), 21 May 1999.

5. FALTA (Feminist Alternative; *Feministskaia alternativa*). Marina Regentova and Natalia Abubikirova, co-chairs, 25 May 1999.

6. Goluba Service for Assistance to Adolescent Women (*Sluzhba pomoshchi nesovershennoletnim zhenshchinam "Goluba"*). Marianna Vronskaia, head of organization, 23 May 1999.

7. Information Center of the Independent Women's Forum (*Inform tsentr nezavisimogo zhenskogo foruma*). Elizaveta Bozhkova, director, 1 April 1999.

8. Lady-Leader (*Ledi-Lider*), Moscow division of Club L International. Maria Kliusa, deputy director, 12 May 1999.

9. Modern Woman Center (*Tsentr "Sovremennaia zhenshchina"*). Zoia Molokova, president, 22 March 1999.*

10. Moscow Center for Gender Studies (*Moskovskii tsentr gendernykh issledovanii*). Zoia Khotkina, senior research affiliate (former co-chair), 26 March 1999; Ol'ga Voronina, co-chair, 24 May 1999.

11. NIS-US Women's Consortium (*Konsortsium zhenskikh nepravitel'stvennykh ob'edinenii*). Elena Ershova, coordinator, 24 March 1999.

12. Syostry [Sisters] Independent Philanthropic Association for Assistance to Victims of Sexual Assault (*Nezavisimyi blagotvoritel'nyi tsentr pomoshchi perezhivshim seksual'noe nasilie "Sestry"*). Irina Chernenkaia, board of directors member and former executive director, 5 April 1999; 23 February 2000.

13. Union of Lawyers Commission on the Legal Status of Women (*Komissiia po pravovomu polozheniiu zhenshchin mezhdunarodnogo nepravitel'stvennogo ob'edineniia "Soiuz iuristov"*). Svetlana Polenina, commission chair, 17 May 1999.

14. Union of Russian Women (*Soiuz zhenshchin Rossii*). Irina Vladimirova, 31 March 1999.

15. Women of Russia Movement (*Obshchestvenno-politicheskoe dvizhenie zhenshchin Rossii*). Tat'iana Grantseva, press secretary and chief editor of *Women of Russia* (newspaper), 10 February 2000.

16. Iaroslavna Center for Psychological Support to Women (*Tsentr psikhologicheskoi pomoshchi zhenshchinam "Iaroslavna"*). Albina Pashina, director, 28 May 1999.

Soldiers' Rights Organizations

1. Antimilitarist Radical Association (ARA) (*Antimilitaristskaia radikal'naia assotsiatsiia*). Nikolay Khramov, secretary, 9 August 2000; Vladimir Oivin, member, 13 May 1999.

2. Committee of Soldiers' Mothers of Russia (*Komitet soldatskikh materei Rossii*). Fliora Salikhovskaia, deputy director, 10 August 2000.

3. Glasnost Foundation (*Obshchestvennyi Fond "Glasnost"*). Vladimir Oivin, deputy director, and Nikolai Gudskov, 13 May 1999.

4. International Ongoing Conference "Women for Life Without Wars and Violence!" (*Mezhdunarodnaia postoianno deistvuiushchiaia konferentsiia "Zhenshchiny za zhizn' bez voin i nasiliia!"*). Marina Sallier, co-chair, and Natalia Mikhailova, executive director, 21 May 1999.

5. Memorial Human Rights Center (*Pravozashchitnyi tsentr Memorial*). Tat'iana Kasatkina, executive director, 5 April 1999.

6. Mother's Right (*Pravo materi*). Valeriia Pantiukhina, press secretary, 23 March 1999.

7. Order of Mercy (*Orden miloserdiia*). Evgeniia Poplavskaia, president, 25 May 1999.

8. Union of Committees of Soldiers' Mothers (*Soiuz komitetov soldatskikh materei Rossii*). Coordinating council members Ida Kuklina, 29 March and 27 May 1999; Kuklina and Valentina Melnikova, 9 February 2000.

Foreign/Transnational Actors

1. Foreign State Agencies

   (a) Delegation of the European Commission: European Initiative for Democracy and Human Rights. Dr. Simon Cosgrove, manager, Moscow office, 1 April 1999.

   (b) Delegation of the European Commission: political section, Moscow. Two anonymous specialists, 7 April 1999.*

   (c) Embassy of Canada, Canadian Technical Cooperation Program. Solveig Schuster, first secretary, and Evgenia Israelian, program consultant to Canadian Fund for Support of Women's Initiatives, 9 February 2000.

   (d) USAID Russia, Office of Democratic Initiatives and Human Resources. Anonymous specialist, 18 May 1999.*

2. Intergovernmental Organizations

   (a) United Nations Development Programme (UNDP). Frederic Claus, program officer and assistant resident representative, 24 and 26 May 1999.

3. Nongovernmental Granting Organizations

   (a) Ford Foundation. Christopher Kedzie, program officer, 29 March 1999.

4. Technical Assistance and Support Organizations

   (a) American Bar Association, Central and East European Law Initiative (ABA/ CEELI). Dianne Post, legal specialist for gender issues, 25 March 1999.

   (b) World Learning NGOSS Program. Mary Heslin, project director, 8 February 2000.

Russian State or Government Organs

1. Committee for Public and Interregional Relations, Government of Moscow (*Komitet obshchestvennykh i mezhregional'nykh sviazei Pravitel'stva Moskvy*). Eleonora Luchnikova, head specialist, 19 May 1999.

2. Department for Family, Women, and Children, Russian Ministry of Labor and Social Development (*Departament po delam sem'i, zhenshchin and detei*). Ol'ga Samarina, deputy director responsible for relations with nongovernmental organizations, 26 May 1999.

3. State Duma Committee on Women, Family, and Youth (*Komitet po delam zhenshchin, semi i molodyozhi*). Zinaida Suslova, consultant to the committee staff, 1 April 1999.

ST. PETERSBURG

Russian Women's Organizations

1. Aleksandra Legal Aid Society for Domestic Violence and Sexual Assault Cases (*Sluzhba sotsial'no-iuridicheskoi pomoshchi postradavshim ot nasiliia "Aleksandra"*). Larisa Korneva, executive director and psychologist; Elena Zabadykina; and Anna Shunkova, 10 August 1999.

2. Alternativa (employment retraining organization for women) (*Tsentr sotsial'noi zashchity zhenshchin "Al'ternativa"*). Leonarda Pchelina, director, 5 and 12 October 1999.*

3. Business and Professional Women's Clubs (BPW) (*Klub professional'no aktivnykh zhenshchin*). Elena Voloshenko and Elena Khiltova, presidents, and other club members, 7 October 1999.*

4. Gloria Women's Center for Social Initiatives (*Zhenskii tsentr sotsial'nykh initsiativ "Gloriia"*). Galina Rusinova, deputy chair, 6 August 1999.*

5. Institute for Development of International Enterprise (*Institut razvitiia mezhdunarodnogo predprinimatel'stva*), member of NIS-US Women's Consortium. Galina Elistratova, director, 11 August 1999.

6. League of Women Voters of St. Petersburg (*Liga izbiratel'nits Sankt-Peterburga*). Tat'iana Dorutina, chair; Tat'iana Matveeva and Elena Diachkova, coordinators, 5 October 1999.

7. Mothers Against Narcotics (*Materi protiv narkotiki*). Liubov Spizharskaia, chair, and other members, 11 October 1999.*

8. Nadezhda Association (social-psychological support for women with breast disease) (*Assotsiatsiia "Nadezhda"*). Nelli Andronova, co-president, 11 August 1999.

9. Petersburg Center for Gender Issues (*Peterburgskii tsentr gendernykh problem*). Ol'ga Lipovskaia, director, 4 October 1999.

10. Psychological Crisis Center for Women (*Krizisnyi psikhologicheskii tsentr dlia zhenshchin*). Natalia Khodyreva, director, 6 October 1999.

11. Union of Disabled Women (*Soiuz zhenshchin-invalidov*). Maria Makhorskova, head, 4 August 1999.

12. Women and Business in Russia Association (*Assotsiatssiia "Zhenshchiny i biznes v Rossii"*). Liudmila Chubatiuk, president, 12 August 1999.

13. Women of Leningrad Oblast (*Zhenshchiny Leningradskoi oblasti*) (member organization of Union of Russian Women). Irina Shirokova, co-chair, and Natalia Grafova, Kirovskii Raion committee chair, 9 August 1999.

14. Women of St. Petersburg (*Zhenshchiny Sankt-Peterburga*) and Woman-21st Century (*Zhenshchina—XXI vek*). Svetlana Skorniakova, 6 August 1999.

15. Women's Christian-Democratic Social-Political Movement Mariia (*Zhenskii Khristiansko-demokraticheskoe obshchestvenno-politicheskoe dvizhenie "Mariia"*). Galina Grigor'eva, leader, 5 October 1999.*

Soldiers' Rights Organizations

1. Soldiers' Mother Committee of St. Petersburg (*Komitet "Soldatskaia Mat'"*). Marina Averkina, chair, 14 October 1999.

2. Soldiers' Mothers of St. Petersburg (*Soldatskie materi Sankt Peterburga*). Elena Vilenskaia and Ella Poliakova, co-chairs, 12 August and 11 October 1999.

3. St. Petersburg Independent Group for Human Rights. Anonymous member, 13 August 1999, telephone interview.*

Other NGOs

1. Citizens'Watch (*Grazhdanskii kontrol'*). Boris Pustintsev, president, 13 August 1999.
2. Russian Center for Citizenship Education. Igor Nagdas'ev, director, and Irina Mirnaia, deputy director, 14 August 1999.
3. St. Petersburg Division of Moscow Memorial (archival-historical division) (*Sankt-Peterburgskoe otdelenie Moskovskogo "Memorial"*). Viacheslav Dolinin, historian, 9 October 1999.*

Russian Resource/Research/Educational Centers for NGOs

1. Strategiia Humanities and Political Science Center of St. Petersburg (*Sankt-Peterburgskii Gumanitarnyi i politologicheskii tsentr "Strategiia"*). Mikhail Gornyi, executive director, and Evgenii Bestuzhev, program officer, 3 August 1999.

Foreign/Transnational Actors

1. Foreign State Agencies
   (a) British Know-How Fund. Victoria Fantseva, program associate, 13 October 1999.
   (b) United States Consulate. Anonymous staff member, 14 October 1999.*
2. Nongovernmental Granting Organizations
   (a) Open Society Institute (Soros Foundation). Oleg Leikind, coordinator of civil society and East-East programs, 7 October 1999.
3. Technical Assistance and Support Organizations
   (a) National Democratic Institute (NDI). Tim Russo, field officer Eurasia, 13 August 1999.

Russian State or Government Organs (Regional and Federal)

1. City Center for Social Assistance to Women (crisis center for domestic violence victims) (*Gorodskoi tsentr sotsial'noi pomoshchi zhenshchinam*). Natalia Shekodina, director, 6 August 1999.
2. Committee for Public Relations of the City of St. Petersburg (*Komitet po sviaz'iam s obshchestvennost'iu goroda Sankt Peterburga*). Dmitrii Solonnikov, specialist, 8 October 1999.
3. St. Petersburg City Commission on Improving the Status of Women. (*Kommissiia po voprosam uluchsheniia statusa zhenshchin administratsii Sankt Peterburga*). Svetlana Iakovleva, head, 12 October 1999.

EKATERINBURG

Russian Women's Organizations

1. Christian Women (*Khristianskie zhenshchiny*). Elena Tishchen'ko, president, 17 April 2000.

2. Ekaterina Crisis Center for Women (*Krizisnyi tsentr dlia zhenshchin "Ekaterina"*). Liudmila Ermakova, director, 20 April 2000.

3. Ekaterina Women's Center (*Tsentr dlia zhenshchin "Ekaterina"*). Nadezhda Golubkova, 6 April 2000.

4. Regional Foundation for Support of Women in Business (*Regional'nyi fond podderzhki zhenskogo predprinimatel'stva*). Vera Samsonova, director, 17 April 2000.

5. Urals Association of Women (*Ural'skaia assotsiatsiia zhenshchin*). Tamara Alaiba, former vice-president, 5 April 2000; Liudmila Novikova, council member, 5 April 2000.

Soldiers' Rights Organizations

1. Committee of Soldiers' Mothers of Ekaterinburg (*Komitet soldatskikh materei Ekaterinburga*). Dina Salokhina, chair, 16 and 19 April 2000 (telephone interviews).*

2. Ekaterinburg Movement Against Violence (*Ekaterinburgskoe dvizhenie protiv nasilie*). Gleb Edelev, consultant, 18 April 2000; anonymous member, 7 April 2000.

Russian Resource/Research/Educational Centers for NGOs

1. Good Will (*Oblastnaia obshchestvennaia organizatsiia "Dobraia Vol'ia"*). Elena Zyrina, director, 19 April 2000.

Foreign/Transnational Actors

1. Foreign State Agencies

    (a) United States Consulate General, Ekaterinburg. Elena Alfyorova, public affairs section officer, 6 April 2000.

2. Nongovernmental Granting Organizations

    (a) Open Society Institute. Andrei Atmanskikh, regional coordinator, 7 April 2000.

Russian State or Government Organs (Regional and Federal)

1. Directorate for Social Communications, Public Relations Department, Sverdlovsk Oblast Administration (*Upravlenie sotsial'nykh kommunikatsii otdela po sviaz'iam s obshchestvennost'iu*). Marina Chashchina, specialist, 7 April 2000.

2. Division for Relations with Social and Religious Organizations, Committee on Social Communications, City of Ekaterinburg (*Otdel po sviaz'iam s obshchestvennymi i religioznymi organizatsiiami komiteta po sviaz'iam s obshchestvennost'iu*). Maia Mikhailova, division head, 18 April 2000.

VLADIVOSTOK

Russian Women's Organizations

1. Amazonka Youth Athletics School (self-defense classes) (*Detsko-iunosheskii sportivnyi klub "Amazonka"*). Oksana Faleeva, director, 2 March 2000.*

2. Bluebird (*Siniaia ptitsa*). Marina Kazakova, former leader, 3 March 2000.

3. Far Eastern Confederation of Businesswomen (*Dal'nevostochnaia konfederatsiia delovykh zhenshchin*). Irina Tumanova, chair, and Natalia Goncharova, assistant, 15 March 2000.

4. International Women's Club (*Internatsional'nyi zhenskii klub*). Galina Nazdraten'ko, president and Nina Sadomskaia, vice-president, 14 March 2000.

5. Pan Pacific and Southeast Asia Women's Association (PPSEAWA), Russian Division. Liudmila Trofimova, president, and Ol'ga Shmelkova, vice-president, 7 March 2000.

6. Primorskii Krai Women's Union (*Soiuz zhenshchin Primorskogo kraia*). Zinaida Iovkova, chair, 27 March 2000.

7. Vladivostok City *Zhensovet* (*Sovet zhenshchin goroda Vladivostok*). Natalia Shcherbakova, chair, 7 March and 28 April 2000.

8. Women of Primorie (*Zhenshchiny Primor'ia*). Anonymous member, 10 November 1999.*

9. Women's Business Club (*Zhenskii biznes klub*). Elena Kurakulova, president, 9 November 1999.*

Foreign/Transnational Actors

1. Nongovernmental Granting Organizations

   (a) Institute for Social Action and Renewal in Eurasia (ISAR). Natalia Proskurina, director, 10 November 1999.*

2. Technical Assistance and Support Organizations

   (a) Institute for Social Action and Renewal in Eurasia (ISAR). Natalia Proskurina, director, 10 November 1999*; Marina Kazakova, program officer, 3 March 2000.

   (b) International Research and Exchanges Board (IREX). Tat'iana Zaitseva, program associate, 10 November 1999.*

Russian State or Government Organs (Regional and Federal)

1. Division for Relations with Public Organizations, Administration of Primorskii Krai (*Otdel po sviaz'iam s obshchestvennymi organizatsiiami Primorskogo kraia*). Tat'iana Filonova, head, and another staff specialist, 16 May 2000.

KHABAROVSK

Russian Women's Organizations

1. Lebedushka [Swan] Women's Club (*Zhenskii klub "Lebedushka"*). Tat'iana Shepel, president, 13 December 1999.*

2. Union of Businesswomen (*Soiuz delovykh zhenshchin*). Svetlana Zhukova, president, 17 November 1999.*

3. Union of Women of Khabarovsk Krai (*Soiuz zhenshchin Khabarovskogo kraia*). Galina Turkova, president, 2 December 1999.*

Soldiers' Rights Organizations

1. Khabarovsk Committee of Soldiers' Mothers (*Khabarovskii komitet soldatskikh materei*).Valentina Reshetkina, chair, 29 November 1999.*

Other NGOs

1. Khabarovsk Division of All-Russia Movement for Human Rights (*Khabarovskoe otdelenie Vserossiiskogo dvizheniia "Za pravo cheloveka"*), regional coordinator for Russian Coalition "Civil Society and Elections" (*Koalitsiia "Grazhdanskoe obshchestvo i vybory"*).Aleksandr Bekhtold, 15 December 1999 and 16 March 2000.*

2. Khabarovsk Krai Lawyers' Association (*Khabarovskaia kraevaia assotsiatsiia iuristov*). Liudmila Gros', chair, 6 December 1999.*

Russian Resource/Research/Educational Centers for NGOs

1. Far Eastern People's Academy of Sciences' Center for Social Information (*Tsentr sotsial'noi informatsii Dal'nevostochnoi narodnoi akademii nauk*). Dmitrii Serbzhinskii, specialist-consultant, 16 November 1999.*

2. NKO-Amur Association of Non-Profit Organizations of Khabarovsk Krai (*Assotsiatsiia nekommercheskikh organizatsii Khabarovskogo kraia "NKO-Amur"*). Evgenii Shar'ko, president, 22 November 1999 (also president of regional division of All-Russia network Narodnyi Dom). *

3. Russian-American Education Center (*Rossiisko-Amerikanskii Uchebno-Nauchnii Tsentr*).Tamara Silukova, director, 23 November 1999.*

Russian State or Government Organs (Regional and Federal)

1. Justice Department of Khabarovsk Krai (*Upravlenie iustitsii Khabarovskogo kraia*). Viacheslav Fain, former staff member, 8 December 1999.

IZHEVSK

Russian Women's Organizations

1. Club for Breast Cancer Patients, Izhevsk Mammological Center (*Klub patsientok Mammologicheskogo tsentra*).Tat'iana Koposova, head physician, and Liudmila Rudol'skaia, coordinator, 11 April 2000.

2. Izhevsk City *Zhensovet* (*Sovet zhenshchin goroda Izhevska*). Liudmila Vedernikova, chair, 10 April 2000.

3. Regional Division of the Women of Russia Movement (*Regional'noe otdelenie dvizheniia Zhenshchin Rossii*). Klara Serebrennikova, leader, and Elena Shesh'ko, Secretary, 11 April 2000.

4. Rifeia-Art Artists' Association (*Tvorcheskoe ob'edinenie "Rifeia-Art"*). Irina Zvarygina, head, 14 April 2000.

5. Union of Women of the Udmurt Republic (*Soiuz zhenshchin Udmurtskoi respubliki*). Zoia Stepnova, chair, 13 April 2000; Marina Zhilina, responsible secretary, 10, 12, and 13 April 2000.

6. Warm Home Municipal Crisis Center (*Gorodskoi krizisnyi tsentr "Teplyi dom"*). Maria Likhacheva, head specialist on social-psychological work, 14 April 2000.

Soldiers' Rights Organizations

1. Izhevsk Committee of Soldiers' Mothers (*Komitet soldatskikh materei goroda Izhevsk*). Liudmila Akat'eva, chair, 13 April 2000.

Other NGOs

1. Vozrozhdenie [Revival] Cultural-Educational Movement (*Obshchestvennoe kul'turno-prosvetitel'skoe ob'edinenie "Vozrozhdenie"*). Tat'iana Komleva, leader, 13 April 2000.*

Foreign/Transnational Actors

1. Nongovernmental Granting Organizations
   (a) Open Society Institute. Aleksandr Stashenko, regional coordinator, 13 April 2000.

Russian State or Government Organs (Regional and Federal)

1. Balizino Raion Administration (*Administratsiia raiona Balizino*). Deputy head on Social Issues, 12 April 2000.

2. Committee on Family, Women's, and Children's Affairs, Izhevsk City Administration (*Komitet po delam sem'i, zhenshchin i detei goroda Izhevsk*). Galina Shamshurina, chair, 12 April 2000.

3. Social Chamber of the Udmurt Republic (*Obshchestvennaia palata Udmurtskoi respubliki*). Tat'iana Kardapolova, press secretary, 12 April 2000.

NOVGOROD AND STARAIA RUSSA, NOVGOROD OBLAST

Russian Women's Organizations

1. Faith, Hope, and Love (*Vera, Nadezhda, Liubov'*), Staraia Russa. Liubov' Solovieva, chair, and other members, 21 February 2000.

2. League of Businesswomen (*Liga delovykh zhenshchin*). Alevtina Novikova, chair, 17 February 2000.

3. Novgorod City *Zhensovet* (*Gorodskoi sovet zhenshchin*). Zinaida Fokina, responsible secretary, 16 February 2000.

4. Novgorod Oblast *Zhensovet* (*Oblastnoi sovet zhenshchin*). Evgeniia Ivanova, responsible secretary, 16 February 2000.

5. Novgorod Women's Parliament (*Novgorodskii Zhenskii Parlament*). Irina Urtaeva, chair, 22 February 2000; Tat'iana Mal'kova, director of Home Labor Exchange Program, 14 February 2000.

6. Success Center for Support of Women in Business (*Tsentr podderzhki zhenskogo predprinimatel'stva Uspekh*), Staraia Russa. Irina Shul'ga, director, 21 February 2000.

7. Trust Psychological–Educational Center and Sisters Hotline (*Gorodskoi psikhologichesko-pedagogicheskii tsentr 'Doverie' i Goriachaia liniia Sestri*). Nadezhda Lisitsina, director, 18 February 2000.

Other NGOs

1. Novgorod Consumers' Society (*Novgorodskoe obshchestvo potrebitelei*). Antonella Strokova, chair, 17 February 2000.

2. Russa Organization for the Disabled (*Organizatsiia dlia invalidov "Russa"*), Staraia Russa. Svetlana Lenok, director, 21 February 2000.

Russian Resource/Research/Educational Centers for NGOs

1. Novgorod NGO Support Center (*Novgodorodskii tsentr podderzhki NKO*). Roman Zolin, director, 14 February 2000.

Foreign/Transnational Actors

1. Foreign State Agencies

   (a) Novgorod-the-Great Regional Initiative (U.S. Department of State). Alla Putii, coordinator, 15 February 2000.

Russian State or Government Organs (Regional and Federal)

1. Municipal Council of the City of Staraia Russa (*Munitsipal'nyi sovet goroda i raiona Staraia Russa*). Aleksandr Vasil'ev, first deputy head, 21 February 2000.

2. Public Relations Division, Novgorod Oblast Administration (*Otdel po sviaz'iam s obshchestvennost'iu Novgorodskoi oblasti*). Dmitrii Zavedovskii, division head, 16 February 2000.

Total number of interviews = 145
Total number of interview subjects = 158
Total number of organizations = 124
Of which Russian NGOs (including resource centers) = 90

July–September 1998

MOSCOW

Russian Women's Organizations

1. Association of Women Journalists (*Assosiatsiia zhurnalistok*). Irina Iurna, co-president, 28 July.

2. Conversion and Women (*Konversiia i zhenshchin*). Eleonora Ivanova, founder, 29 July.

3. Feminist Orientation Center (*Feministskii orientatsionnyi tsentr*). Marina Liborakina, director, 23 July.

4. Information Center of the Independent Women's Forum (*Inform tsentr nezavisimogo zhenskogo foruma*). Lidia Iurovskaia, staff member, 29 July.

5. Moscow Center for Gender Studies (*Moskovskii tsentr gendernykh issledovanii*). Zoia Khotkina, co-chair, 24 July.

6. NIS-US Women's Consortium (*Konsortsium zhenskikh nepravitel'stvennykh ob'edinenii*). Elena Ershova, coordinator, 21 July.

7. Union of Russian Women (*Soiuz zhenshchin Rossii*). Elena Boshun, consultant-coordinator, July 27.

8. Women's Information Network (*Zhenskaia informatsionnaia set'*). Tat'iana Troinova, 21 July.

9. Women's Unity (*Zhenskoe edinstvo*). Lusia Kabanova, member and former director; also chief of the Division for Social Rehabilitation of Women, Bureau of Labor and Employment, Northern Administrative Okrug, Moscow City Government (*Upravlenie truda i zaniatosti severnogo administrativnogo okruga, Otdel sotsial'noi reabilitatsii zhenshchin*), 27 July.

Other NGOs

1. Center for the Development of Democracy and Human Rights. Iurii Dzhibladze, director, 30 July.

2. New Perspectives Foundation (*Fond "Novye Perspektivy"*). Nadia Ser'iakova, president, 23 July.

Foreign/Transnational Actors

1. Foreign State Agencies

(a) USAID Russia, Office of Democratic Initiatives and Human Resources. Anonymous specialist, 30 July.

2. Nongovernmental Granting Organizations

(a) American Bar Association, Central and East European Law Initiative (ABA/CEELI). Dianne Post, legal specialist for gender issues, 31 July.

(b) Eurasia Foundation. Chris Barkidjia, deputy director, 22 July.

(c) Ford Foundation. Christopher Kedzie, program officer, 16 July; Irina Iurna, scholar in residence, 28 July.

(d) International Research and Exchanges Board (IREX). Stewart Chisholm, representative, Project for Institutional Partnerships with Russia and Ukraine, 22 July.

(e) MacArthur Foundation. Tat'iana Zhdanova, director, 24 July; Susan King, associate director, and Galina Ustinova, program assistant, 28 July.

(f) Open Society Institute. Anonymous staff member, Civil Society Program, 30 July.

3. Technical Assistance and Support Organizations

(a) Charities Aid Foundation (CAF). Jenny Hodgson, co-director, 17 July.

(b) League of Women Voters. Svetlana Kupriashkina, 24 July.

(c) National Democratic Institute. Anonymous representatives, 17 and 28 July.

(d) Women, Law, and Development. Gabi Fitchett, attorney, 22 July.

EKATERINBURG

Russian Women's Organizations

1. Mariia Publishing Center (*Izdatel'skii dom "Mariia"*). Elena Goncharova, director, 27 August.

2. Regional Foundation for Support of Women's Entrepreneurship (*Regional'nyi fond podderzhki zhenskogo predprinimatel'stva*). Vera Samsonova, director, and Galina Kondrashkina, assistant director, 10 August.

3. Social Scientific Center Women of Russia (*Obshchestvennyi nauchnyi tsentr "Zhenshchini Rossii"*), Ekaterinburg filial of national organization. Evgeniia Barazgova, president, and Ol'ga Kozlovskaia, vice-president, 10 August.

4. Sverdlovsk Oblast Union of Russian Women (*Sverdlovskii Oblastnoi Soiuz zhenschin Rossiiskoi Federatsiii*). Ol'ga Leonova, chair; also chair of city *zhensovet,* September 3.

5. Uralmash Factory *Zhensovet* (*Sovet zhenshchin zavoda Uralmash*). Ekaterina Moskvina, chair, 17 August.

6. Urals Association of Women (*Ural'skaia Assotsiatsiia Zhenshchin*). Valentina Der'iabina, vice-president, 7 August; Liudmila Novikova, council member, 7 August; Evgeniia Barazgova, president, 10 August.

7. Valentina. Valentina Karpovich, leader, 26 August (telephone interview).

Soldiers' Rights Organizations

1. Ekaterinburg Committee of Soldiers' Mothers (*Komitet soldatskikh materei goroda Ekaterinburg*). Dina Salokhina, chair, 2 and 3 September.

Other Russian NGOs

1. Association of Victims of Political Repression of Ekaterinburg (*Assotsiatsiia zhertv politicheskikh repressii Ekaterinburga*). Ol'ga Zubareva, chair, and representatives of 7 raions of Ekaterinburg, 2 September; Elizaveta Zyr'ianova, chair, Chkalov Raion Division, 7 August.

2. Center for Charitable Foundations and Organizations (*Tsentr blagotvoritel'nikh fondov i organizatsii*). Nikolai Khomets, vice-president; also president of the Urals Center for Social Adaptation of War Veterans (*Ural'skii tsentr cotsial'noi adaptatsii voennosluzhashchikh*), 7 August.

3. Children's Health through Physical Fitness and Sport (*Zdorov'e detei cherez fizicheskuiu kul'turu i sport*), Sverdlovsk Regional Association. Evgenii Kalegin, president, 11 August.

4. Ekaterinburg Division of Memorial. (*Ekaterinburgskoe otdelenie "Memoriala"*). Anna Pastukhova and Lena Makkei, members, 13 August.

5. Good Will (*"Dobraia Vol'ia"*). Nikolai Geller, co-director (also local regional representative of Eurasia Foundation 1996–98), 8 September (telephone interview).

6. Russian Union of Youths (*Rossiiskii Soiuz Molodezhi*), Sverdlovsk Regional Committee. Elena Zvereva, secretary, 11 August.

7. Sutiazhnik. Sergei Beliaev, president, 11 August.

8. Sverdlovsk Oblast Association of Students (*Sverdlovskaia oblastnaia assotsiatsiia uchashchikhsia molodyozhi*). Andrei Shirokov, president, 11 August.

9. Urals Ecological Foundation (*Ural'skii Ekologicheskii Fond*). Gennadii Rashchupkin, executive director, 17 August.

Foreign/Transnational Actors

1. Foreign State Agencies

    (a) TACIS Technical Office. Peter Wedemeyer, team leader; Evgenii Gaidyshev, local expert, 25 August.

2. Nongovernmental Granting Organizations

    (a) Local representative (former, 1996–98) for Eurasia Foundation. Nikolai Geller (also of Good Will), 8 September.

3. Technical Assistance and Support Organizations

    (a) Business Cooperation Center. Anatolii Plotkin, director (also director of umbrella organization, International Consulting Center), 14 August.

    (b) Center for Citizen Initiatives. Lena Novomeiskaia, director, 13 August.

    (c) Friedrich-Naumann Foundation, Urals Bureau. Vladimir Bykodorov, director, 26 August.

IZHEVSK

Russian Women's Organizations

1. Confederation of Businesswomen of the Russian Federation, Udmurt Division (*Udmurtskoe otdelenie Konfederatsii delovykh zhenshchin Rossiiskoi federatsii*). Ol'ga Gurina, director (also deputy in Izhevsk City Duma and director of Social-Rehabilitational Consultative Women's Center ReSCow), 19 August.

2. International Women's Club (*Mezhdunarodnyi zhenskii klub*). Numerous members, 20 August.

3. Izhevsk Radio Plant *Zhensovet* (*Sovet zhenshchin Izhevskogo Radiozavoda*). Valentina Shamsutdinova, chair, 21 August.

4. Regional Division of Women of Russia Movement (*Udmurtskoe regional'noe otdelenie dvizheniia Zhenshchin Rossii*). Elena Reffel, assistant director, 22 August.

5. Women of Science of the Udmurt Republic (*Zhenshchiny nauki Udmurtskoi Respubliki*). Natalia Ladyzhets, former director, 19 August.

Other Russian Organizations and Individuals

1. Apparatus of the Udmurt Republic State Council. Sergei Bekhterev, head specialist, Sociopolitical Analysis Division. 20 August.

2. Committee on Family, Women's, and Children's Affairs, Izhevsk City

Administration (*Komitet po delam sem'i, zhenshchin i detei goroda Izhevsk*). Galina Tseneva, committee specialist, 21 August.

3. Higher Women's Courses Program, Faculty of Social Communications, Udmurt State University. Galina Merzliakova, president, 20 August.

Total number of interviews = 60
Total number of interview subjects = 57
Total number of organizations = 42
Of which Russian NGOs (including resource centers) = 27

Interviews typically lasted between one and two hours, and occasionally up to four hours. In several cases I conducted multiple interviews with subjects. Interviews with Russian nationals were conducted in Russian unless the interviewee expressed a preference to conduct it in English.

The interviews had a semistructured format. Starting with a prepared set of interview questions and depending on the flow of the conversation and information during the course of the interview, in most cases questions were modified by adding some and deleting others. The order in which I asked questions was not always the same as that listed below. After a few initial exploratory questions, I attempted to introduce questions in an order related to the statements offered by the subjects, to give the conversation a natural flow and gain a sense not only of what I thought was important about their experience, but also of what information the subjects themselves wished to volunteer. I sought their independent confirmation or rejection of the importance of foreign donors and other transnational actors to their general work environment, while also leaving the research open to the emergence of unanticipated hypotheses.

Questions for Russian NGOs

1. When was your organization founded?

2. What does the organization do? In what activities and/or projects has your organization engaged? When have they begun and ended?

3. How many members are in your organization? How do you define who is counted as a member? Are you trying to increase membership? If so, how?

4. How would you say that your organization's focus has changed, if at all, since it was founded?

5. Do you engage in any activities to produce and spread information about your organization or other NGOs, or about issues that concern your organization? If so, what kind of information? How and to whom is it distributed?

6. Do you and/or other divisions of your organization have e-mail capabilities? How often do you use it for communication?

7. Do you know anything about other organizations like yours in the city, oblast, country, or internationally? How do you find out such information? Do you maintain communication with other organizations? Which ones? By what methods? How often?

8. Where do you obtain financial resources to maintain your organization?

    (a) International foundations?

    (b) Federal, oblast, or city government?

    (c) Contributions from private individuals or businesses?

    (d) Other sources?

9. (Depending on answer to #8) Why one source more than the others? How did you find out about and succeed in obtaining these funding sources?

10. For which of your projects have you received funding?

11. Does your organization spend time writing analyses or reports on social issues that concern your organization and/or producing newsletters? What portion of your time would you say is spent on such activities?

12. What portion of the organization's time is spent working directly with members of society whom your organization represents—i.e., working to solve their problems at the local level?

13. How much time do you spend on seeking and applying for funding?

14. How much time do you spend attending seminars/conferences? What kinds of conferences have you attended?

15. What kinds of contact have you had with international organizations, people, or events?

16. Have you ever been overseas? For what purpose? What were your impressions? Did the trip affect your work in any way?

17. What aspect of your contact with foreigners do you feel has most affected you, if at all?

18. (If have contact with international organizations) How have you found out about the programs of various international organizations? Do you receive any information or publications from any of them?

19. Have you attended any seminars or conferences hosted by international organizations? (If yes) What was the topic? What if any benefits did this bring to you?

20. Do you believe in acting politically—such as by communicating with parties, politicians, or government officials to achieve your organization's goals? Have you ever done so? Why/why not?

21. How clear is it to you which areas of the state or government are responsible for listening to issues related to NGO status? To the social issues that concern your organization? Federal, oblast, or city organs? Do they work effectively in doing so? Is there any coordination among different levels of government in working with NGOs?

22. Do you ever consider using the mass media as a vehicle to get the attention of powerful people and the public? Have you ever done so? Why/why not?

23. Do you ever hold any public events such as exhibitions, rallies, or publishing articles/announcements in the media? (If yes) What has this accomplished for you? (If no) Why not?

24. What would you say are the biggest obstacles to your organization in working toward its goals?

25. How do you picture your organization's role in society? How do you think society relates to your organization and its goals?

Questions for Foreign Donors

1. What is the mission of your organization in Russia? Do you have any informational brochures and/or websites containing such information?

2. Have your organization's goals, strategy, or decision-making process changed over time? If so, why and how?

3. How would you say your organization is different from others, such as [name a few competitors] that do similar work in Russia in regard to civil society?

4. Does your organization focus on particular kinds of organizations and/or particular locations in Russia? How were these sectors/locations chosen?

5. Do you maintain any informational publications and/or websites about your programs for NGOs? How is such information distributed, and to whom?

6. Does your organization sponsor projects of information dissemination among or about NGOs? If so, where and through which NGOs? To whom is the information disseminated? What is the aim of such projects? Do you see that their aims are being accomplished?

7. Why does your organization emphasize development of civil society in its mission? What does the organization view as being the role of civil society?

8. What impact do you see your organization or other international organizations having on Russian civil society? Do developments that you see conform with the goals that your organization has set out for itself?

9. How does your organization look upon the idea of projects or programs aimed at increasing Russian NGOs' involvement in politics? (If positively) Do you have any such programs? (If yes) Describe them. Why do you think, then, that so few Russian NGOs get involved at all politically? (If negatively) Why?

10. Do you have a list of organizations and projects funded by your organization with the dates, locations, and amounts of the grants? Could I have a copy of this information? Are there any reports following up from projects that I could look at?

11. Would you say that any particular types of NGOs or regions dominate in the list of those that you have funded/assisted? For example, are there a lot of women's organizations but not many disabled persons' organizations? (If yes) Would you say that this is due to a strategic mandate of the foundation, or does it simply reflect the distribution of organizational types among applicants, or do certain organizations just write better grant proposals?

Questions for Government/State Officials

1. Does your ministry/committee interact at all with NGOs? If so, how? Do you have any mechanisms for communicating with NGOs on a regular basis?

2. Can you give me one or more examples of situations in which NGOs have worked with you and your committee/ministry? Did you find any benefits or drawbacks that resulted from such work with NGOs?

3. (If there has been interaction) What made the government decide to include NGOs in your policy process?

4. How do you decide which NGOs to work with? How do you maintain contact with them?

5. Has the (regional/city) government had any interaction with foreign or international organizations such as USAID or TACIS or the UN? What interactions have you had with them? What kinds of programs, if any, have you engaged in with international organizations?

6. What in your opinion is the proper role of NGOs in politics? What kind of relationship should NGOs have with the state?

7. In your experience, how well do different levels and branches of government coordinate specifically regarding their work with NGOs?

State Foreign Assistance Agencies

Foreign governments are the largest funders of Russian NGO development. Yet many government programs are contracted out to Western organizations for implementation, such as to grant foundations and technical assistance NGOs.

This appendix describes the programs that several key foreign government donors had implemented for developing Russian NGOs through the year 2000, in terms of their goals and approaches, as well as the advantages and drawbacks of those varying approaches. The United States and the European Union had the largest NGO development initiatives, but smaller donors also implemented significant programs. In addition to discussing the largest donors, I compare the programs of Great Britain, Canada, the Netherlands, and Germany to demonstrate the range of approaches that donors adopted in their assistance programs.

1. THE UNITED STATES

The vast majority of official U.S. assistance to Russian NGO development was located within the budgets of the United States Agency for International Development (USAID) and the Department of State. Within the Department of State, programs were located mostly within the Bureau of European and Eurasian Affairs, Bureau of Educational and Cultural Affairs, and the Bureau of Democracy, Human Rights, and Labor. Smaller amounts came from other agencies such as the United States Information Agency (USIA), which closed in 1999, and whose programs were mostly amalgamated into the Department of State's Bureau for Educational and Cultural Affairs. Several large exchange programs, in which Russian citizens travel to the United States to learn about democratic civil society and government, operated through USAID and the Cultural and Educational Affairs bureau of the Department of State (many programs formerly managed by USIA). In the Department of State, one of the largest exchange programs was the International Visitor Program, through which American Foreign Service Officers chose candidates from various professions in Russia to visit their counterparts in the United States. These funds nearly all came from budget funds allocated according to the 1992 FREEDOM Support Act. Overall, between 1992 and 1999, USAID spent $133.8 million in the category of

"Democratic Reform," $26.2 million on the Eurasia Foundation (an organization that implements grants to Russian organizations for NGO development, business sector, and government reforms), and $88.5 million on "Exchanges and Training" (Office of the Coordinator, 2000). Some of the assistance from each of these categories was directed toward NGO development.

Based on information taken largely from the year 2000 annual report on assistance activities in the NIS (Coordinator of U.S. Assistance to the NIS, 2001), some of the major U.S. government programs working with Russian NGOs that were ongoing in 2000 included:

a. Regional Initiative (RI) (formerly Regional Investment Initiative)

In 2000, the RI continued its activities in Novgorod, Samara, and Sakhalin/ Khabarovsk. It was beginning to wind down activities in Novgorod, with RI closure in that region planned for 2001. The RI was a program that coordinated activities among several U.S. government-funded donors, such as USAID, Department of Agriculture, and the U.S. Russia Investment Fund. While RI programs generally focused on economic development much more than on democratic development, a few programs were still involved that related to democracy, such as ones that promoted civil society development, Internet access, and rule of law.

b. U.S. Department of State—Internet Access and Training Program (IATP), administered by the Bureau of Educational and Cultural Affairs

Sought to expand Internet access throughout Russia's regions and encourage the development of the Russian-language Internet by providing free and open Internet access and targeted training to alumni of U.S. government-funded exchange programs and other targeted audiences. IATP provided training, professional workshops, and online events.

c. USAID Independent Media Programs

Assistance for the development of independent media in Russia ranging from professional journalism training to media-related business and legal support activities. One subcontractor organization that was conducting much of this work was Internews-Russia.

d. U.S. Department of State—Media Programs

The U.S. Embassy's Public Affairs Section implemented a $900,000 media assistance program, which was part of the $10 million media assistance package announced by Secretary of State Albright in January 1999. Projects included many small and large grants, some of which were for media coverage of civic education and civil society (for example, to a television station in Ekaterinburg to produce a program on this topic).

e. USAID Support for Human-Rights Monitoring

Support for a human-rights monitoring program that covered sixty regions and produced reports for those regions, as well as a report about Russia's national human rights situation. Other programs offered to NGOs working on issues such as the rights of minorities, refugees, and psychiatric patients.

f. USAID Political Process Programs

The USAID-supported International Republican Institute (IRI) and the National Democratic Institute for International Affairs (NDI) worked on strengthening Russia's "democratically oriented" political parties. IRI and NDI trained political party leaders and civic and political activists in twelve regions. IRI provided grants to Russian NGOs with the mission of promoting democratic development. USAID funded NDI in supporting a coalition of national NGOs to organize and coordinate election-oriented advocacy activities.

g. USAID NGO Development Programs

Through its grantees World Learning and the Initiative for Social Action and Renewal in Eurasia (ISAR), USAID provided training and small grants to NGOs through forty NGO resource centers operating in twenty-five of Russia's regions. Save the Children was the American subcontractor in the Civic Education Program prior to World Learning's involvement. These programs also supported information exchange among NGOs through the Internet.

h. USAID Support for Trade Union Development

USAID-supported American Center for International Labor Solidarity (ACILS) conducted training seminars on basic trade unionism, collective bargaining, and labor dispute resolution for trade union activists across Russia. Note that in an incident that attracted great attention in the Western assistance community, the Russian government refused to allow the head of ACILS to reenter Russia (despite holding a valid visa) in December 2002 after her organization's involvement in advising the Russian air-traffic controllers' union as they planned a strike.

i. USAID Domestic Violence and Gender Equality Programs

A small-grant program implemented by the International Research and Exchanges Board (IREX) provided support to women's crisis centers in Russia. USAID also contributed to strengthening the Russian Association of Crisis Centers. Other USAID programs for civil society and human rights also supported NGOs that defended women's rights at the policy level.

j. USAID Institutional Partnerships

USAID's Sustaining Partnerships into the Next Century (SPAN) Project supported partnerships between Russian and American organizations in the areas of business development, civil society, health, environment, and the rule of law.

k. Democracy Fund Small-Grants Program

The U.S. Embassy's Democracy Commission, administered by the Public Affairs Section, awarded grants in areas including human rights advocacy, civic education, public policy, volunteerism, media, and environment. The Democracy Commission awarded small grants of up to $24,000 directly to NGOs in Russia, enabling these institutions to develop their own programs and become self-sustaining over the long run.

l. U.S. Department of State

Women's Leadership Programs Within the Embassy's Public Affairs Section, the Democracy Commission awarded grants to NGOs led by women, and the NIS

Training Grants Program awarded grants to projects implemented by female NGO activists and community leaders. These programs focused on transferring organizational skills, establishing links among NGOs, encouraging grassroots activism, establishing training centers, and training in how to mount public awareness campaigns and work with volunteers. Project topics included women's legal rights and combating domestic violence and the trafficking of women.

2. EUROPEAN UNION

The major EU body that granted assistance to Russia is the European Commission (EC), and until the late 1990s, all democracy assistance was channeled through the EC's TACIS (Technical Assistance to the CIS) program. Until the late 1990s, the EU had a very unclear policy with regard to democracy assistance in Russia. According to Richard Sakwa (2000, p. 292), the EU did not create any formal policy on democracy assistance to countries that were not slated for imminent accession into the Union, including Russia, until 1999.

The TACIS program of the early 1990s experienced serious problems of incoherent goals and extremely cumbersome and bureaucratic project approval regulations (Santiso, 2002; Youngs, 2001). Both internal and external observers sharply criticized the program, with one evaluation even calling it "one of the worst managed aid programs of all" (quoted in Sakwa, 2000, p. 291; see also Santiso, 2002, p. 107). In 1999, TACIS and its approach to democratic initiatives underwent a major overhaul, associated with the introduction of a new EC regulation governing the program (EC, 1999). Part of the overhaul involved moving TACIS's democracy component, which was renamed the European Initiative for Democracy and Human Rights (EIDHR), outside of TACIS, to report directly to the European Commission's Delegation to Russia, according to Simon Cosgrove, manager of the Moscow Office, EU European Initiative for Democracy and Human Rights (1 April 1999).

a. European Initiative on Democracy and Human Rights (EIDHR)

EIDHR grants were of three types, called targeted projects, micro-projects, and macro-projects. Targeted projects were administered by organizations from EU member states, to pursue specific priority activities on which the EC had decided to focus in any given year. The macro-projects, as their name indicates, were much larger than micro-projects, ranging in value typically from 500 thousand to one million Euros. An outside contractor in Brussels, the European Human Rights Foundation, managed the decision-making procedures for these projects, with oversight from the EC central office in Brussels. The decision process for these projects, from proposal submission to project start, was extremely long: on average, it took eighteen months but could continue as long as three years (ISA Consult et al., 1997, p. 79).

Smaller micro-projects (initially with a maximum value of ten thousand Euros but raised to fifty thousand Euros in 2000) were administered by the EIDHR Moscow office. The decision time line for these projects was much shorter, since the entire process occurred in Moscow. According to the Moscow EIDHR office manager, only five to six months passed between the grant application deadline and actual receipt of money by successful NGO applicants. The budget for the program as a whole in 2000 was one million Euros.

The micro-projects program was largely demand driven, especially in comparison with most other donors' grant programs. Within the broad realm of topics dealing with rule of law, parliamentarism, independent media, and NGO development, Russian NGOs applied with their own ideas for projects, rather than the EIDHR deciding in advance what the funding priorities for that year would be (interview with Simon Cosgrove, 1 April 1999).

b. LIEN Program (Linking Inter European NGOs) (under TACIS)

Another EU program for assistance to Russian NGOs was located directly under TACIS, and was called the LIEN Programme (Linking Inter European NGOs). It required participation of partner NGOs from both Russia and a European Union member state. A peculiarity of the LIEN grants was that they required the NGO partners to contribute at least 20 percent of the project costs (10 percent can be in-kind contributions). LIEN projects could receive TACIS funding in amounts from ten thousand to one hundred thousand Euros. The program focused particularly on providing assistance to improve the status of disadvantaged women and to promote the social reintegration or health and welfare of socially marginalized groups.

3. GREAT BRITAIN

Like the U.S. government, the British government tended to contract its programs out to British nongovernmental organizations for implementation through programs such as Partnerships in the Non-Profit Sector, Charity Know-How, and the Democratic Institutions Small Projects Scheme.

a. Partnerships in the Non-Profit Sector (PNPS)

Funded by DFID and implemented by the British-based NGO, Charities Aid Foundation (CAF), the program required a partnership between a British organization and a Russian NGO for the purpose of transferring expertise in areas such as improving services and organizational skills, enhancing mutual cooperation, and improving Russian NGO legislation. Projects were to benefit the overall NGO community, rather than individual NGOs. The maximum grant amount was fifty thousand pounds (approximately US$72,000) (DFID, n.d.).

b. The Charity Know How (CKH) program

Also implemented by CAF, this program offered three types of smaller grants for knowledge exchange and development of partnerships between NGOs from different countries. The CKH differed from the PNPS grant program in that it increasingly encouraged partnerships between NGOs from different post-Communist countries (so-called East-East partnerships) more than partnerships between UK and Russian organizations (CAF, 2001).

c. Democratic Institutions Small Projects Scheme (DISPS)

Managed by the British Council, and the grants could be up to fifty thousand pounds. They required partnership with a British organization and focused on training courses, study visits, and consultancy advice (British Council, 2001).

4. CANADA

The government agency that delivers nearly all assistance to Russian NGOs is the Canadian International Development Agency (CIDA). Annually, a few million additional dollars in assistance to Russia originated outside CIDA's standard technical cooperation and humanitarian assistance budget, in programs such as the Trust Funds for the Yeltsin Democracy Fellowship, a Russia nuclear safety program, and CIDA regional programs (CIDA, 2001). The 2001 CIDA budget for technical cooperation and humanitarian projects in Russia was 24 million Canadian dollars (approximately US$15.6 million) (CIDA 2001).

At the time of the study, the Canadian government had three basic programs that provided grants to Russian NGOs, all operating using CIDA funds. The total grant disbursement budget for these programs in 2000 was approximately 1 million Canadian dollars, according to Solveig Schuster, first secretary of the Canadian Cooperation Program at the Canadian Embassy in Moscow (interview with author, 9 February 2000). The Canadian government also had a number of programs for training NGO activists, including a program that requires Canadian partner organizations, and another that focuses on training human rights activists.

a. Canada Fund

   Began initially in 1993 by providing only equipment, rather than liquid funds, to Russian NGOs and other organizations. Canadian embassies in developing and transitional countries around the world have their own Canada Funds, with emphases that vary depending on local conditions. The program later developed into a more standard grants scheme, which focuses on funding material purchases, community socioeconomic development projects, production of information materials, and training. Examples of such projects are production of prosthetic devices and establishment of a prenatal educational center (Canadian Embassy, n.d.). The maximum grant amount was twenty thousand Canadian dollars (approximately US$13,000).

b. Canadian Fund for Support of Russian Women

   Launched in late 1999. Grants under this program ranged in value from twenty thousand to fifty thousand Canadian dollars (Canadian Embassy, 2000). The fund supported initiatives such as coalitions among NGOs, distribution of information about women's human rights, improvement of women's professional qualifications, and publication of information on women's issues in the mass media. Not only NGOs, but also academic institutions and state institutions that had joint programs with NGOs could apply for these grants.

c. Elections Fund

   Launched in 1999, the program was intended to strengthen the activities of nongovernmental groups and institutions to work toward a free, fair, and transparent election process, and to improve voter information. The maximum grant size under the Elections Fund was twenty-five thousand Canadian dollars.

d. Partnerships for Tomorrow Program

The Partnerships for Tomorrow Program supported travel by Russian and Canadian organizations in order to establish partnerships between Canadian and East
European countries and to train Russian NGOs and other kinds of organizations.

e. Promoting Human Rights in Post-Soviet Societies

Implemented by the Canadian Human Rights Foundation, this program mainly
funded projects for Canadian activists to train Russian activists in human rights
law, protection techniques, and organizational management.

5. THE NETHERLANDS

The official Netherlands assistance program that was relevant for interactions with
Russian NGOs was called the Matra program, which stands for "social transformation." Like most other donors, the Netherlands attempted to promote the rule of law,
public participation in decisions, and proliferation of NGOs. Like the larger EIDHR
of the EU, the Netherlands' program contained a specific focus on the role of armed
forces in a democratic society. And like the Canada Fund, there was a significant
emphasis on welfare and health care service provision.

a. Matra Projects Programme

The program consisted of the Matra Projects Programme, the Small Embassy
Projects Programme (MatraKAP), and Matra Training Programme. In 1996, the
government allocated 37.5 million Netherlands guilders (approximately US$15.4
million) to Matra programs throughout the Central and East European region,
including the former Soviet Union. The Matra program included strategies for
working with both governmental and nongovernmental organizations in Russia,
and the essential criterion stated for choosing activities to support is that they
"should promote public involvement in the shaping of society" (Netherlands
Ministry, 2000).

b. MatraKAP

This program gave small grants for projects to NGOs, with a maximum value of
11,345 Euros (approximately US$13,000). These grant projects did not require a
Dutch partner's participation and focused more on knowledge transfer, public
information, and education than the larger Matra Projects Programme did.
Among the NGO leaders in Moscow and St. Petersburg whom I interviewed for
this study, the MatraKAP program was one of the most frequently cited sources
from which they had received foreign funding.

c. Matra Training Programme

This program focused specifically on funding Russian representatives of governmental, educational, and nongovernmental institutions to undertake specialized
training courses in Dutch educational institutions. This differed from most
donors, who tended to support internships or brief tours in governmental and
nongovernmental institutions in their training programs. Some typical study topics were international law, health care, and environmental management (Netherlands Ministry, 2000).

GERMANY

Germany was unique as a foreign government donor, in that nearly all of its NGO development funding was channeled through foundations, or *Stiftungen,* that are closely associated with particular German political parties. The amount of funding that each *Stiftung* received from the German state budget depended on the size of its affiliated party in the parliament. Their allocations came from the Ministries of Home Affairs, Economic Cooperation, Education, and the Foreign Ministry. These funds supported the *Stiftungen* both in their domestic work in civic education and political party functions, and in their international programs. The foundations, at their peak of funding in the mid-1990s, received approximately 4 percent of Germany's total foreign aid budget. In 1996, they received US$237 million for overseas programs (Phillips, 1999, p. 81). After that, funding for the *Stiftungen* declined significantly, and by 2000 they were receiving approximately 120 million Euros (around US$137 million) per year from the German budget for their international work (Mair, 2000, p. 130). Yet this was still much more than the congressional budget allocations of the analogous American political foundations, the National Endowment for Democracy (NED), National Democratic Institute for International Relations (NDI), and the International Republican Institute (IRI), which received a total combined overseas program budget of US$54.5 million in 1996 (Phillips, 1999, p. 81) and only US$31 million in 2001 (Congressional Research Service, 2001, p. 6).

The first foundation created was the Friedrich Ebert *Stiftung,* associated with the German Social Democratic Party, more than seventy years ago. It began conducting international activities in 1957. The Konrad Adenauer *Stiftung* of the conservative Christian Democratic Union and the Friedrich Naumann *Stiftung* of the Free Democratic Party were both created in the late 1950s. These were followed by the Hanns Seidel *Stiftung* (1960s) of the Christian Social Union, the Heinrich Böll *Stiftung* (1980s) of the Green Party, and the Rosa Luxemburg *Stiftung* of the Party of Democratic Socialism (1990).

According to Stefan Mair, there was a significant difference between the Heinrich Boll *Stiftung* and the other, older foundations: it professed to devote much less importance to political party work and established interest groups, and instead focused on advocacy and self-help groups as its main beneficiary (Mair, 2000, p. 134).

Foreign Nongovernmental Organizations

Many granting foundations and training organizations working with Russian NGOs received a great deal of their funding from government agencies. In doing so, by necessity, their programs closely followed the priorities and types of mechanisms that their government funders preferred. Foundations that received their resources entirely from private sources were significantly more diverse in their approaches to Russian NGO development.

I. GOVERNMENT-FUNDED GRANTING ORGANIZATIONS

Many granting foundations that were nongovernmental nonetheless received a considerable amount of funding from governmental sources. Some of these organizations, such as the American Eurasia Foundation and NED, Germany's *Stiftungen,* and the British Westminster Foundation for Democracy received annual allocations directly from government budgets. Others with more mixed funding bases, such as Initiative for Social Action and Renewal (ISAR) and International Research and Exchanges Board (IREX), competed constantly with similar organizations for government program contracts. Because the U.S. government has been by far the largest funder of overseas democracy assistance, American nongovernmental organizations dominated in this category of government-funded granting organizations. Due to the conditions that the U.S. government specified in its contracts to these organizations, their programs closely resembled U.S. government priorities for NGO assistance. Human rights and interest group advocacy, civic education, training in NGO management techniques, and efforts to improve the legal environment of the NGO sector were common themes in the granting programs of these NGOs.

The U.S.-based Eurasia Foundation was one of the most heavily government-funded granting foundations. Although it is a nongovernmental organization, Eurasia received nearly all of its funds from USAID through the study period, and was initially created for the purpose of executing USAID's small grants programs for civil society and business development in Russia. Eurasia began making grants in 1993 with an initial allocation of US$75 million from USAID, and received continued funding of approximately US$420 million annually after that. By 2001, the foundation had raised an additional US$36 million from non-U.S. government sources (Eurasia Foundation, 2002, p. 23).

The NED is another case of a government-funded granting organization, although it operates worldwide and funds only a small number of organizations in Russia. U.S. congressional legislation created NED in 1983. Although it is funded by an annual allocation from Congress, and depends on White House and Congress support for continuation of its funding, NED claims to be autonomous in its program development and has the legal status of a nongovernmental organization. In Russia, it most often gave grants for projects on human rights monitoring and education, civic education, and encouragement of constructive dialogue between NGOs and government (NED, 2000).

There were similar examples among granting organizations from other countries. For example, the British Westminster Foundation for Democracy is funded mainly by the British Foreign and Commonwealth Office, and at the time of the study was receiving approximately four million pounds per year in government funds (WFD, 2001b). Germany's *Stiftungen,* discussed above, were another obvious example.

Several other nongovernmental foundations had a more mixed funding base, receiving support from both private and state funding sources. ISAR represented one example of this kind of arrangement: it ran various small-grants programs for NGOs and was financed by U.S. government agencies as well as by private sponsors such as the MacArthur and Mott Foundations and individual member donations. IREX, which provided travel and project grants to Russian NGOs, was another example. IREX was financed not only by U.S. government agencies, but also by private organizations like the Pew Charitable Trust and Carnegie Corporation. The majority of IREX's programming focused on academic exchanges and scholarships rather than on activists, but it did offer some technical assistance exchanges and partnering programs to NGOs. The Community Connections program provided internships for leaders of NGOs and other private or governmental organizations with relevant organizations in the United States. The Sustaining Partnerships into the Next Century (SPAN) program provided funding for joint American-Russian projects, in which—like the EU LIEN program—the partners were obligated to provide a small portion of project financing themselves.

2. LARGE PRIVATE FOUNDATIONS

The other major granting organizations for NGOs in Russia were the large private charitable foundations. The main foundations involved in Russia were the Ford Foundation, the MacArthur Foundation, and the Soros Foundation (called the Open Society Institute [OSI] in the post-Communist region). The MacArthur Foundation established a Moscow office earlier than the other foundations, opening an office in Moscow in 1992 and officially launching its grants program in 1993. George Soros' Open Society Institute opened its offices in Russia in 1995, but prior to that had been working for several years through the international Cultural Initiative Fund (*Mezhdunarodnyi fond "Kul'turnaia Initsiativa"*) and the International Scientific Fund (*Mezhdunarodnyi Nauchnyi Fond*) (OSI, 2001). Although the Ford Foundation began granting to Russian organizations in 1989 from its New York office, it only opened a representative office in Moscow in 1996.

Despite OSI's massive network, and the praise that it often received for being the most Russified and locally knowledgeable foreign donor, many Russian NGO activists complained about the way in which the foundation was run. Several NGO leaders I interviewed, in different cities, complained that OSI's grant competition process was far from transparent and that projects appeared to be chosen not on the basis of merit, but rather by some other semiclientelistic method. They also complained that OSI's programmatic focus changed dramatically from year to year. For example, in one year, OSI would fund projects for soldiers' rights, but in the next, OSI staff would state that soldiers' rights were no longer "this year's priority."

The Ford and MacArthur Foundations instead had much broader and more permanent program emphases. MacArthur was known as more of a "scientist's" foundation, supporting a great deal of academic work, including the work of individual researchers. However, MacArthur's mandate was to support research that aims to improve the human condition. In accordance with this, the foundation's Program on Global Security and Sustainability focused on topics including human rights, international justice, and new governance arrangements to address the consequences of globalization. MacArthur grants were often awarded to Russian NGOs in these areas.

The Ford Foundation, in contrast, was more of an activist-focused foundation, and its worldwide goals were to "strengthen democratic values, reduce poverty and injustice, promote international cooperation, and advance human achievement" (Ford Foundation, 2000). In Russia, its priorities were human rights and legal reform, independent analysis of economic and social policies, improving Russian social science education, and regional civic initiatives. Under both the civic initiatives and human rights programs, most grants were awarded to NGOs.

3. SMALL PRIVATE GRANTING FOUNDATIONS

Two examples of small, issue-focused private foundations that supported Russian NGOs were the U.S.-based Global Fund for Women and the Netherlands-based Mama Cash Foundation. Both of these foundations were nonendowed—thus, they depended on constant fundraising from individuals, corporations, and/or other foundations—and they worked specifically in the area of women's rights.

The Global Fund for Women (GFW) was founded in 1987 by three women in Palo Alto, California. Between then and 2001, the foundation had granted more than US$19.5 million to over 1,800 women's organizations around the world. GFW focused on various aspects of promoting women's human rights, such as increasing women's economic opportunity and independence, improving girls' access to education, stopping violence against women, and supporting lesbians' rights. GFW was particularly proud of what it called a "flexible, respectful, and responsive style of grantmaking" (GFW, 2001). Indeed, GFW was an early and important supporter of several of the women's NGOs I interviewed. For many, a grant from GFW was the first foreign grant they received, and in this sense, GFW was known in the Russian women's NGO community for "taking risks" with young NGOs that large foundations were not yet willing to support. This opinion was expressed in interviews with the author by subjects including Marina Liborakina, director of the Feminist Orientation Center (Moscow, 23 July 1998), and Olga Lipovskaia, director of the Petersburg Center for Gender Issues (St. Petersburg, 4 October 1999).

Mama Cash in the Netherlands is an example of a small, nongovernmental European foundation. Mama Cash was financed by private donations and loans from individuals and operated with a total staff and board of twenty people. The foundation supported "feminist groups that want to change for women oppressive traditional norms and work for a society in which there is equal access to wealth, (natural) resources, education, and health care." The organization specifically placed priority on "groups that encounter difficulties in raising money for controversial issues from other sources" (Mama Cash, 2000).

GFW and Mama Cash were typical of other small, private Western foundations in that they did not possess a large enough financial base to support overseas offices. Instead, nearly all of their communications with Russian NGOs were by e-mail, fax, and regular mail. Naturally, those Russian NGOs that had Internet access were much more likely to discover small-grant opportunities of this sort. Nonetheless, an amazing number of NGOs in my study learned of GFW in particular by simple word of mouth from a successful grantee.

TRAINING ORGANIZATIONS

Two of the most prominent democracy training organizations in transitional countries around the world are NDI and IRI. They work chiefly with political parties and on electoral system design; however, they also work with civic groups on topics such as organizational management, coalitional skills, lobbying techniques, and civic education (NDI, 2001; IRI, 2001). The foundations were mandated by the U.S. Congress in 1983, as part of the creation of the NED, and they were modeled closely on the experience of the German *Stiftungen,* discussed above. Unlike the *Stiftungen,* however, NDI and IRI were much less ideologically tied to their associated political parties; their advocates vehemently defended their reputations as autonomous and nonpartisan organizations (Brock, 1983; Mair, 2000, pp. 130–31). In fact, the programs of IRI and NDI resembled each other fairly closely, despite drawing staff from two ideologically different parties.

Other organizations worked as NGO resource centers and headquarters for NGO management training. A prominent example of this was World Learning's NGO Sector Support (NGOSS) program, which worked to develop regional Russian NGO resource centers in Samara, Novgorod, southern Russia, and Siberia. The program was wholly funded by USAID, as a follow-up from the earlier Civic Initiatives Program, which was contracted by USAID to the NGO Save the Children. The goal, as project director Mary Heslin stated in an interview with the author (Moscow, 8 February 2000), was "to make sure everyone has basic management training." The program focused on imparting models that had been found to work elsewhere in Russia. For example, according to Heslin, the idea of holding yearly NGO Fairs in cities to improve the public image and awareness of NGOs, initially successful in Siberia, caught on quickly in other regions through NGOSS trainings.

Other organizations that trained Russian NGOs focused on more specialized topics, rather than on general NGO development questions. ISAR adopted a mix of the two strategies, providing both NGO management training and an especially strong focus on environmental issues. It also worked both by providing a great deal of training for NGOs on Russian soil and by offering occasional overseas exchanges for ISAR clients to develop partnerships with American NGOs. In addition, as mentioned earlier in the section on granting organizations, ISAR gave hundreds of small-project grants to Russian NGOs. ISAR was known for working at a relatively grassroots level with Russian NGOs, employing many local staff members and developing priorities from below. For example, by the late 1990s, the Vladivostok office was entirely run by Russian staff, who conducted all of the trainings throughout the Russian Far East region. Recent examples of ISAR's environmentally focused programs were a week-long training course in making environmental documentary films, and production of a regular journal for Far Eastern environmental educators. More general programs included running information centers for NGOs and operating a network of NGO management trainers.

Another example of a more specialized technical assistance provider is the American Bar Association's Central and East European Law Initiative (ABA-CEELI). CEELI was closely involved with training Russian women's NGOs, lawyers, and state officials such as prosecutors, judges, and police regarding legal approaches to the problem of domestic violence. ABA-CEELI's office in Moscow had a specialist on gender issues and organized bimonthly roundtables on domestic violence topics. The gender specialist throughout most of the study period, Dianne Post, traveled extensively around Russia to encourage the organization of local NGO coalitions to work on the problem of domestic violence and to urge relevant officials to become involved.

Note that the following list is not exhaustive. It only includes those assistance providers which have had contact with the Russian NGOs in the study sample. Some are direct donors of funding, while others are nongovernmental providers of training, often subcontracted by government donors.

MOSCOW

Granting Organizations

1. Nongovernmental Granting Foundations with Offices in City

    (a) Ford Foundation (USA)

    (b) MacArthur Foundation (USA)

    (c) OSI (USA)

    (d) Eurasia Foundation (USA)

    (e) Charities Aid Foundation (CAF) (UK)

    (f) IREX (USA)

    (g) Counterpart International (USA)

    (h) Center for Citizen Initiatives (USA)

    (i) Action for Russian Children (UK)

    (j) International Women's Club (transnational, located in Moscow)

2. Foreign State Agencies or Embassies with Grant Programs—Offices in City

    (a) United States Embassy: USAID, U.S. Information Agency (former; now part of the Department of State), PROWID (USA)

    (b) Embassy of the Netherlands

    (c) Embassy of Canada

    (d) Embassy of Great Britain (British Council, British Know-How Fund)

    (e) Embassy of Switzerland

    (f) TACIS Democracy Program (EU)

3. Nongovernmental Granting Foundations without Offices in City, from whom interview subjects have received grants

   (a) Global Fund for Women (USA)

   (b) Westminster Foundation (UK)

   (c) Winrock International (USA)

   (d) Institute for Women, Law, and Development (USA)

   (e) OWEN (Germany)

   (f) Pew Charitable Trust (USA)

   (g) Sam Rubin Fund (USA)

   (h) *Frauenanstiftung* (German women's party fund, merged to become part of Heinrich Böll *Stiftung* of the German Green Party in 1997)

   (i) Right Livelihood Foundation (Sweden)

   (j) National Endowment for Democracy (USA)

   (k) KARAT Coalition (Poland)

   (l) Mama Cash (Netherlands)

   (m) Mott Foundation (USA)

   (n) Guggenheim Foundation (USA)

   (o) Center for Development and Population Activities (CEDPA) (USA)

4. Foreign State or Interstate Organizations from whom interview subjects have received grants—without office in city

   (a) Senate of City of Berlin (Germany)

   (b) United Nations: UNIFEM (project grants), UNESCO (program and travel grants)

Training Organizations (nongranting)

1. Nongovernmental Organizations with Offices in City

   (a) National Democratic Institute (USA; training seminars, overseas training)

   (b) IRI (USA; training seminars, overseas training)

   (c) American Bar Association (USA; training seminars)

   (d) Urban Institute (USA; training seminars, conferences)

   (e) World Learning (USA; administers' network of NGO support centers around Russia, consultations for NGOs)

   (f) Charities Aid Foundation (CAF) (UK; trainings and consultations for NGOs, NGO support library)

   (g) Center for Peacemaking and International Development (Chris Hunter, UK; overseas exchange)

2. Nongovernmental Organizations without Offices in City, which have offered programs for interview subjects

   (a) OWEN (Germany; training course and overseas training)

(b) Mediawatch (Canada; travel to overseas conference)

(c) Counterpart International (USA; training seminars)

(d) Center for Citizen Initiatives (USA; overseas training internships)

(e) Women's World Banking (USA; training course)

(f) Peace Links (USA; early perestroika citizen exchanges)

(g) Global Citizens' Network (USA; exchange trips)

(h) British and Swedish divisions of European Union of Women (UK, Sweden; visits, conferences, information exchange)(i) Social Democratic Party of Germany (travel to overseas conference)

(j) Konrad Adenauer *Stiftung* (foundation of German Christian Democratic Party) (Germany; overseas training exchange)

(k) Polish Helsinki Foundation (Poland; overseas training courses)

(l) Family Violence Prevention Fund (USA; training seminars)

(m) Women for World Peace (Sweden; training seminars, overseas exchanges)

(n) Association of Women in Development (AWID) (USA; overseas conference)

(o) Mitterand-Gorbachev Foundation (France; overseas educational program)

(p) MiraMed Institute (USA; information exchange, conferences, trainings)

Total number of transnational actors for Moscow: 56
Number of transnational actors per NGO interviewed: 56/35 = 1.6

ST. PETERSBURG

Granting Organizations

1. Nongovernmental Granting Foundations with Offices in City

    (a) OSI (USA)

    (b) Russian-German Exchange (Germany)

2. Foreign State Agencies or Embassies with Grant Programs—Offices in City

    (a) TACIS (EU)

    (b) British Consulate (British Know-How Fund, British Council—all applications forwarded to Moscow) (UK)

    (c) United States Consulate (USIS, USAID—all applications forwarded to Moscow) (USA)

    (d) Consulate of the Netherlands

    (e) Royal Danish Consulate (Denmark)

3. Nongovernmental Granting Foundations without Offices in City, from whom interview subjects have received grants

    (a) Ford Foundation (USA)

    (b) National Endowment for Democracy (USA)

    (c) Eurasia Foundation (USA)

    (d) Global Fund for Women (USA)

    (e) Heinrich Böll *Stiftung* (Germany)

    (f) *Frauenanstiftung* (Germany)

    (g) Freedom House (USA)

    (h) Mama Cash (Netherlands)

    (i) Center for Research on European Women

    (1j) Mott Foundation (USA)

    (k) Witness (USA)

    (l) Fukabori Foundation (Japan)

    (m) Konrad Adenauer *Stiftung* (Germany)

4. Foreign State or Interstate Organizations from whom interview subjects have received grants—without office in city

    (a) United Nations Population Fund (conference)

    (b) Council of Europe, Department for Human Rights (EU)

Charitable Donations

1. Caritas (international Catholic charity with office in St. Petersburg) (Vatican; material donations)

2. Burda Moden (German fashion magazine) (Germany; material donations)

Training Organizations (primarily nongranting)

1. Nongovernmental Organizations with Offices in City

    (a) NDI (USA; training seminars, also some grants)

    (b) IRI (formerly in city) (USA; training seminars, also some grants)

    (c) AIDA (women's business association) (Italy; overseas internship, training)

    (d) Burda Moden (German fashion magazine) (Germany; training)

2. Nongovernmental Organizations without Offices in City, which have offered programs for interview subjects

    (a) American Civil Liberties Union (USA; publications and overseas exchanges)

    (b) Center for National Security Studies (USA; conferences, information exchange)

    (c) International Helsinki Foundation (Austria; overseas conferences)

    (d) Library of Congress (USA; overseas lectures)

    (e) MiraMed Institute (USA; information exchange, conferences, trainings)

    (f) Central European University (Hungary; overseas education program)

    (g) International Research and Exchanges Commission (IREX) (USA; overseas education program)

(h) Kettering Foundation (USA; conferences, training, overseas education)

(i) Reach to Recovery (breast cancer association) (USA; training, overseas conferences)

(j) Pax Christi (Catholic peace organization) (Belgium; overseas lecture tour)

(k) SOS Mothers Center (USA; overseas conference)

(l) International School for Human Rights (Poland; overseas training)

(m) Marta (women's organization) (Finland; overseas travel exchange)

(n) Esquinore (women's division of Swedish Social Democratic Party) (Sweden; overseas training)

(o) Association of Women with University Education (USA; seminars)

(p) Peace Links (USA; citizen exchanges)

(q) Greenpeace (Finland; student overseas conferences)

3. Foreign State or Intergovernmental Organizations with Offices in City

(a) Consulate of Poland (space for organization meetings, trainings)

Total number of transnational actors for St. Petersburg: 46
Number of transnational actors per NGO interviewed: 46/22 = 2.1

EKATERINBURG

Granting Organizations

1. Nongovernmental Granting Foundations with Offices in City

(a) Eurasia Foundation (no office in city since 1998) (USA)

2. Foreign State Agencies or Embassies with Grant Programs—Offices in City

(a) British Consulate (British Know-How Fund; joint EU-USA "Democracy and Civil Society Award" to Urals Association of Women, nominated by British Consulate) (UK)

3. Nongovernmental Granting Foundations without Offices in City, from whom interview subjects have received grants

(a) Ford Foundation (USA)

(b) Friedrich Naumann *Stiftung* (Germany)

(c) USAID/IRIS (Center for Institutional Reform and the Informal Sector) (USA)

(d) Bear Trust (UK)

(e) Mott Foundation (USA)

4. Foreign State or Interstate Organizations from whom interview subjects have received grants—without office in city

(a) TACIS (EU)

(b) United Nations (travel grants to Beijing)

Training Organizations (nongranting)

1. Nongovernmental Organizations with Offices in City
    (a) Center for Citizen Initiatives (USA) (training trips overseas)
    (b) Friedrich Naumann *Stiftung* (Germany) (training seminars)
    (c) Citizens Democracy Corps (USA; training by foreign volunteers)
    (d) Center for Business Support) (no longer with office in city) (USA; training)
2. Nongovernmental Organizations without Offices in City, which have offered programs for interview subjects
    (a) IREX Business for Russia program (USA; overseas internships)
    (b) NDI (USA; training seminars)
3. Foreign State or Intergovernmental Organizations with Offices in City
    (a) TACIS (EU; overseas internships)
    (b) United States Consulate (USA; training seminars by visiting experts)
    (c) British Know-How Fund (UK; overseas internships)
    (d) Library of Congress (USA; overseas internships)

Total number of transnational actors for Ekaterinburg: 19
Number of transnational actors per NGO interviewed: 19/25 = 0.76

IZHEVSK

Granting Organizations

1. Nongovernmental Granting Foundations with Offices in City
    (a) OSI (regional representative only) (USA)
2. Nongovernmental Granting Foundations without Offices in City, from whom interview subjects have received grants
    (a) IREX (USA)
    (b) Russia 01 (American birth control program, Magee-Women's Hospital) (USA)
    (c) CEDPA (USA)
3. Foreign State or Interstate Organizations from whom interview subjects have received grants—without office in city
    (a) TACIS (EU)

Training Organizations (nongranting)

1. Nongovernmental Organizations without Offices in City, which have offered programs for interview subjects
    (a) Southern Maine University (USA; academic internship)
    (b) University of Kent (UK) (academic partnership with Kazan University)

(c) Central European University (Hungary; paid trips for study)

(d) CEDPA (USA; training seminars)

(e) National Peace Foundation (USA; training seminar)

2. Foreign State or Intergovernmental Organizations without Offices in City

(a) USAID/AED (USA; overseas training)

Total number of transnational actors for Izhevsk: 11
Number of transnational actors per NGO interviewed: 11/13 = 0.85

VLADIVOSTOK

Granting Organizations

1. Nongovernmental Granting Foundations with Offices in City

(a) Eurasia Foundation (USA)

(b) Initiative for Social Action and Renewal (ISAR) (USA)

(c) Project on Environmental Policy and Technology (no longer with office in city) (USA)

2. Nongovernmental Granting Foundations without Offices in City, from whom interview subjects have received grants

(a) Institute for Sustainable Communities ROLL (Replication of Lessons Learned) Program (USA)

(2) Pacific Environment and Resources Center (PERC) (USA)

(3) Caritas (Vatican)

3. Foreign State or Interstate Organizations from whom interview subjects have received grants—without office in city

(a) USAID/IRIS (USA)

Training Organizations (nongranting)

1. Nongovernmental Organizations with Offices in City

(a) IREX (USA; overseas internships)

(b) ISAR (USA; training seminars, information provision)

2. Nongovernmental Organizations without Offices in City, which have offered programs for interview subjects

(a) International Bahai Community (transnational; overseas conference)

3. Foreign State or Intergovernmental Organizations with Offices in City

(a) USAID (no longer with office in city)

(USA; training seminars, overseas trainings)

Total number of transnational actors for Vladivostok: 11
Number of transnational actors per NGO interviewed: 11/9 = 1.2

KHABAROVSK

Granting Organizations

1. Nongovernmental Granting Foundations without Offices in City, from whom interview subjects have received grants

  (a) Eurasia Foundation (USA)

  (b) Counterpart International (USA)

  (c) OSI (USA)

  (d) ISAR (USA)

2. Foreign State or Interstate Organizations from whom interview subjects have received grants—without office in city

  (a) USAID (USA)

Training Organizations (nongranting)

1. Nongovernmental Organizations with Offices in City

  (a) Citizens Democracy Corps (no office in city since 1999) (USA; training by foreign volunteers)(b) IREX (regional representative only) (USA; overseas internships)

  (c) Winrock International (USA; training by foreign consultants)

2. Nongovernmental Organizations without Offices in City, which have offered programs for interview subjects

  (a) Counterpart International (USA; overseas training and organizational support)

  (b) Pacific Environment and Resources Center (PERC) (USA; training seminars)

  (c) Bear Trust (UK; training seminars)

  (d) Foundation for Russian American Economic Cooperation (USA; training seminars)

  (e) University of Alaska American-Russian Center (USA; overseas training)

  (f) Community Connections Program (USA; overseas exchange and training)

  (g) Peace Links (USA; overseas exchange)

  (h) NDI (USA; overseas training)

3. Foreign State or Intergovernmental Organizations without Offices in City, which have offered programs for interview subjects

  (a) Portland, Oregon sister city (USA; overseas exchanges)

  (b) USAID (USA; Moscow conference)

  (c) British Know-How Fund (UK; training conferences)

Total number of transnational actors for Khabarovsk: 19
Number of transnational actors per NGO interviewed: 19/10 = 1.9

Novgorod

Granting Organizations

1. Nongovernmental Granting Foundations with Offices in City
   (a) IREX (regional representative only) (USA)
   (b) OSI (regional representative only) (USA)
2. Foreign State Agencies or Embassies with Grant Programs—Offices in City
   (a) TACIS (EU)
   (b) United States Regional Investment Initiative (coordinates U.S. assistance in the region) (USA)
3. Nongovernmental Granting Foundations without Offices in City, from whom interview subjects have received grants
   (a) Eurasia Foundation (USA)
   (b) World Learning (USA; overseeing local NGO support center)
   (c) Winrock International (USA)
4. Foreign State or Interstate Organizations from whom interview subjects have received grants—without office in city
   (a) Embassy of Canada
   (b) Embassy of Netherlands

Training Organizations (nongranting)

1. Nongovernmental Organizations with Offices in City
   (a) IREX (USA; overseas internships, training seminars)
2. Nongovernmental Organizations without Offices in City, which have offered programs for interview subjects
   (a) Swedish crisis center (Sweden) (overseas exchanges and internships, conferences)
   (b) Citizen Democracy Corps (USA; training seminars)
   (c) Opportunity International (USA; training seminars)
   (d) Miramed Institute (USA; information exchange, conferences, trainings)
   (e) NDI (USA; overseas training)
   (f) Library of Congress (USA; overseas training)
   (g) Winrock International (USA; training seminars)
   (h) Women's World Bank (USA; training seminar in Moscow)
3. Foreign State or Intergovernmental Organizations with Offices in City
   (a) United States Regional Investment Initiative (USA; training seminars, conferences)

Total number of transnational actors for Novgorod: 19
Number of transnational actors per NGO interviewed: 19/10 = 1.9

Calculating NGO populations is difficult, since official statistics given by regional governments are often counted in different ways: some, for example, include political parties, others include state-formed organizations (often called GONGOs, or government organized NGOs, in Western literature), and still others include both. Where possible, I tried to determine what the tallies included, and to remove the counts of political parties and GONGOs from the total. It was not always possible to obtain this level of detail, however. Typically, regional-level divisions of the Ministry of Justice had statistics available for locally based organizations registered at the regional level (but not at the national or municipal level). By using the statistics on officially registered NGOs, I hoped to obtain a relatively comparable count of organizations across regions.

As noted elsewhere, though, not all organizations that are officially registered are actually active, and many active NGOs have chosen not to register officially. Research indicates that approximately only 25 percent of all officially registered organizations are active (research conducted by the Center for Development of Democracy and Human Rights in Moscow, cited in Sevortian, 2000).

Thus, the official statistics do not give an adequate picture of the number of existing, active NGOs. For a more accurate picture, I consulted with local experts at NGO resource centers. This method has the serious defect of being inconsistent across regions, since different experts and NGO resource centers gather their information in different ways, and some counts were conducted more recently than others.

At the aggregate national level, counts of NGOs are equally disputed. Most recent estimates of the numbers of NGOs existing in Russia range from 135,000 to approximately 570,000 (Federal News Service, 2003). In 2001, Mariia Slobodskaia of Moscow's Institute of Problems of Civil Society cited a total of 300,000 NGOs (Liubin, 2001).

Table A5.1 gives both kinds of measures for each of the seven cities. Beside the official and unofficial counts, it also lists the NGO density per thousand residents that results from dividing the NGO counts by the city population. In the case of official statistics, I use the city population, although the statistics generally include all regional-level organizations (which might be located in other towns of the region), because the vast majority of NGOs in the regions studied were located in the regional capitals.

TABLE A5.1. Estimates of NGO populations, by region.

City	Officially registered NGOs at regional level	City population (thousands)[1]	Resulting NGO density per 1,000 residents	Local alternative estimates of number of active NGOs	Resulting NGO density per 1,000 residents
Moscow	24,000	10,102	2.4	15,000[2]	1.5
St. Petersburg	12,044	4,669	2.6	8,000–9,000[3]	1.7–1.9
Ekaterinburg	2,000	1,293	1.5	1,500[4]	1.2
Vladivostok	2,232	592	3.8	170[5]	0.3
Khabarovsk	850	583	1.5	100–200[6]	0.2–0.3
Izhevsk	400	632	0.6	n/a	n/a
Novgorod	1,040	217	4.8	500[7]	2.3

SOURCES:

1. Federal Service of State Statistics (2002)

2. CAF (1997)

3. Russian-German Exchange NGO Center (*Tsentr RNO*) (2000)

4. Good Will NGO Directory (1999)

5. ISAR-RFE NGO Directory (2001)

6. Far Eastern People's Academy of Sciences Center for Social Information, Russian-American Education Center (1999)

7. Novgorod Center for NGO Support

Notes

Preface

1. With some exceptions, such as Carothers (1999); Carothers and Ottaway (2000); Mendelson and Glenn (2002); Mendelson (2001); Henderson (2003); Sperling (1999).

2. Carothers (1999, p. 50) cites the total of worldwide assistance to civil society from USAID alone from 1991 to 1999 as being US$1.1 billion. One estimate of worldwide government expenditures on civil society assistance states that in the years 1993–94 alone, the United States spent just over US$100 million on civil society assistance worldwide, or one-third of its democracy-aid spending. During the same period, the EU, Sweden, and the UK together spent approximately US$60 million on civil society assistance worldwide, while in 1993–95 Canada spent CA$13.5 million (or 28 percent of its democracy assistance) on civil society projects (Van Rooy and Robinson, 1998, pp. 60–61).

3. I differentiate the terms "international" and "transnational" in the following, widely accepted manner: "International" is a broader umbrella term that includes relations between governments or state structures, as well as nongovernmental relations. "Transnational" refers more particularly to relations conducted across international borders, in which one or more of the actors involved is a non-state actor (see, for example, Keck and Sikkink, 1998, p. 1; Tarrow, 1998; Evangelista, 1995, p. 1). Thomas Risse-Kappen defines transnational relations as "regular interactions across national boundaries when at least one actor is a non-state agent or does not operate on behalf of a national government or an intergovernmental organization" (1995, p. 3).

4. Examples include Evans, Henry, and Sundstrom (2005); Sperling (1999); Gibson (2001); Hale (2002); Mendelson and Glenn (2002); Richter (2002); Henderson (2003); Howard (2003); Hemment (2004).

Chapter 1

1. Keck and Sikkink use data collected by Jackie Smith to document the proliferation of international nongovernmental organization (INGOs) committed to social change (1998, p. 11). For example, women's rights INGOs have grown in num-

ber from 10 in 1953, to 25 in 1983, to 61 in 1993. Human rights INGOs have multiplied even more rapidly, from 33 in 1953, to 79 in 1983, and 168 in 1993.

2. Aleksandr Bekhtold, regional coordinator for the Russian coalition Civil Society and Elections, Khabarovsk division of the All-Russia Movement "For Human Rights," interviews with author, Khabarovsk, 15 December 1999 and 16 March 2000. See further details in Chapter Four.

3. The term "resurrecting civil society" is borrowed from O'Donnell and Schmitter's famous outline of the paradigmatic pattern of transition from authoritarian rule (1986, ch. 5).

4. Some authors have pointed out the significant political role of transnational contacts between scientists and technical specialists much earlier in the Soviet period. For example, contacts between nuclear scientists through the medium of professional journals as early as the Khrushchev era were important in developing a Soviet movement of scientists who favored ending the nuclear arms race (Evangelista, 1999, pp. 39–40, 82–89).

5. Olga Leonova, chair, Sverdlovsk Oblast Union of Russian Women, interview with author, Ekaterinburg, 3 September 1998; Ekaterina Moskvina, chair, *zhensovet* of Uralmash Factory, interview with author, Ekaterinburg, 17 August 1998.

6. Zoia Khotkina, senior research affiliate and former co-director, Moscow Center for Gender Studies, interview with author, Moscow, 27 March 1999.

7. CAF International (1997, p. 2.6).

8. However, it is generally agreed that *associations* of businesses, to promote their group interests, are certainly part of civil society.

9. Fish (1995) is one of the few authors who implicitly include political parties by largely studying political opposition groups in his study of perestroika-era Russian civil society.

10. Elena Vilenskaia, co-chair, Soldiers' Mothers of St. Petersburg, interview with author, St. Petersburg, 12 August 1999.

11. Incidentally, as Carothers points out, "boosters of civil society aid often cite Putnam as support for their approach," even though they miss a large part of his argument (1999a, p. 212).

12. Liah Greenfeld, for example, charts discussions among the Russian intelligentsia regarding the regime transition over the course of the 1990s and argues that the intelligentsia were dismayed to discover that democratization "mixed them with hoi polloi. This was the crux of the problem. Much of the discussion about the essence and the role of the intelligentsia focused precisely on this aspect of it, and numerous attempts to define the group, which were, in effect, attempts to distinguish it from the so-called 'masses' and prove its superiority, suggested that its crisis of identity was caused not by the introduction of market mechanisms and the materialism they fostered, but by democratization and by the fact that the Russian intelligentsia as a group was inherently, fundamentally opposed to democracy" (Greenfeld, 1996).

13. This figure was derived from compiling relevant funds expended from the Freedom Support Act (FSA); the Department of State's Bureau of Democracy, Human Rights, and Labor and Bureau for European Affairs; the U.S. Justice Department's Criminal Law Assistance program; and the Open World Program of the Center for Russian Leadership Development (compiled from the annual fiscal year re-

port, *U.S. Government Assistance to and Cooperative Activities with Eurasia* (U.S. Department of State, 2001, 2002, 2003).

14. Longtime leaders in Russian feminist movement, interview with author, Moscow, 25 May 1999.

15. Donor funding profiles are discussed in greater detail in Chapter Two.

16. Staff member, Civil Society Program, Open Society Institute, interview with author, Moscow, 30 July 1998.

17. Christopher Kedzie, program officer, Ford Foundation, interview with author, Moscow, 16 July 1998.

18. Chapter Three discusses public opinion on this issue in detail.

19. Regional Initiative is the new name of the program formerly called Regional Investment Initiative. The name was changed to reflect a transition to broader assistance aside from economic investment to the designated regions.

20. Statistics from the 2002 Russian census indicated that the percentage of the urban population aged fifteen or older with mid- or higher-level professional (post-secondary) education was 61.4 percent in Moscow and 58.5 percent in St. Petersburg, and ranged between 45.5 and 53.2 percent in the other five regions studied (Federal Service of State Statistics, 2004).

21. Indeed, Ruble (1987, p. 181) states that even in the late Soviet period, "expanding private markets (both legal and illegal) for housing and consumer goods" increased employees' independence from their employers.

22. The database program used was QSR NUD*IST 4, by Qualitative Solutions and Research Pty Ltd.

23. The only exception to this was the use of information about transnational funding and training frequencies from an additional eleven interviews from 1998, in order to compare NGO communities across regions in Chapter Four. This was done in order to provide as full a picture as possible of how regional locations compared in their transnational interactions, since such information was available from those 1998 interviews.

Chapter 2

1. For accounts of this early, short-lived effort at forming an independent women's organization, see *Maria* (1981); Waters (1993); and Dyukova (1998).

2. Beginning in 1975, the Netherlands achieved the internationally agreed aim of allocating at least 0.7 percent of GNP to official development aid, making it the second country after Sweden to achieve this target (Netherlands Ministry of Foreign Affairs, 2000). By 1997, the proportion had reached 0.81 percent (North-South Institute, 1999, p. 123).

3. Boris Pustintsev, president, Citizen Watch, interview with author, St. Petersburg, 13 August 1999.

4. For more information on these organizations, see Chapter 3. Other detailed sources are Sperling (1999) and Henderson (2003).

5. The conference, "Development of the Nonprofit Sector in the Far East and Baikal Regions of Russia," was held in Khabarovsk on 31 March to 2 April 1999 and was funded by the Mott and Eurasia foundations.

6. Anonymous leader of a local NGO, interview with author, Khabarovsk, 13 December 1999.

7. Elena Potapova, executive director, ANNA Crisis Center, interview with author, Moscow, 12 May 1999.

8. Irina Chernenkaia, Syostry Center for Assistance to Victims of Sexual Assault, interview with author, Moscow, 23 February 1999.

9. Natalia Abubikirova and Marina Regentova, Feminist Alternative (FALTA), interview with author, Moscow, 25 May 1999.

10. See Nelson (2000, p. 15) also regarding a foundation program evaluator's finding that a high percentage of e-mail addresses of NGOs subscribing to national networks were either defunct or rarely checked by their owners.

11. The Russian Far East (RFE) RI is headquartered in the city of Yuzhno-Sakhalinsk on Sakhalin Island.

12. Solveig Schuster, first secretary, Canadian Embassy, interview with author, Moscow, 9 February 2000.

13. Elena Zabydykina, Anna Shunkova, and Larisa Korneva, Aleksandra Legal Aid Society for Domestic Violence and Sexual Assault Cases, interview with author, St. Petersburg, 12 August 1999.

Chapter 3

1. Sarah Mendelson and John Glenn, in their conclusions from a research project concerning democracy assistance and NGO strategies in the post-Communist region, do briefly make a similar argument to the frame resonance approach (Mendelson and Glenn, 2002, p. 23). Marina Ottaway (2000) makes a similar point concerning foreign assistance to African civil society organizations. Aside from these examples, very few authors have examined in detail why certain specific transnationally promoted norms transfer successfully to local contexts, while others do not.

2. Also, author's interviews with Elena Ershova, NIS-US Women's Consortium, Moscow, 24 March 1999; Elizaveta Bozhkova, Information Center of the Independent Women's Forum, Moscow, 1 April 1999; and Maria Likhacheva, Warm Home Crisis Center, Izhevsk, 14 April 2000.

3. Stated by Flyora Salikhovskaia, deputy chair, Committee of Soldiers' Mothers of Russia, interview with author, 10 August 2000. Also confirmed in CSMR (1999).

4. UCSMR records show an increase in soldiers' appeals (*obrashcheniia*) to them from 1,400 in 1994 to 7,000 in 1995, and an increase in the number of consultations given to draftees and their parents from 5,200 in 1994 to 11,000 in 1995. By 1998, the number of appeals had settled to 2,600, and the number of consultations to 10,000 (CSMR, 1999). In 2001, the numbers had increased again as a result of the second Chechen campaign: the UCSMR reported that over 15,000 soldiers and parents had appealed to them for assistance (RFE/RL, 2001c).

5. The Right Livelihood Award is granted by a foundation that Jakob von Uexkull, a writer and former European Parliament member, created in 1980. It is intended to spread the recipients' knowledge and to show that small numbers of mobilized people can confront difficult problems (Right Livelihood Foundation, 2000).

6. Valeria Pantiukhina, press secretary, Mother's Right Foundation, interview with author, Moscow, 23 March 1999.

7. Maria Averkina, chair, Soldier's Mother Committee, interview with author, St. Petersburg, 14 October 1999. It is doubtful that the mother in question was lying to Averkina, since I observed no fewer than four other mothers who came to the committee that day with similar complaints about their sons from the very same division.

8. Nikolai Khramov, secretary, ARA, interview with author, Moscow, 9 August 2000.

9. Khramov, interview.

10. Pantiukhina, interview.

11. Elena Vilenskaia and Ella Poliakova, co-chairs, Soldiers' Mothers of St. Petersburg, interview with author, St. Petersburg, 12 August 1999.

12. Vilenskaia and Poliakova, interview.

13. Valentina Melnikova, coordinating council member, Union of Committees of Soldiers' Mothers of Russia, interview with author, Moscow, 9 February 2000.

14. In certain cases, however, ARA's leaders have approved of NATO's military operations in Yugoslavia, stating that "if you aren't strong enough to oppose violence by nonviolent means, then it is preferable to oppose it by violence rather than doing nothing . . . We're not pacifists, but proponents of aggressive nonviolence" (Khramov, interview).

15. Article 59, clause 3 of the Russian Constitution states that "a citizen of the Russian Federation has the right to replace army service with alternative civil service in the case that his convictions or religious beliefs contradict the conduct of military service, as well as in other circumstances established by federal law."

16. Khramov, interview; Vladimir Oivin, deputy director, Glasnost Foundation, and ARA member, interview with author, Moscow, 13 May 1999.

17. Leaders of the Russian Committee of Soldiers' Mothers, interview with author, Moscow, 10 August 2000; and leaders of the Union of Committees of Soldiers' Mothers, interview with author, Moscow, 27 May 1999.

18. Valentina Reshetkina, chair, Khabarovsk Committee of Soldiers' Mothers, interview with author, Khabarovsk, 29 November 1999.

19. According to the Union of Soldiers' Mothers of Russia, fifteen thousand soldiers and parents had turned to them for assistance during the year prior to September 2001 (RFE/RL, 2001c).

20. Vilenskaia, interview.

21. Pantiukhina, interview. Also see RFE/RL (1999).

22. According to the Russian Ministry of Defense, among conscripts in autumn 1999, 57.6 percent fell under the category of only "partially fit" for service due to medical problems. In 1989, this figure was only 4 percent (Yegorov, 2000). Moreover, officials at the Defense Ministry's chief medical administration report that in the years 1999–2001, every third draftee has been excused from service because of poor health (RFE/RL, 2001b).

23. On the land mines campaign, see Rutherford (2000), Price (1998), and Cameron, Lawson, and Tomlin (1998). On torture, see Risse and Sikkink (1999) and Keck and Sikkink (1998). On the issues of violence against women and rainforest destruction, see Keck and Sikkink (1998).

24. Khramov, interview.

25. For example, in 1998 Sergeev stated "I'm convinced only a professional army can meet today's requirements. Unfortunately, there are doubts about our ability to

comply with the presidential decree as early as 2000. This would need an additional outlay of at least six billion roubles" (Reuters, 12 August 1998).

26. The survey was multiple choice without a specific option to choose "opposition to militarism" as an answer. This omission in itself is revealing of Russian elite views on the military. However, only 5 percent of respondents fell under the residual categories "other reasons" and "cannot name reasons."

27. Nonetheless, soldiers' rights NGOs do report some instances of falling out of fashion with foreign donors. For example, the SMSP reports that they received a three-year grant from OSI, after which OSI refused to grant them any more funding, saying that they thought they had "done enough" for soldiers' rights groups and would now focus on children's issues (Vilenskaia and Poliakova, interview).

28. Schuster, interview.

29. Mikhail Gornyi, executive director, Strategiia Humanities and Political Science Center of St. Petersburg, interview with author, St. Petersburg, 3 August 1999.

30. Prominent examples are ARA, SMSP, UCSMR, and Memorial.

31. See also the quote in Chapter One by Zoia Khotkina, senior research affiliate and former co-director, Moscow Center for Gender Studies, interview with author, Moscow, 27 March 1999.

32. The members of SAFO included Marina Regentova and Natalia Abubikirova of FALTA, and Olga Lipovskaia of the Petersburg Center for Gender Issues. LOTOS's founders included Anastasia Posadskaia and Olga Voronina of MCGS.

33. Marina Regentova and Natalia Abubikirova, *Feministskaia alternativa* (FALTA), interview with author, Moscow, 25 May 1999.

34. Regentova and Abubikirova, interview.

35. Khotkina, interview.

36. The ICIWF was formed in 1994 by a small number of participants from the Dubna Forums. The Independent Women's Forum itself never developed into a formal organization.

37. The authors exclude nearly all of the vast network of *zhensovet* organizations on the basis that most of these groups are tied closely with the state.

38. For example, the list of registered NGOs in Khabarovsk Krai includes just 41 NGOs in the combined category of "women, family, and youth," but 124 sports organizations, 137 religious organizations, 49 organizations for the disabled, 49 environmental organizations, and 51 veteran and charity organizations, among others (Khabarovsk Krai, 2000). An independent study by the Charities Aid Foundation found that 30 percent of Russian NGOs were social welfare organizations, 24 percent clubs and "interest groups," and 10 percent each environmental, human rights, and cultural. Women's organizations comprised only 1 percent (CAF International, 1997, pp. 2.8–2.9).

39. See interview with Anastasia Posadskaia in Waters (1993, p. 294).

40. Senior member of the Union of Russian Women, interview with author, Moscow, summer 1998.

41. Sperling (1999, pp. 48–49) also notes this difference between Moscow and other regions and its effect on levels of conflict within local women's movements.

42. Azhgikhina is co-president of the Russian Association of Women Journalists, in addition to being a regular columnist.

43. For example, one episode of the wildly popular police drama series, *Ulitsa razbitykh fonarei* [Street of broken streetlamps], was devoted to a case of domestic violence and portrayed the issue in a way that was in keeping with the views of anti–domestic violence NGOs. The episode featured hotline posters produced by ANNA. Larisa Ponarina, executive director, ANNA National Center for Violence Prevention, interview with author, Moscow, 1 July 2005.

44. Elena Ershova, coordinator, NIS-US Women's Consortium, interview with author, Moscow, 21 July 1998.

45. These statistics are based on data from the All-Russia Center for the Study of Public Opinion (VTsIOM).

46. Zoia Khotkina states that this phenomenon was almost universal among women's job advertisements in 1996 (Khotkina, 1996b, p. 15). My own search of a major source for job advertisements, the Russian newspaper *Iz ruk v ruki*, in July 2002 revealed that eleven out of twenty-eight "seeking work" ads submitted by women in the office work section included phrases signaling rejection of "intimate relations." Data from http://www.win.izrukvruki.ru, retrieved 31 July 2002.

47. Zinaida Suslova, Duma Committee on Women, Family, and Youth, interview with author, Moscow, 1 April 1999.

48. Olga Samarina, deputy director, Department for Family, Women, and Children, Russian Ministry of Labor and Social Development, interview with author, Moscow, 26 May 1999; Sperling (1999, p. 131).

49. Ershova, interview, 24 March 1999. Similar sentiments were also voiced in author's interviews with Suslova and Samarina.

50. Ershova, interview, 21 July 1998.

51. Ershova, e-mail communication with author, 13 April 2004.

52. Ershova, e-mail communication.

53. I found only two examples of Russian women's NGOs that had received foreign assistance for employment search and job retraining programs, both in Moscow: Conversion and Women headed by Eleonora Ivanova, and Women's Unity (*Zhenskoe Edinstvo*) headed by Lusia Kabanova. Each of these NGOs participated in a project funded by the German organization OWEN (East European Women's Center) in 1994–95. Lusia Kabanova, member and former director, Women's Unity, interview with author, Moscow, 27 July 1998; Eleonora Ivanova, founder, Conversion and Women, interview with author, Moscow, 29 July 1998.

54. Olga Khasbulatova, interview with Valerie Sperling, 6 April 1995. Cited in Sperling (1999, p. 65).

55. Russia was the country with the third-highest approval of this statement, behind Lithuania (97 percent) and Czechoslovakia (93 percent), and tied with India. Vannoy et al. also found that "public opinion is hostile to the idea that a woman cannot find satisfaction and self-realization totally within the family" (1999, p. 53).

56. Ershova, interview, 21 July 1998.

57. Chernenkaia, interview, Moscow, 23 February 2000.

58. Dianne Post, legal specialist for gender issues, American Bar Association, Central and East European Law Initiative (ABA/CEELI), interview with author, 25 March 1999.

59. Chernenkaia, interview, 23 February 2000.

60. Post, interview; Chernenkaia, interview, 23 February 2000.

61. Chernenkaia, interview, 23 February 2000.

62. Moscow and St. Petersburg figures cited in Human Rights Watch (1997). Izhevsk statistics cited by Marina Likhacheva, head specialist for Socio-Psychological Work, Warm Home Municipal Crisis Center, interview with author, Izhevsk, 14 April 2000.

63. Director of a St. Petersburg women's NGO, interview with author, St. Petersburg, 5 October 1999.

64. Samarina, interview.

65. Ershova, interview, 21 July 1998. Bureaucrats who admitted these weaknesses of the national machinery during interviews were Samarina of the Ministry of Labor and Social Development and Suslova of the Duma Committee on Women, Family, and Youth.

66. Olga Lipovskaia, chair, Petersburg Center for Gender Issues, interview with author, St. Petersburg, 4 October 1999. Similar statements were made by many others, including Dina Salokhina, chair, Ekaterinburg Committee of Soldiers' Mothers, interview with author, Ekaterinburg, 19 April 2000; Marina Kazakova, Bluebird, interview with author, Vladivostok, 3 March 2000; and Olga Voronina, co-chair, Moscow Center for Gender Studies, Moscow, 24 May 1999.

67. Abubikirova and Regentova, interview.

68. This basic pattern of personal history arose in interviews with Elena Ershova, Natalia Abubikirova, and Olga Voronina.

Chapter 4

1. Note that for the purposes of this chapter, the term "local government" refers to both regional and city governments.

2. The term "decoupling" is frequently used by authors in the world polity institutionalist school of sociology. See Meyer et al. (1997); Boli and Thomas (1999), 1997; Meyer (1994).

3. Population figures cited in this chapter are taken from official Russian government (Goskomstat) statistics from 2002 (Federal Service of State Statistics, 2004). See Appendix 5 for the population statistics for all seven cities.

4. Note that Russian citizens from other cities had difficulty moving permanently to Moscow, due to a very strict system of residency permits (*propiska*) that was heavily enforced by the Moscow government.

5. The Soviet statistics on military production cited in this chapter are taken from a compilation of official Soviet statistics collected by the Brookings Institution (1998). Note that these statistics on defense-related production are highly inaccurate and are likely to severely underestimate the actual proportion of the labor force employed in the defense industry. Many Soviet factories that declared themselves civilian-related production sites to the outside world actually conducted a considerable amount of military production (Fish, 1995, pp. 138, 164). Nonetheless, the rank order of the regions presented by official statistics is likely to be accurate, given common assessments of military production levels in the various locations by both Westerners and local residents.

6. For an excellent discussion of these battles, and differences among regions with "uniactor" versus "multiactor" regional political environments, see Lankina (2004, ch. 7).

7. On this situation, see Sergievskii (2001); also see discussion on the website of *Mestnoe upravlenie* [Local government] at http://www.rels.obninsk.com/rels/lg/. It is important to note that in 2003, legislation was passed to reform local government powers as a result of recommendations from a presidential commission led by Dmitrii Kozak. These reforms, which began to be implemented in 2006 but now have an extension on implementation to 2009, significantly curb local government powers and financial capabilities and make local mayors more answerable to regional leaders and the central government (see Lankina, 2005; RFE/RL, 2005).

8. Another hypothesis from social movement theory is that social movements experience greater difficulty penetrating centralized, "strong" states than decentralized states with multiple access points. Once penetrated, though, such centralized systems with strong policy-making capacities are better able to implement major changes than decentralized political systems (see Kitschelt, 1986; Jenkins, 1995; Evangelista, 1995). Nonetheless, that hypothesis is more concerned with centralization within a single level of government than across levels of federalist systems. Moreover, Russian NGOs have been so weak in affecting public policy at all levels that the hypothesis is thus far moot.

9. Note that, due to the financial crisis that hit Russia in August 1998, the value of these grant monies would have plummeted soon after organizations received them. For example, a grant of 30,000 rubles that was worth US$4,800 when awarded in July 1998 would have been worth only about US$2,300 in late August.

10. Information also from Eleonora Luchnikova, chief expert, Committee for Public and Interregional Relations, Government of Moscow, interview with author, Moscow, 19 May 1999.

11. Evgeniia Poplavskaia, president, Order of Mercy (*Orden Miloserdiia*), interview with author, Moscow, 25 May 1999.

12. Those who doubted the city grant program's objectivity included Marianna Vronskaia, leader, Goluba Service for Assistance to Adolescent Women, interview with author, Moscow, 23 May 1999; and Albina Pashina, director, Iaroslavna Center for Psychological Support to Women, interview with author, Moscow, 28 May 1999. Elena Ershova of the Consortium of Women's Nongovernmental Organizations argued that grants from the mayor's office demanded political loyalty as a condition. Interview with author, Moscow, 24 March 1999.

13. Maria Makhorskaia, chair, Union of Disabled Women of St. Petersburg, interview with author, St. Petersburg, 4 August 1999.

14. Luchnikova, interview.

15. Irina Chernenkaia, member of Board of Directors and former executive director, Syostry Center for Victims of Sexual Assault, interview with author, Moscow, 5 April 1999.

16. Nadezhda Lisitsina, director, Doverie Psychological-Educational Center and Syostry Hotline, interview with author, Novgorod, 18 February 2000.

17. Olga Lipovskaia, chair, Petersburg Center for Gender Issues, interview with author, St. Petersburg, 4 October 1999.

18. Tatiana Matveeva, coordinator, League of Women Voters of St. Petersburg, interview with author, St. Petersburg, 5 October 1999.

19. "Travel overseas," unless otherwise noted, refers to travel for training, formal exchanges, or other work-related purposes. Obviously, if tourist travel were included, the proportion of NGO activists who have traveled would be larger.

20. Lipovskaia, interview.

21. Dmitrii Solonnikov, director, Committee for Press and Public Relations, Administration of St. Petersburg, interview with author, St. Petersburg, 8 October 1999.

22. Lipovskaia, interview.

23. Solonnikov, interview.

24. Natalia Khodyreva, director, St. Petersburg Psychological Crisis Center, interview with author, St. Petersburg, 6 October 1999.

25. Solonnikov, interview.

26. Solonnikov, interview.

27. These organizations were Women of St. Petersburg, headed by Elena Kalinina, and the Association of Women with University Education, led by Nina Andreeva.

28. An alternative estimate, according to Steven Fish's conversations with Ekaterinburg residents, is that military production in the late Soviet period accounted for 75–85 percent of industrial output in Ekaterinburg (Fish, 195, p. 138).

29. Maia Mikhailova, head of the Division for Relations with Public and Religious Organizations, Committee for Public Relations, Ekaterinburg City Administration, interview with author, Ekaterinburg, 18 April 2000.

30. Reported by Liudmila Ermakova, director, Ekaterina Crisis Center for Women, interview with author, Ekaterinburg, 20 April 2000.

31. Stated by Tamara Alaiba, former vice-president, Urals Association of Women, interview with author, Ekaterinburg, 5 April 2000; also Nadezhda Golubkova, Ekaterina Women's Center, interview with author, Ekaterinburg, 6 April 2000.

32. Golubkova, interview.

33. Vera Samsonova, director, Regional Foundation for Support of Women in Business, interview with author, Ekaterinburg, 17 April 2000.

34. Maria Chashchina, specialist, Directorate for Social Communications, Public Relations Department, Sverdlovsk Oblast Administration, interview with author, Ekaterinburg, 7 April 2000.

35. They included Elena Tishchenko, president, Christian Women, interview with author, Ekaterinburg, 17 April 2000; Samsonova, interview; and Valentina Deriabina, vice-president, Urals Association of Women, interview with author, Ekaterinburg, 7 August 1998.

36. The UAW and the Sverdlovsk administration claim that the 1996 agreement was the first of its kind in all of Russia. This was stated at a ceremony held at the governor's residence to congratulate women deputies newly elected to the Oblast Duma, Ekaterinburg, 18 April 2000.

37. Liudmila Novikova, council member, Urals Association of Women, interview with author, Ekaterinburg, 5 April 2000; Tamara Alaiba, former vice-president, Urals Association of Women, interview with author, Ekaterinburg, 5 April 2000; and Chashchina, interview.

38. The still-official president of the UAW, Galina Karelova, has a poor relationship with the governor and tried to forge alliances with Ekaterinburg's mayor instead during the UAW's early years. In recent years, though, as Karelova has spent more and more time in Moscow, the locally based leaders of the UAW, who are close to the oblast government, have played a more influential role.

39. Golubkova, interview.

40. Anna Pastukhova, Ekaterinburg division of Memorial, interview with author, Ekaterinburg, 13 August 1998. Note that several types of organizations coexist within the Memorial network: some work on human rights and democratization; others work primarily on historical research; and still others focus on philanthropic work.

41. Elena Zyrina, director, Good Will (*Dobraia Vol'ia*), interview with author, Ekaterinburg, 19 April 2000. Others who praised the work of the city administration included Ermakova, interview; and Samsonova, interview.

42. Mikhailova, interview.

43. Eurasia Foundation representative, interview cited by Henderson (1998, p. 75).

44. For news background on this rivalry, see EastWest Institute (1999).

45. Staff member of the Committee on Family, Women's, and Children's Affairs, Izhevsk City Administration, interview with author, Izhevsk, 21 August 1998.

46. A member of the Udmurt Regional Division of the Women of Russia Movement, Elena Reffel, commented that "maybe if either Fedulova and Lakhova hadn't split up, or the local governments hadn't entered into conflict, we could have worked better as organizations together [with the Union of Women]" (Elena Reffel, assistant director, Udmurt Regional Division of the Women of Russia Movement, interview with author, Izhevsk, 22 August 1998).

47. Stated by Maria Likhacheva, head specialist for Social-Psychological Work, Warm Home Municipal Crisis Center, interview with author, Izhevsk, 14 April 2000; Klara Serebrennikova, chair, Udmurt Regional Division of the Women of Russia Movement, interview with author, Izhevsk, 11 April 2000; Liudmila Vedernikova, chair, Izhevsk City Zhensovet, interview with author, Izhevsk, 10 April 2000; Galina Merzlyakova, president, Higher Women's Courses Program, Faculty of Social Communications, Udmurt State University, interview with author, Izhevsk, 20 August 1998.

48. Galina Shamshurina, chair, Committee on Family, Women's, and Children's Affairs, Izhevsk City Administration, interview with author, Izhevsk, 12 April 2000.

49. Serebrennikova, interview; Elena Sheshko, secretary, Udmurt Regional Division of the Women of Russia Movement, interview with author, Izhevsk, 11 April 2000.

50. Tatiana Komleva, leader, Vozrozhdenie [Revival] Cultural-Educational Movement, interview with author, Izhevsk, 13 April 2000.

51. Elena Sheshko, secretary, Regional Division of the Women of Russia Movement, interview with author, Izhevsk, 11 April 2000.

52. Galina Tseneva, committee specialist, Committee on Family, Women's, and Children's Affairs, Izhevsk City Administration, interview with author, Izhevsk, 21 August 1998.

53. Natalia Ladyzhets, former director, Women of Science of the Udmurt Republic, interview with author, Izhevsk, 19 August 1998.

54. Tatiana Filonova, head, Division for Relations with Public Organizations, Administration of Primorskii Krai, interview with author, Vladivostok, 16 May 2000.

55. Liudmila Trofimova, president, and Olga Shmelkova, vice-president, Vladivostok Division of the Pan Pacific and Southeast Asia Women's Association (PPSEAWA), interview with author, Vladivostok, 7 March 2000; Natalia Shcherbakova, chair, Vladivostok City Zhensovet, interview with author, Vladivostok, 7 March 2000; and anonymous leader of a women's NGO, interview with author, Vladivostok, November 1999.

56. Anonymous leader of a women's NGO, interview.

57. Trofimova and Shmelkova, interview; Shcherbakova, interview, 28 April 2000.

58. ISAR-RFE (1999) stated that the Russian Far East has a relatively small number of NGOs compared to much of the rest of Russia. According to its database of NGOs, there were approximately 170 NGOs in Primorskii Krai (ISAR-RFE, 2001).

59. Tatiana Shepel, Lebedushka Women's Club, interview with author, Khabarovsk, 13 December 1999.

60. Valentina Reshetkina, chair, Khabarovsk Committee of Soldiers' Mothers, interview with author, Khabarovsk, 29 November 1999.

61. This account is based on statements by Aleksandr Bekhtold, Khabarovsk Division of the All-Russia Movement "For Human Rights," interview with author, Khabarovsk, 15 December 1999.

62. The article in question appeared in *Khabarovskii ekspress* 42, 18−25 (October 1997) and questioned the veracity of the governor's recent receipt of a doctoral degree. Bekhtold reported his subsequent loss of work in *Khabarovskii ekspress* 45, 8−15, (November 1997). The editor of the newspaper, which was frequently critical of the government, also paid a high price: his printing house had been set on fire twice in suspicious circumstances and he had been beaten up twice (see EastWest Institute, 2001).

63. Information based on author's interview with staff member of a Khabarovsk NGO resource center, 1 December 1999.

64. Anonymous staff member of a Khabarovsk NGO resource center, interview with author, Khabarovsk, 1 December 1999.

65. Anonymous staff member of a Khabarovsk NGO resource center, interview; also Tatiana Silukova, director, Russian American Education Center, interview with author, Khabarovsk, 23 November 1999.

66. The EastWest Institute stated that "Viktor Ishaev is known as a pillar of stability standing against the stormy gales of Far Eastern politics" (EastWest Institute, 2000b). The Moscow Carnegie Center has given a similar assessment (McFaul and Petrov, 1998, 413−14).

67. Filippov resigned in July 2000, and a new mayor, Aleksandr Sokolov, who was a deputy mayor prior to 1994, ran for the office at the governor's invitation and was elected to the post in September 2000 (see EastWest Institute, 2001). As a reason for resigning, Filippov stated that he "was tired of an endless search for money to buy coal and maintain the city" (Interfax, 2000). For a short résumé of Sokolov's career, see the city of Khabarovsk website (http://khb.ru/City/Admin/mer.htm).

68. See Chapter Two and Appendix 3 for a description of the RI program.

69. One organization involved in NGO development that abandoned its office in Khabarovsk was the Citizens' Democracy Corps. Technical assistance organizations involved with Khabarovsk NGOs that became "Russified" in their staff included Ecolinks and Counterpart International.

70. Women's NGOs that have participated in exchanges with Asian NGOs include the Primorskii Krai *zhensovet*, the Khabarovsk Krai *zhensovet*, the Vladivostok city *zhensovet*, and the International Women's Club in Vladivostok. Most of the organizations with Asian ties are descendents from Soviet-era *zhensovety* because such contacts were often formed with women's organizations in Asian countries during the Soviet period, as part of the internationalist mandate of the CSW.

71. According to the ISAR-RFE (2001) database of NGOs, there are approximately 120 active NGOs in Khabarovsk Krai.

72. Anonymous staff member of a Khabarovsk NGO resource center, interview, 1 December 1999. He stated also that several foreign granting organizations, including CAF, TACIS, and the British Council, had told him that NGOs from the RFE "should not bother applying for grants," since they have no resources to dedicate to the region.

73. In 1999, Prusak was reelected to a second term as governor with 91.6 percent of the vote (EastWest Institute, 2000c).

74. Lisitsina, interview. Similar statements were made by Roman Zolin, director, NGO Support Center, interview with author, Novgorod, 14 February 2000. A report on the region aimed at foreign investors made a related point regarding the investment climate: "Succeeding in Novgorod depends on having good personal ties with the governor. While such ties are useful while the governor is in office, they will likely become meaningless when Prusak is no longer there. If another leader came to power in the region, conditions could change dramatically" (EastWest Institute, 2000c).

75. Faith, Hope, and Love in Staraia Russa and the Novgorod Consumer's Society had received free office space from a theater and an institute, respectively, while the Success Center for Support of Women in Business paid rent for office space, and the League of Businesswomen had no office.

76. Dmitrii Zavedovskii, head of Public Relations Department, Novgorod Oblast Administration, interview with author, Novgorod, 16 February 2000.

77. Zolin, interview.

78. Stated by Lisitsina, interview; and Irina Urtaeva, chair, Novgorod Women's Parliament, interview with author, Novgorod, 22 February 2000.

79. Urtaeva, interview.

80. For example, a member of the Novgorod Women's Parliament stated that "They are more positive than negative. They help us sometimes, and at the very least, they don't bother us." (Staff member of the Novgorod Women's Parliament, interview with author, Novgorod, 14 February 2000).

81. Lyubov Soloveva, chair, Faith, Hope, and Love, interview with author, Staraia Russa, 21 February 2000; and Irina Shulga, Success Center for Support of Women in Business, interview with author, Staraia Russa, 21 February 2000.

82. Larisa Korneva, Elena Zabadykina, and Anna Shunkova, Aleksandra Crisis Center, interview with author, St. Petersburg, 10 August 1999.

83. Khodyreva, interview.

84. Ershova, interview, 24 March 1999.

85. Tishchenko, interview.

86. Zinaida Iovkova, chair, Primorskii Krai Union of Women, interview with author, Vladivostok, 27 March 2000.

87. Two well-publicized examples are the government-initiated cases against the environmentalists Grigorii Pasko and Aleksandr Nikitin, who published reports on radioactive pollution from Russia's navy. Environmentalists have frequently been attacked in recent years as spies or agents of the West (see Henry, 2001, pp. 13–14). In the area of human rights, there have been numerous cases of harassment, including authorities barring a prominent human rights activist from traveling to a conference abroad (see Mendelson, 2002, p. 49). Russian journalist Anna Politkovskaya of *Novaya Gazeta* has been threatened repeatedly for her critical reporting on Chechnya (see Hodgson, 2001; www.gazeta.ru news website, 17 October 2001).

88. On basic legal obstacles for NGOs, see Sevortian (2000). Regarding the 1999 government law requiring that all Russian NGOs re-register themselves (with some politically challenging NGOs being refused registration or being required to change their legally permitted activities), see ICIWF (1999a) and Information Center of the Human Rights Movement and the Center for Development of Democracy and Human Rights (2000). Many NGOs claimed that the express purpose of the re-registration law was to decrease the number of NGOs in Russia (see Mendelson, 2000; Henry, 2001). A member of the UCSMR in Moscow claimed that an official in the president's administration had told her this directly (Ida Kuklina, member of Coordinating Council, Union of Committees of Soldiers' Mothers of Russia, interview with author, Moscow, 29 March 1999).

89. See Henry (2001); Mendelson (2002); and Evans (2005b) for excellent discussions of these barriers to NGO collaboration with government in Russia, despite foreign-donor encouragement.

90. I use the term "foreign assistance providers" rather than "foreign donors" for this particular measure since this category also includes organizations that may be training NGOs under contracts from governmental donors, but who are not themselves donors of assistance (such as MiraMed or Counterpart International).

91. Elizaveta Bozhkova, director, ICIWF, interview with author, Moscow, 1 April 1999.

92. Voluminous discussions appeared on several NGO information websites, such as Human Rights On-Line (www.hro.org), We, Citizens! (*My, grazhdane!*) (www.citizens.ru), and the Agency for Social Information (www.asi.org.ru). The ICIWF (2001b) listserv also devoted considerable discussion to the debate.

93. Lipovskaia, interview.

94. Leader of Moscow women's organization, interview with author, Moscow, May 1999. The interview subject reported that following her delivery of a report on violence against women at a conference, several soldiers' mothers approached her and said, "What the heck are you talking about? You are talking about sex all the time, when we need to think about our children, our boys who are dying at war and in the army! Girls, don't wear short skirts, and then there won't be any rape—that's the end of the story!"

95. Lipovskaia, interview; Natalia Khodyreva, director, Psychological Crisis Center for Women, interview with author, St. Petersburg, 6 October 1999.

96. Korneva, Zabadykina, and Shunkova, interview.

97. Nadezhda Golubkova, director, Ekaterina City Women's Center, interview with author, Ekaterinburg, 6 April 2000.

98. This account is based on interviews with Tamara Alaiba, former member of the UAW, and with another current member of the Council of the UAW, both in Ekaterinburg, 5 April 2000.

99. Tamara Alaiba, former vice-president, Urals Association of Women, interview with author, Ekaterinburg, 5 April 2000.

100. Liudmila Novikova, council member, Urals Association of Women, interview with author, Ekaterinburg, 5 April 2000.

101. Elena Zyrina, director, Good Will, interview with author, Ekaterinburg, 19 April 2000.

102. Zoia Stepnova, chair, Union of Women of the Udmurt Republic, interview with author, Izhevsk, 13 April 2000.

103. Maria Zhilina, responsible secretary, Union of Women of the Udmurt Republic, interview with author, 13 April 2000.

104. Iovkova, interview.

105. Members of four different women's NGOs in Vladivostok made comments to this effect.

106. Anonymous member of a women's organization, interview, November 1999. The other clear case of such incongruity between an NGO's actual position and its leader's preferences was a women's organization in St. Petersburg.

107. Iovkova, interview.

108. Marina Kazakova, program officer, ISAR-RFE, and former leader, Bluebird, interview with author, Vladivostok, 3 March 2000.

109. Kazakova, interview.

110. Shcherbakova, interviews, 7 March and 28 April 2000.

111. Shcherbakova, interview, 7 March 2000.

112. Shcherbakova, interview, 28 April 2000.

113. Shcherbakova, appearance on local television program *Allo! Studiia*, OTV-Prim television station, Vladivostok, 25 July 2000.

114. Elena Kurakulova, president, Women's Business Club, interview with author, Vladivostok, 9 November 1999; also *Vestnik* (Vladivostok), 8–16 March 2000, p. 5.

115. Statement on nonpolitical character made by Svetlana Zhukova, chair, Union of Businesswomen, interview with author, Khabarovsk, 17 November 1999. On the gubernatorial elections, see EastWest Institute (2000d). Ishaev won the election with 88 percent of the vote.

116. Shepel, interview.

117. Anonymous staff member of Khabarovsk NGO resource center, interview with author, 1 December 1999.

118. Evidence of the friction among the organizations came from interviews with one of the resource center leaders and the head of the NGO association, as well as with several NGO leaders, including Reshetkina of the CSM and Shepel of Lebedushka.

119. Alevtina Novikova, chair, League of Businesswomen, interview with author, Novgorod, 17 February 2000.

120. Evgenia Ivanova, responsible secretary, Novgorod Oblast *Zhensovet* (*Oblast-noi sovet zhenshchin*), interview with author, Novgorod, 16 February 2000.

121. Zolin, interview.

122. Average income and unemployment rankings were taken from Goskomstat statistics (Federal Service of State Statistics, 2004); also compiled in McFaul and Petrov (1998).

123. Kathryn Hendley used the term "ticking boxes" in making this point at a conference in 1999 (presentation to MacArthur Consortium Summer Institute, "Evaluating Non-Governmental and International Organizations," 17–20 June 1999, Stanford University, Palo Alto, California). This kind of approach was visible in donor reports measuring results of civil society programs. For example, the American NGO Save the Children reported from its Civic Initiatives Program that "10 legal education books for NGOs and government officials were produced" and "on-line access to NGO data and technical assistance was provided" (Save the Children, 1998, p. 18). USAID reported its progress toward the objective of increased citizen participation as follows: "6,500 political party activists have been trained in party development" (USAID, 1999b).

Chapter 5

1. Marina Regentova, co-chair, FALTA, interview with author, Moscow, 25 May 1999.

2. For a full discussion on the Public Chamber, see Evans (2005b).

Bibliography

Abdullaev, Nabi. 2005. Public Chamber Bill Gets Bad Marks. *Moscow Times* (19 January).

Abubikirova, N. I., et al. 1998. *Spravochnik: Zhenskie nepravitel'stvennye organizatsii Rossii i SNG* [Directory: Women's NGOs in Russia and the CIS]. Moscow: Women's Information Network.

Agence France-Presse (AFP). 2002. Russian Parliament Approves Alternative Military Service Bill. AFP (28 June). Reprinted 28 June 2002 in *Johnson's Russia List* #6327. Available at http://www.cdi.org/russia/johnson/.

Alexander, James. 2000. *Political Culture in Post-Communist Russia: Formlessness and Recreation in a Traumatic Transition*. New York: St. Martin's Press.

Anheier, Helmut, Marlies Glasius, and Mary Kaldor. 2001. Introducing Global Civil Society. In *Global Civil Society 2001*. Oxford, UK: Oxford University Press, 2001.

Applebaum, Anne. 2003. *Gulag: A History*. New York: Doubleday.

ARA (Antimilitarist Radical Association). 2000. Chto takoe ARA? [What is ARA?]. Retrieved 28 July 2000 from http://www.ara.ru/whatsara.html.

Arendt, Hannah. 1963. *On Totalitarianism*. New York: Viking Press.

ASI (Agency for Social Information) (Agenstvo sotsial'noi informatsii). 2004a. Lobbirovanie interesov NKO v oblasti nalogooblozheniia [Lobbying the interests of NGOs in the area of taxation]. (15 June). Retrieved 31 March 2005 from http://asi.org.ru/ASI3/main.nsf/0/81C097952EACA723C3256EB4004282E0.

———.2004b. Poiasnitel'naia zapiska k voprosu o vnesennoi Pravitel'stvom RF popravke k stat'e 251 Nalogovogo Kodeksa v chasti, kasaiushcheisia nalogooblozheniia grantov [Note of clarification on the question of amendments inserted by the Russian government in Article 251 of the Tax Code in the area concerning taxation of grants]. 23 September. Retrieved 31 March 2005 from http://asi.org.ru/ASI3/main.nsf/0/5E76556954C1A07FC3256F1800336926.

Ayvazova, Svetlana. 1998. *Russkie zhenshchiny v labirinte ravnopraviia* [Russian women in the labyrinth of equal rights]. Moscow: RIK Rusanova.

Azhgikhina, Nadezhda. 2000. Zolushki perestroiki i rynochnykh reform [The Cinderellas of Perestroika and market reforms]. *Nezavisimaia gazeta*, 7 March. Retrieved 5 June 2001 from http://www.ng.ru/politics/2000–03–07/1_cinderellas.html.

Bahry, Donna, and Lucan Way. 1994. Citizen Activism in the Russian Transition. *Post-Soviet Affairs* 10(4): 330–66.

Baskakova, Marina. 1998. *Ravnye vozmozhnosti i gendernye stereotipy na rynke truda* [Equal opportunities and gender stereotypes in the labor market]. Gender Expertise Project of the Moscow Center for Gender Studies. Moscow: MCGS.

———.2000. Gender Aspects of Pension Reform in Russia. In *Making the Transition Work for Women in Europe and Central Asia*. Edited by Marnia Lazreg. World Bank Discussion Paper on. 411. Europe and Central Asia Gender and Development Series. Washington, D.C.: World Bank.

Bekhtold, Aleksandr Fedorovich. 2000. *Doklad ? sobliudenii izbiratel'nykh prav grazhdan v Khabarovskom krae* [Report on observance of citizens' electoral rights in Khabarovsk Krai]. Khabarovsk: For Human Rights Movement.

Belyaeva, Nina Y. 1995. Charity of Strangers? Philanthropy in the Russian Commercial Sector. Edited by Franklin M. Parlamis. Moscow: Interlegal Foundation. Available on the Center for Civil Society International website: http://solar.rtd.utk .edu/ccsi/resource/chrtystr.htm.

Bialer, Seweryn. 1988. Gorbachev's Program of Change: Sources, Significance, Prospects. In *Gorbachev's Russia and American Foreign Policy*. Edited by Seweryn Bialer and Michael Mandelbaum. Boulder, Colo.: Westview Press.

Bivens, Matt. 2003. A Glum Report Card on Russia. *Moscow Times* (2 June). Reprinted 2 June 2003 in *Johnson's Russia List* #7205. Available at http://www.cdi.org/ russia johnson/.

Black, Antony. 1988. *State, Community and Human Desire: A Group-Centred Account of Political Values*. New York: Harvester Wheatsheaf.

Boli, John, and George M. Thomas. 1997. World Culture in the World Polity: A Century of International Non-Governmental Organization. *American Sociological Review* (April): 171–90.

———.1999. Introduction. In *Constructing World Culture: International Nongovernmental Organizations since 1875*. Edited by John Boli and George M. Thomas. Stanford, Calif.: Stanford University Press.

Bransten, Jeremy. 2005. Russia: New Public Chamber Criticized as "Smokescreen." RFE/RL (17 March). Accessed 28 April 2005 at http://www.rferl.org/features article/2005/03/3283f57c-12e6-48f8-acf0-87a0f31accf8.html.

Bredun, Yulia. 1999. Pomoshch' idet peshkom [Help arrives on foot]. *Itogi* (19 January): 40–41.

Bridger, Sue, Rebecca Kay, and Kathryn Pinnick. 1996. *No More Heroines? Russia, Women and the Market*. London: Routledge.

British Council. 2001. Democratic Institutions Small Projects Scheme (DISPS). Retrieved 25 April 2001 from http://www.britishcouncil.ru/work/wodisps.htm.

Brock, Bill. 1983. The Democracy Program and the National Endowment for Democracy. *Commonsense* 6(1) (December): 85–121. Retrieved 28 April 2001 from http://www.iri.org/common1.asp.

Brookings Institution. 1998. *Brookings Institution Regional Statistical Database for the Russian Federation/RSFSR*. Compiled by Clifford Gaddy and Melanie Allen. Washington, D.C.: Brookings Institution. Available at http://www.brookings .org/fp/projects/russdata.htm.

Browning, Genia K. 1987. *Women and Politics in the USSR: Consciousness Raising and Soviet Women's Groups*. New York: St. Martin's Press.

Buckley, Mary. 1989. *Women and Ideology in the Soviet Union*. Toronto: Harvester Wheatsheaf.

———. 1997. Women and Public Life. In *Developments in Russian Politics 4*. Edited by Stephen White, Alex Pravda, and Zvi Gitelman. Durham, N.C.: Duke University Press.

Bunce, Valerie. 2000. Comparative Democratization: Big and Bounded Generalizations. *Comparative Political Studies* 33(6/7): 703–34.

Bunch, Charlotte. 1990. Women's Rights as Human Rights: Toward a Revision of Human Rights. *Human Rights Quarterly* 12: 486–98.

Burnell, Peter. 2000. Democracy Assistance: The State of the Discourse. In *Democracy Assistance: International Co-operation for Democratization*. Edited by Peter Burnell. Portland, Ore.: Frank Cass.

CAF (Charities Aid Foundation) International. 1997. *Working with the Nonprofit Sector in Russia*. London: Basic Work.

———. 2001. Charity Know How: Grants Programmes. Retrieved 25 April 2001 from http://www.cafonline.org/charityknowhow/default.cfm.

Caiazza, Amy. 2002. *Mothers and Soldiers: Gender, Citizenship, and Civil Society in Contemporary Russia*. New York: Routledge.

Cameron, Maxwell A., Robert J. Lawson, and Brian W. Tomlin, eds. 1998. *To Walk Without Fear: The Global Movement to Ban Landmines*. Toronto: Oxford University Press.

Canadian Embassy, Moscow. n.d. Canada Fund. Canadian Embassy, Moscow. Photocopy.

———. 2000. Fund Announcement: Elections Fund. Canadian Embassy, Moscow. Photocopy.

Carothers, Thomas. 1999. *Aiding Democracy Abroad: The Learning Curve*. Washington, D.C.: Carnegie Endowment for International Peace.

Carothers, Thomas, and Marina Ottaway. 2000. The Burgeoning World of Civil Society Aid. In *Funding Virtue: Civil Society Aid and Democracy Promotion*. Washington, D.C.: Carnegie Endowment for International Peace.

Checkel, Jeffrey T. 1998. The Neoliberal Moment in Sweden: Economic Change, Policy Failure or Power of Ideas. Paper presented at the Ideas, Culture and Political Analysis Workshop, Princeton University, 15–16 May, Princeton, N.J. Retrieved 7 December 2000 from https://wwwc.cc.columbia.edu/sec/dlc/ciao/conf/ssr01/ssr01al.html.

———. 1999. Norms, Institutions and National Identity in Contemporary Europe. *International Studies Quarterly* 43: 83–114.

Chilton, Patricia. 1995. Mechanics of Change: Social Movements, Transnational Coalitions, and the Transformation Processes in Eastern Europe. In *Bringing Transnational Relations Back In*. Edited by Thomas Risse-Kappen. Cambridge, UK: Cambridge University Press.

CIDA (Canadian International Development Agency). 2001. Russia: Canadian Assistance. Retrieved 26 April 2001 from http://www.acdi-cida.gc.ca/cidaweb/web country.nsf/VLUDocEn/Russia-Canadianassistance

Clark, Ann Marie, Elisabeth J. Friedman, and Kathryn Hochstetler. 1998. The Sovereign Limits of Global Civil Society: A Comparison of NGO Participation in UN World Conferences on the Environment, Human Rights, and Women. *World Politics* 51 (October): 1–35.

Congressional Research Service, Library of Congress. 2001. *State Department and Related Agencies: FY2001 Appropriations*. Washington, D.C.: Library of Congress. Retrieved 15 May 2003 from http://www.globalsecurity.org/military/library/report/crs/RL30591.pdf.

Conroy, Mary Schaeffer. 2005. Civil Society in Late Imperial Russia. In *Russian Civil Society: A Critical Assessment*. Edited by Alfred B. Evans, Laura A. Henry, and Lisa McIntosh Sundstrom. Armonk, N.Y.: M.E. Sharpe.

Consortium of Women's Nongovernmental Organizations. 2004a. O Konsortsiume [The consortium]. Retrieved 11 April 2004 from http://www.wcons.org.ru/ru/page.php?page_id=131&page_up=0.

———. 2004b. Zamechaniia zhenskikh nepravitel'stvennykh organizatsii k trudovomu zakonodatel'stvu [Remarks of women's nongovernmental organizations to the labor legislation]. Photocopy.

Cortell, Andrew P., and James W. Davis, Jr. 2000. Understanding the Domestic Impact of International Norms: A Research Agenda. *International Studies Review* 2(1):65–87.

CSMR (Committee of Soldiers' Mothers of Russia), Coordinating Committee. 1999. Glavnoe—ne opozdat'! Molodye soldaty "golosuiut nogami" za voennuiu reformu [Most important—don't be late! Young soldiers "vote with their feet" for military reform]. Press release distributed at press conference of Committee of Soldiers' Mothers of Russia and the Moscow Solidarity Movement, National Press Institute, Moscow, 25 March.

Della Porta, Donatella, and Mario Diani. 1999. *Social Movements: An Introduction*. Oxford, UK: Blackwell.

DFID (Department for International Development). n.d. Two Opportunities for Central and Eastern European Funding . . . Partnerships in the Non-Profit Sector, Charity Know How. London: DFID. Pamphlet.

Diamond, Larry. 1996. Toward Democratic Consolidation. In *The Global Resurgence of Democracy*. 2nd ed. Edited by Larry Diamond and Marc F. Plattner. Baltimore, Md.: Johns Hopkins University Press.

Diligenskii, G. G. 2001. Putin i Rossisskaia demokratiia [Putin and Russian democracy] (18 January). Retrieved 4 June 2001 from the Fond Obshchestvennogo Mneniia [Public Opinion Foundation] website at http://www.fom.ru/reports/frames/do10130.html.

Donors' Forum. 2005. Donorskie i nekommercheskie organizatsii: chto my o nikh znaem [Donor and nonprofit organizations: What we know about them]. Moscow: Donors' Forum.

Drakulic, Slavenka. 1993. *How We Survived Communism and Even Laughed*. New York: Harper Perennial.

Durkheim, Emile. 1960. *The Division of Labor in Society*. Glencoe, Ill.: Free Press.

Dyukova, Natalya. 1998. Istoriia sozdaniia feministskogo dvizheniia v nachale 80-kh godov [History of formation of the feminist movement in the early 1980s]. Paper presented at conference, Society and Totalitarianism: First Half of the 1980s, November, St. Petersburg.

EastWest Institute. 2000a. *Russian Regional Report* 5(1) (12 January). Retrieved 12 January 2000 from listserv RRR@iews.org.

———.2000b. Russian Regional Database. Profile of Viktor Ivanovich Ishaev: Khabarovsk Krai. Retrieved 13 February 2001 from the EastWest Institute website: http://www.iews.org/rrrabout.nsf/pages/russian+regional+database.

———.2000c. Mikhail Mikhailovich Prusak: Novgorod Oblast. Retrieved 13 February 2001 from the EastWest Institute website: http://www.iews.org/rrrabout.nsf/pages/russian+regional+database.

———.2000d. *Russian Regional Report* 5(46) (13 December). Retrieved 14 December 2000 from listserv RRR@iews.org.

———.2001. *Russian Regional Report* 6(29) (22 August). Retrieved 22 August 2001 from listserv *RRR@iews.org*.

EC (European Commission of the European Union). 1996. *The European Union's Phare and Tacis Democracy Programme: Projects in Operation 1996*. Brussels: European Commission.

———.1999. EU Cooperation with the New Independent States and Mongolia: Explanatory Memorandum. Retrieved 4 May 1999 from http://europa.eu.int/comm/dg1a/nis/reg99_memo/index.htm.

———.2001. Country Strategy Paper 2002–2006; National Indicative Programme 2002–2003: Russian Federation. Retrieved 25 October 2005 from http://europa.eu.int/comm/external_relations/russia/csp/02–06_en.pdf.

Economist. 2004. Russia: Who Needs Democracy? *The Economist* (UK), 22–28 May.

Eurasia Foundation. 2000a. Description of grantmaking program in civil society of the Eurasia Foundation. Retrieved 31 August 2000 from http://www.eurasia.org/grant.html.

European Union, Delegation of the European Commission in Russia. 1999. European Initiative for Democracy and Human Rights: Full List of Micro-Projects approved by the Facility Steering Committee. Moscow: European Initiative for Democracy and Human Rights Micro-Project Facility. Photocopy.

Evangelista, Matthew. 1995. The Paradox of State Strength: Transnational Relations, Domestic Structures, and Security Policy in Russia and The Soviet Union. *International Organization* 49(1) (Winter): 1–38.

———.1999. *Unarmed Forces: The Transnational Movement to End the Cold War*. Ithaca, N.Y.: Cornell University Press.

Evans, Alfred B., Jr. 2005a. Civil Society in the Soviet Union? In *Russian Civil Society: A Critical Assessment*. Edited by Alfred B. Evans, Laura A. Henry, and Lisa McIntosh Sundstrom. Armonk, N.Y.: M.E. Sharpe.

———.2005b. Vladimir Putin's Design for Civil Society. In *Russian Civil Society: A Critical Assessment*. Edited by Alfred B. Evans, Laura A. Henry, and Lisa McIntosh Sundstrom. Armonk, N.Y.: M.E. Sharpe.

Evans, Alfred B., Jr., Laura A. Henry, and Lisa McIntosh Sundstrom. 2005. *Russian Civil Society: A Critical Assessment*. Armonk, N.Y.: M.E. Sharpe.

Fajth, Gaspar. 2000. Themes of the UNICEF MONEE Project. In *Making the Transition Work for Women in Europe and Central Asia*. Edited by Marnia Lazreg. World

Bank Discussion Paper no. 411. Europe and Central Asia Gender and Development Series. Washington, D.C.: World Bank.

Federal News Service. 2003. Press Conference with a Group of Experts Regarding the Results of Social Research on Democracy in Russia. Reprinted 3 November 2003 in *Johnson's Russia List* #7399. Available at http://www.cdi.org/russia/johnson/.

Federal Service of State Statistics (Goskomstat). 2004. *Vserossiskaia perepis' naseleniia 2002 goda* (All-Russia Population Census 2002). Retrieved 10 January 2005 from http://www.perepis2002.ru/index.html?id=40.

Felgenhauer, Pavel. 2000. Defense Dossier: True Numbers, No Reform. *Moscow Times*, 5 October. Retrieved 21 May 2001 from http://www.cdi.org/russia/122 .html##3.

Fish, M. Steven. 1995. *Democracy from Scratch: Opposition and Regime in the New Russian Revolution.* Princeton, N.J.: Princeton University Press.

——. 1996. Russia's Fourth Transition. In *The Global Resurgence of Democracy.* 2nd ed. Edited by Larry Diamond and Marc F. Plattner. Baltimore, Md.: Johns Hopkins University Press.

Fong, Monica S. 1993. *The Role of Women in Rebuilding the Russian Economy.* Studies of Economies in Transformation 10. Washington, D.C.: The World Bank.

Ford Foundation. Moscow Office. n.d. Fond Forda: Moskovskoe predstavitel'stvo [Ford Foundation: Moscow Office]. Pamphlet.

——. 2001. Programs in This Office. Retrieved 3 May 2001 from http://www.ford found.org/global/moscow/frame2.cfm.

Funk, Nanette. 1993. Introduction: Women and Post-Communism. In *Gender Politics and Post-Communism: Reflections from Eastern Europe and the Former Soviet Union.* Edited by Nanette Funk and Magda Mueller. New York: Routledge.

Gelb, Joyce. 1990. Feminism and Political Action. In *Challenging the Political Order: New Social and Political Movements in Western Democracies.* Edited by Russell J. Dalton and Manfred Kuechler. Oxford: Polity Press.

Gelb, Joyce, and Marian Lief Palley. 1987. *Women and Public Policies.* Revised and expanded edition. Princeton, N.J.: Princeton University Press.

Gerber, Theodore P., and Sarah E. Mendelson. 2003. Strong Public Support for Military Reform in Russia. Program on New Approaches to Russian Security Policy Memo 288 (May). Retrieved 30 June 2003 from http://www.csis.org/ruseura/ ponars/.

Gessen, Masha. 1997. *Dead Again: The Russian Intelligentsia After Communism.* New York: Verso.

Gibson, James L. 2001. Social Networks, Civil Society, and the Prospects for Consolidating Russia's Democratic Transition. *American Journal of Political Science* 45(1): 51–68.

Giugni, Marco. 1999. How Social Movements Matter: Past Research, Present Problems, Future Developments. In *How Social Movements Matter.* Edited by Marco Giugni, Doug McAdam, and Charles Tilly. Minneapolis: University of Minnesota Press.

Goble, Paul. 1999. Russia: Analysis from Washington—A Threat to the Growth of Civil Society. *RFE/RL* (24 May). Reprinted 25 May 1999 in *Johnson's Russia List* #3304. Available at http://www.cdi.org/russia/johnson/.

Government of the Russian Federation. 1995. Conception for the Improvement of the Status of Women in the Russian Federation. Available on the Womenwatch website of the U.N. Division for the Advancement of Women: gopher://gopher .un.org:70/00/conf/fwcw/natrep/NatActPlans/rusia.txt.

Greenfeld, Liah. 1996. The Bitter Taste of Success: Reflections on the Intelligentsia in Post-Soviet Russia. *Social Research* 63(2) (Summer): 416–39.

Hale, Henry. 2002. Civil Society from Above? Statist and Liberal Models of State-Building in Russia. *Demokratizatsiya* 10(3) (Summer): 306–21.

Hall, Macer. 2001. Russians Call in our Army over Suicides. *Telegraph* (London) (5 August). Reprinted in *Post-Soviet Armies Newsletter* (November 1999). Retrieved 17 September 2001 from www.psan.org.

Hearn, Julie, and Mark Robinson. 2000. Civil Society and Democracy Assistance in Africa. In *Democracy Assistance: International Co-operation for Democratization*. Edited by Peter Burnell. Portland, Ore.: Frank Cass.

Hemment, Julie. 2004. The Riddle of the Third Sector. *Anthropological Quarterly* 77(2) (Spring): 215–42.

Henderson, Sarah L. 2000. Importing Civil Society: Foreign Aid and the Women's Movement in Russia. *Demokratizatsiya* 8(1): 65–82.

———.2002. Selling Civil Society: Western Aid and the Nongovernmental Organization Sector in Russia. *Comparative Political Studies* 35(2): 139–67.

———.2003. *Building Democracy in Contemporary Russia: Western Support for Grassroots Organizations*. Ithaca, N.Y.: Cornell University Press.

Henry, Laura A. 2001. The Greening of Grassroots Democracy? The Russian Environmental Movement, Foreign Aid, and Democratization. Berkeley Program in Soviet and Post-Soviet Studies. Working Paper. Berkeley: University of California, Berkeley. Retrieved 26 June 2001 from http://socrates.berkeley.edu/bsp/.

———.2002. Two Paths to a Greener Future: Environmentalism and Civil Society Development in Russia. *Demokratizatsiya* 10(2) (Spring): 184–206.

———.2005. Russian Environmentalists and Civil Society. In *Russian Civil Society: A Critical Assessment*. Edited by Alfred B. Evans, Laura A. Henry, and Lisa McIntosh Sundstrom. Armonk, N.Y.: M.E. Sharpe.

Hoare, Anna. 1998. In Search of Russia's "Strong Sex." *Russian Life* 41(5): 8–16.

Hodgson, Jessica. 2001. Russian Writer Warns of Attacks on Press Freedom. *The Guardian* (UK) (3 May). Reprinted 4 May 2001 in *Johnson's Russia List* #5237. Available at http://www.cdi.org/russia/johnson/.

Hough, Jerry. 1990. *Russia and the West: Gorbachev and the Politics of Reform*. New York: Simon & Schuster.

Howard, Marc Morjé Howard. 2002. The Weakness of Postcommunist Civil Society. *Journal of Democracy* 13(1) (January): 157–69.

———.2003. *The Weakness of Civil Society in Post-Communist Europe*. Cambridge, UK: Cambridge University Press.

Human Rights Watch. 1995. Neither Jobs Nor Justice: State Discrimination Against Women in Russia. *Human Rights Watch Report* 7(5). Retrieved 29 May 2001 from http://www.hrw.org/reports/1995/Russia2a.htm.

———.1997. *Russia—Too Little, Too Late: State Response to Violence Against Women*. *Human Rights Watch Report* 9(13). Retrieved 29 May 2001 from http://www.hrw .org/reports97/russwmn/.

———.2000. What Will It Take? Stopping Violence Against Women: A Challenge to Governments. Human Rights Watch Backgrounder (June). Retrieved 29 May 2001 from http://www.hrw.org/backgrounder/wrd/fiveplus.htm.

———.2004a. Human Rights Watch Honors Russian Activist. Retrieved 27 April 2005 from http://hrw.org/english/docs/2004/11/05/russia9609.htm.

———.2004b. The Wrongs of Passage: Inhuman and Degrading Treatment of New Recruits in the Russian Armed Forces. Retrieved 27 April 2005 from http://hrw .org/reports/2004/russia1004/.

ICIWF (Information Center of the Independent Women's Forum). 1999a. Nachalo vtorogo etapa kampanii "My ne prosim l'got, my trebuem spravedlivykh nalogov!" [Beginning of the second step of the campaign "We aren't asking for benefits, we're demanding fair taxes!"] *Informatsionnyi listok* 34(130) (4 October). Retrieved 4 October 1999 from listserv iciwf@glas.apc.org.

———.1999b. Predstavliaem organizatsiiu: Tsentr zhenskikh issledovanii (Tomsk) [Introducing an organization: Women's Research Center (Tomsk)]. *Informatsionnyi listok* 16(112) (5 May). Retrieved 5 May 1999 from listserv iciwf@glas.apc.org.

———.2001. *Informatsionnyi listok* 36(222) (27 September). Retrieved 27 September 2001 from listserv iciwf@glas.apc.org.

Information Center of the Human Rights Movement and the Center for Development of Democracy and Human Rights. 2000. Doklad o faktakh narushenii v khode pervichnoi registratsii i pereregistratsii obshchestvennykh organizatsii v Rossiiskoi federatsii v 1999 gody [Report on the facts of violations in the process of initial registration and re-registration of public organizations in the Russian Federation in 1999]. Retrieved 16 May 2001 from http://www.hro.org/docs/ reps/ngo/index.htm.

Inglehart, Ronald, Miguel Basanez, and Alejandro Moreno. 1998. *Human Values and Beliefs: A Cross-Cultural Sourcebook.* Ann Arbor: University of Michigan Press.

Interfax. 2000. Khabarovsk Mayor Resigns. Interfax (23 June). Retrieved 15 October 2001 from http://vn.vladnews.ru/Arch/2000/iss219/text/news5.htm.

IRI (International Republican Institute). 2001. IRI in Russia. Retrieved 28 April 2001 from http://www.iri.org/countries.asp?id=6134613543.

ISA Consult, European Institute of Sussex University, and GJW Europe. 1997. *Final Report: Evaluation of the PHARE and TACIS Democracy Programme, 1992–1997.* Brighton and Hamburg: ISA Consult.

ISAR-RFE (Initiative for Social Action and Renewal, Russian Far Eastern Regional Office). 1999. Analysis of the Third Sector in the Russian Far East. Photocopy.

———.2001. *Katalog organizatsii—po regionam* [Catalog of organizations—by region]. Retrieved 25 September 2001 from http://domino.kuban.net/vra/fair.nsf/ISAR ByRegion.

Ivankovskaia, Svetlana (Soldiers' Mothers of St. Petersburg). 2001. Soldaty—zhertvy nasiliia v Rossiiskoi armii [Soldiers—victims of violence in the Russian army]. Retrieved 16 May 2001 from http://www.hro.org/docs/reps/spbmoth.htm.

Janos, Andrew. 1986. *Politics and Paradigms: Changing Theories of Change in Social Science.* Stanford, Calif.: Stanford University Press.

Jaquette, Jane S., and Sharon L. Wolchik. 1998. Women and Democratization in Latin America and Central and Eastern Europe: A Comparative Introduction. In

Women and Democracy: Latin American and Central and Eastern Europe. Edited by Jane S. Jaquette and Sharon L. Wolchik. Baltimore, Md.: Johns Hopkins University Press.

Jenkins, J. Craig. 1995. Social Movements, Political Representation, and the State: An Agenda and Comparative Framework. In *The Politics of Social Protest: Comparative Perspectives on States and Social Movements.* Edited by J. Craig Jenkins and Bert Klandermans. Social Movements, Protest, and Contention, Vol. 3. Minneapolis: University of Minnesota Press.

Jepperson, Ronald, Alexander Wendt, and Peter J. Katzenstein. 1996. Norms, Identity, and Culture in National Security. In *The Culture of National Security: Norms and Identity in World Politics.* Edited by P. J. Katzenstein. New York: Columbia University Press.

Johnson, Janet Elise. 2004. Sisterhood Versus the "Moral" Russian State: The Post-communist Politics of Rape. In *Post-Soviet Women Encountering Transition: Nation Building, Economic Survival, and Civic Activism,* pp. 217–38. Edited by Kathleen Kuehnast and Carol Nechemias. Baltimore, Md.: Johns Hopkins University Press.

Judis, John B. 1992. The Pressure Elite: Inside the Narrow World of Advocacy Group Politics. *The American Prospect* 9 (Spring): 15–29.

Jurna, Irina. 1995. Women in Russia: Building a Movement. In *From Basic Needs to Basic Rights: Women's Claim to Human Rights.* Edited by Margaret A. Schuller. Washington, D.C.: Women, Law and Development.

Kagarlitsky, Boris. 2002. *Russia Under Yeltsin and Putin: Neo-liberal Autocracy.* London: Pluto Press.

Kay, Rebecca. 2000. *Russian Women and Their Organizations: Gender, Discrimination, and Grassroots Women's Organizations, 1991–1996.* New York: St. Martin's Press.

Keck, Margaret E. 1995. Social Equity and Environmental Politics in Brazil: Lessons from the Rubber Tappers of Acre. *Comparative Politics* (July): 409–24.

Keck, Margaret, and Kathryn Sikkink. 1998. *Activists Beyond Borders.* Ithaca, N.Y.: Cornell University Press.

Khabarovsk Krai. Directorate of Justice. 2000. Spisok politicheskikh obshchestven-nykh ob"edinenii, proshedshikh registratsiiu v Glavnom upravlenii iustitsii Khabarovskogo kraia [List of political social organizations registered in the main directorate of justice of Khabarovsk Krai]. Photocopy.

Khotkina, Zoia. 1996a. Ot redaktora [From the editor]. In *Seksual'nye domogatel'stva na rabote* [Sexual harassment in the workplace]. Edited by Zoia Khotkina. Moscow: ABA-CEELI.

———. 1996b. Problema seksual'nykh presledovanii v Rossii: Obzor [The problem of sexual harassment in Russia: Overview]. In *Seksual'nye domogatel'stva na rabote* [Sexual harassment in the workplace]. Edited by Zoia Khotkina. Moscow: ABA-CEELI.

———, ed. 1996c. *Seksual'nye domogatel'stva na rabote* [Sexual harassment in the workplace]. Moscow: ABA-CEELI.

Kitschelt, Herbert P. 1986. Political Opportunity Structures and Political Protest: Anti-nuclear Movements in Four Democracies. *British Journal of Political Science* 16 (January): 57–85.

Kowert, Paul, and Jeffrey Legro. 1996. Norms, Identity, and Their Limits: A Theoretical Reprise. In *The Culture of National Security: Norms and Identity in World Politics.* Edited by P. J. Katzenstein. New York: Columbia University Press.

Krestnikova, Irina, and Lyovshina, Ekaterina. 2002. Korporativnaia filantropiia: mify i real'nost' [Corporate philanthropy: Myths and reality]. Moscow: Charities Aid Foundation.

Kubicek, Paul. 2000. *Unbroken Ties: The State, Interest Associations, and Corporatism in Post-Soviet Ukraine.* Ann Arbor: University of Michigan Press.

Kuklina, Ida N. 1997. Soldatskie materi: uroki Chechenskoi voiny [Soldiers' mothers: Lessons of the Chechen war]. In *Mezhdunarodnaia konferentsiia: Zhenshchiny v ekstremal'nykh situatsiiakh: zashchita prav i interesov zhenshchin* [International conference: Women in Extreme Situations: Protecting the Rights and Interests of Women]. Book 2: 98–105. Moscow: Ekonomika i informatika.

Laber, Jeri. 2002. *The Courage of Strangers: Coming of Age with the Human Rights Movement.* New York: Public Affairs.

LaFraniere, Sharon. 2001. Russia's Battered Military: Internal Violence Illuminates Decay. *Washington Post* (20 May).

Laitin, David. 1986. *Hegemony and Culture: Politics and Religion Among the Yoruba.* Chicago: University of Chicago Press.

——.1988. Political Culture and Political Preferences. *American Political Science Review* 82: 589–93.

Lakhova, Ekaterina. 1995. *Moi put' v politiku* [My path to politics]. Moscow: Aurika.

Lambroschini, Sophie. 2000a. Chechnya: Draft Avoidance Rises as Russia Ponders Professional Army. *RFE/RL* (14 July). Reprinted 15 July 2000 in *Johnson's Russia List* #4405, available at http://www.cdi.org/russia/johnson/.

——.2000b. Russia: NGOs Just Beginning to Take Root. RFE/RL (13 October). Reprinted 15 October 2000 in *Johnson's Russia List* #4405, available at http://www.cdi.org/russia/johnson/.

Landsberg, Christopher. 2000. Voicing the Voiceless: Foreign Political Aid to Civil Society in South Africa. In *Funding Virtue: Civil Society Aid and Democracy Promotion.* Edited by Marina Ottaway and Thomas Carothers. Washington, D.C.: Carnegie Endowment for International Peace.

Lankina, Tomila V. 2004. *Governing the Locals: Local Self-Government and Ethnic Mobilization in Russia.* Oxford, UK: Rowman & Littlefield.

——.President Putin's Local Government Reforms. 2005. In *Dynamics of Russian Politics: Putin's Reform of Federal-Regional Relations.* Vol. 2. Edited by Peter Reddaway and Robert Orttung. Lanham: Rowman & Littlefield.

Lapidus, Gail W. 1978. *Women in Soviet Society: Equality, Development, and Social Change.* Berkeley: University of California Press.

Linz, Juan J., and Alfred Stepan. 1996. *Problems of Democratic Transition and Consolidation.* Baltimore, Md.: Johns Hopkins University Press.

Lipman, Masha. 2005. How Russia Is Not Ukraine: The Closing of Russian Civil Society. *Policy Outlook* (January). Washington, D.C.: Carnegie Endowment for International Peace.

Lipschutz, Ronnie. 1992. Reconstructing World Politics: The Emergence of Global Civil Society. In *Millennium* 21(3): 389–420.

Lipset, Seymour M. 1959. Some Social Requisites of Democracy: Economic Development and Political Legitimacy. *American Political Science Review* 53: 245–59.

Liubin,Valery. 2001. Summary of Roundtable at Moscow's President Hotel.Translated by Joan Barth Urban. Reprinted 27 June 2001 in *Johnson's Russia List* #5324. Available at http://www.cdi.org/russia/johnson/.

Mair, Stefan. 2000. Germany's Stiftungen and Democracy Assistance: Comparative Advantages, New Challenges. In *Democracy Assistance: International Co-operation for Democratization.* Edited by Peter Burnell. Portland, Ore.: Frank Cass.

Malyakin, Ilya, and Marina Konnova. 1999.Voluntary Organizations in Russia:Three Obstacle Courses. In *Jamestown Foundation Prism* 8 (23 April). Reprinted in *Post-Soviet Armies Newsletter* (November 1999). Retrieved 15 December 1999 from www.psan.org.

Malysheva, M., E. Ballaeva, E. Tiuriukanova, T. Klimenkova, and V. Konstantinova. 1998. Rossiia-1997: Prava zhenshchin v kontekste sotsial'no-ekonomicheskikh reform [Russia-1997:Women's rights in the context of socioeconomic reforms]. In *Prava zhenshchin v Rossii: issledovanie real'noi praktiki ikh sobliudeniia i massovogo soznaniia* [Women's rights in Russia: Research into the actual practice of their observance and mass consciousness].Vol. 2. Edited by M. M. Malysheva. Moscow: Moskovskii Filosofskii Fond.

Mama Cash. 2000. Mama Cash—Central and Eastern Europe. Retrieved 24 August 2000 from http://www.undp.uz/GID/eng/COMMON/mama_cash.html.

Maria: Zhurnal Rossiiskogo nezavisimogo zhenskogo religioznogo kluba 'Maria' [Maria: Journal of the Russian independent women's religious club Maria]. 1981. Otvety na ankety zhurnala "Alternativy" [Responses to the questionnaire of the journal "Alternativa"]. *Maria* (Leningrad and Frankfurt-on-Main) (1): 22–30.

Mathews, Jessica T. 1997. Power Shift. *Foreign Affairs* 76(1): 50–66.

McAdam, Doug. 1996. Conceptual Origins, Current Problems, Future Directions. In *Comparative Perspectives on Social Movements.* Edited by Doug McAdam, John D. McCarthy, and Mayer M. Zald. Cambridge, UK: Cambridge University Press.

McAdam, Doug, and Dieter Rucht. 1993. The Cross-National Diffusion of Movement Ideas. *Annals of the American Academy of Political and Social Science* 528: 56–74.

McFaul, Michael. 1996. Revolutionary Transformations in Comparative Perspective: Defining a Post-Communist Research Agenda. In *Reexamining the Soviet Experience: Essays in Honor of Alexander Dallin.* Edited by David Holloway and Norman Naimark. Boulder, Colo.:Westview Press.

McFaul, Michael, and Nikolay Petrov, eds. 1998. *Politicheskii almanakh Rossii 1997* [Political almanac of Russia 1997].Vol. 2. Moscow: Moscow Carnegie Center.

MCGS (Moscow Center for Gender Studies). 1998.Vvedenie [Introduction]. In *Prava zhenshchin v Rossii: issledovanie real'noi praktiki ikh sobliudeniia i massovogo soznaniia* [Women's rights in Russia: Research into the actual practice of their observance and mass consciousness].Vol. 1. Moscow: Moskovskii Filosofskii Fond.

Mendelson, Sarah E. 2000. Revealing the Power and Constraints of Norms and Networks: Democracy, Human Rights, and Russia. Paper presented at the annual meeting of the American Political Science Association,August 31–September 3, Washington, D.C.

———.2001. Democracy Assistance and Political Transition in Russia: Between Success and Failure. *International Security* 25(4): 68–106.

———.2002. Russians' Rights Imperiled: Has Anybody Noticed? *International Security* 26(4): 39–69.

Mendelson, Sarah E., and Theodore P. Gerber. 2005. Local Activist Culture and Transnational Diffusion: An Experiment in Social Marketing Among Human Rights Groups in Russia. Paper presented at the annual meeting of the American Political Science Association, September 1–4, in Washington, D.C.

Mendelson, Sarah E., and John K. Glenn. 2000. Democracy Assistance and NGO Strategies in Post-Communist Societies. Democracy and Rule of Law Project of the Carnegie Endowment for International Peace, Working Paper no. 8. Washington, D.C.: Carnegie Endowment for International Peace.

———.2002. Introduction: Transnational Networks and NGOs in Postcommunist Societies. In *The Power and Limits of NGOs: A Critical Look at Building Democracy in Eastern Europe and Eurasia*. Edited by Sarah E. Mendelson and John K. Glenn. New York: Columbia University Press.

Meyer, John W. 1994. The Changing Cultural Content of the Nation-State: A World Society Perspective. For presentation at the University of Chicago, January.

Meyer, John W., and Brian Rowan. 1977. Institutionalized Organizations: Formal Structure as Myth and Ceremony. *American Journal of Sociology* 83(2): 340–63.

Meyer, John W., John Boli, George M. Thomas, and Francisco O. Ramirez. 1997. World Society and the Nation-State. *American Journal of Sociology* 103(1) (July): 144–81.

Mill, John Stuart. 1973. Of the Four Methods of Experimental Inquiry. In *A System of Logic*. Edited by J. M. Robson. Toronto: University of Toronto Press.

Ministry of Defence of the Russian Federation. 1993. Glava 2: Vzaimootnosheniia mezhdu voennosluzhashchimi. Ustav vnutrennei sluzhby [Section 2: Relations among military personnel. Charter of the internal service]. Retrieved 7 April 2004 from http://www.mil.ru/print/articles/article4088.shtml.

———.2004. Osobennosti prizyva grazhdan na voennuiu sluzhbu vesnoi 2004 goda [Particularities of the draft of citizens for military service, spring 2004]. Retrieved 25 May 2004 from http://www.mil.ru/articles/article5379.shtml. Moscow Helsinki Group. Istoriia. Retrieved 11 January 2005 from http://www.mhg.ru/history.

MosNews. 2005. We Have Broken the Silence on Chechnya (1 March). Accessed 27 April 2005 at http://mosnews.com/interview/2005/03/01/soldiersmothers.shtml.

Mother's Right Foundation. 1999. Mosgorsud vpervye udovletvoril zhalobu materi soldata, pogibshego v Chechne [Moscow City Court for the first time conceded to a complaint from the mother of a soldier killed in Chechnya]. Press Release no. 22/170 (22 March). Mother's Right Foundation, Moscow.

———.2001. Napravleniia raboty fonda "Pravo Materi" [Directions of work of the Mother's Right Foundation]. Retrieved 15 May 2001 from http://www.hro.org/ngo/mright/dir.htm.

National Democratic Institute for International Affairs (NDI). 2001. NDI Activities in Eurasia: The Russian Federation. Retrieved 27 April 2001 from http://www.ndi.org/ndi/worldwide/eurasia/russia/russia.htm.

National Report on Institutional Mechanisms for the Advancement of Women in Russia (NGO Alternative Report). 1999. Prepared for 43rd session of Commission on the Status of Women, United Nations, New York (March). Retrieved 29 May 2001 from http://www.iiav.nl/european-womenaction-2000/countries/reports/russia1 .html.

NED (National Endowment for Democracy). 2000. New Independent States Program Highlights. Retrieved 28 April 2001 from http://www.ned.org/grants/ nis_highlights.html.

Nelson, Tina. 2000. Democratization, NGOs and New Technologies: Building Connectivity for Russian Women's Groups. Report prepared for the Columbia University Project on Evaluating Western NGO Strategies for Democratization and the Reduction of Ethnic Conflict in the Former Communist States. Retrieved 15 August 2000 from http://www.ceip.org/programs/democr/NGOs/Nelson.pdf.

Netherlands Ministry of Foreign Affairs. 2000. Dutch Aid to Central and Eastern Europe. Retrieved 26 December 2000 from http://www.netherlands.ru/f_enet scape.html.

North-South Institute. 1999. *Canadian Development Report, 1996–97*. Ottawa: North-South Institute.

Oates, Sarah. 2005. Media, Civil Society, and the Failure of the Fourth Estate in Russia. In *Russian Civil Society: A Critical Assessment*, edited by Alfred B. Evans, Jr., Laura A. Henry, and Lisa McIntosh Sundstrom. Armonk, N.Y.: M.E. Sharpe.

Obraztsova, Lyudmila. 1999. Stat'ia [Article]. Union of Soldiers' Mothers of Russia, Moscow. Photocopy.

O'Donnell, Guillermo, and Philippe C. Schmitter. 1986. *Transitions from Authoritarian Rule: Tentative Conclusions About Uncertain Democracies*. Baltimore, Md.: Johns Hopkins University Press.

OECD. 1997. Statistical Annex. *Development Co-operation: Efforts and Policies of the Members of the Development Assistance Committee*. Paris: OECD Development Assistance Committee.

——.2003. Statistical Annex. *Development Co-operation: Efforts and Policies of the Members of the Development Assistance Committee*. Paris: OECD Development Assistance Committee. Retrieved 24 November 2004 from http://www.oecd.org/.

Office of the Coordinator of U.S. Assistance to the NIS. 2000. *U.S. Government Assistance to and Cooperative Activities with the New Independent States of the Former Soviet Union: FY 1999 Annual Report.* Washington, D.C.: U.S. Department of State.

OSI (Open Society Institute). 2001. Fond Sorosa v Rossii [The Soros Foundation in Russia]. Retrieved 27 April 2001 from http://osi.ru/web/homepage.nsf.

Ottaway, Marina. 2000. Social Movements, Professionalization of Reform, and Democracy in Africa. In *Funding Virtue: Civil Society Aid and Democracy Promotion*. Edited by Marina Ottaway and Thomas Carothers. Washington, D.C.: Carnegie Endowment for International Peace.

Ottaway, Marina, and Thomas Carothers. 2000. Toward Civil Society Realism. In *Funding Virtue: Civil Society Aid and Democracy Promotion*. Edited by Marina Ottaway and Thomas Carothers. Washington, D.C.: Carnegie Endowment for International Peace.

Parchomenko, Walter. 1986. *Soviet Images of Dissidents and Nonconformists.* New York: Praeger.

Patomaki, Heikki, and Christer Pursiainen. 1999. Western Models and the "Russian Idea": Beyond "Inside/Outside" in Discourses on Civil Society. *Millennium: Journal of International Studies* 28(1): 53–77.

Perlin, George. 2003. International Assistance to Democratic Development: A Review. IRPP Working Paper Series no. 2003–4. Montreal: Institute for Research on Public Policy.

Petrescu, Dan. 2000. Civil Society in Romania: From Donor Supply to Citizen Demand. In *Funding Virtue: Civil Society Aid and Democracy Promotion.* Edited by Marina Ottaway and Thomas Carothers. Washington, D.C.: Carnegie Endowment for International Peace.

Petro, Nicolai. 2004. *Crafting Democracy: How Novgorod Has Coped with Rapid Social Change.* Ithaca, N.Y.: Cornell University Press.

Phillips, Ann L. 1999. Exporting Democracy: German Political Foundations in Central-East Europe. *Democratization* 6(2) (Summer): 70–98.

Pilkington, Hilary. 1992. Behind the Mask of Soviet Unity: Realities of Women's Lives. In *Superwomen and the Double Burden: Women's Experience of Change in Central and Eastern Europe and the Former Soviet Union.* Edited by Chris Corrin. London: Scarlet Press.

Politkovskaya, Anna. 1999. *Obshchaia gazeta* (Moscow) (8 April).

Price, Richard. 1998. Reversing the Gun Sights: Transnational Civil Society Targets Land Mines. *International Organization* 52 (Summer).

Przeworski, Adam, and Fernando Limongi. 1997. Modernization: Theories and Facts. *World Politics* 49: 155–84.

Pustintsev, Boris. 2001. The Kremlin and Civil Society. *Moscow Times* (22 October).

Putnam, Robert D. 1993. *Making Democracy Work.* Princeton, N.J.: Princeton University Press.

——.1996. Bowling Alone: America's Declining Social Capital. In *The Global Resurgence of Democracy.* 2nd ed. Edited by Larry Diamond and Marc F. Plattner. Baltimore, Md.: Johns Hopkins University Press.

Quigley, Kevin F. F. 2000. Lofty Goals, Modest Results: Assisting Civil Society in Eastern Europe. In *Funding Virtue: Civil Society Aid and Democracy Promotion.* Edited by Marina Ottaway and Thomas Carothers. Washington, D.C.: Carnegie Endowment for International Peace.

Racioppi, Linda, and Katherine O'Sullivan See. 1997. *Women's Activism in Contemporary Russia.* Philadelphia: Temple University Press.

Reddaway, Peter. 1972. Introduction. In *Uncensored Russia: Protest and Dissent in the Soviet Union.* Edited and translated by Peter Reddaway. New York: American Heritage Press.

RFE/RL (Radio Free Europe/Radio Liberty). 1999. Illegal Draftees File Suit Against Military Commissions (23 August). Reprinted in *Post-Soviet Armies Newsletter* (November 1999). Retrieved 15 December 1999 from www.psan.org.

——.2001a. 5.9 Million Still in Uniform. *RFE/RL (Un)Civil Societies* 2(21) (23 May).

Retrieved 23 May 2001 from http://www.rferl.org/ucs/2001/05/21–230501 .html.

———.2001b. More Generals Become Governors. *RFE/RL (Un)Civil Societies* 2(23) (6 June). Retrieved 6 June 2001 from listserv ucs@list.rferl.org.

———.2001c. 30,000 Russian Soldiers Said Beaten Each Year. *RFE/RL (Un)Civil Societies* 2(35) (13 September). Retrieved 13 September 2001 from listserv ucs@list .rferl.org.

———.2005. Putin Signs into Law Delay of Local Government Reform. *RFE/RL Newsline* (13 October). Retrieved 7 April 2006 from http://www.rferl.org/ newsline/2005/10/1-rus/rus-131005.asp.

Richter, James. 1997. Promoting a Strong Civil Society: U.S. Foreign Assistance and Russian NGOs. Program on New Approaches to Russian Security, Policy Memo Series no. 13. Cambridge, Mass.: Davis Center for Russian Studies, Harvard University.

———.2002. Promoting Civil Society? Democracy Assistance and Russian Women's Organizations. *Problems of Post-Communism* 48(1) (January/February): 30–41.

Right to Life and Civil Dignity (*Pravo na zhizn' i grazhdanskoe dostoinstvo*). 1999. *Za Mirnuiu Rossiiu* [For a peaceful Russia] (Moscow) 1(19) (January).

Right Livelihood Foundation. 2000. About the Award. Retrieved 18 December 2000 from http://www.rightlivelihood.se/about.html.

Risse, Thomas, and Kathryn Sikkink. 1999. The Socialization of International Human Rights Norms into Domestic Practices: Introduction. In *The Power of Human Rights: International Norms and Domestic Change*. Edited by Thomas Risse, Stephen C. Ropp, and Kathryn Sikkink. Cambridge, UK: Cambridge University Press.

Risse, Thomas, Stephen C. Ropp, and Kathryn Sikkink, eds. 1999. *The Power of Human Rights: International Norms and Domestic Change*. Cambridge, UK: Cambridge University Press.

Risse-Kappen, Thomas. 1994. Ideas Do Not Float Freely: Transnational Coalitions, Domestic Structures, and the End of the Cold War. *International Organization* 48 (Spring).

———.1995. Bringing Transnational Relations Back In: Introduction. In *Bringing Transnational Relations Back In*. Edited by Thomas Risse-Kappen. Cambridge, UK: Cambridge University Press.

ROMIR (Russian Public Opinion and Market Research). 2000a. Otnoshenie Rossiian k voennym vo vlasti [Attitudes of Russians to military in government]. Retrieved 24 May 2001 from http://www.romir.ru/socpolit/vvps/11_2000/ power-military.htm.

———.2000b. Rossiiane o blagotvoritel'nosti [Russians on charity]. Retrieved 18 May 2001 from http://www.romir.ru/socpolit/socio/08_2000/charity.htm.

Rose, Richard. 1999. *New Russia Barometer: Trends Since 1992*. Studies in Public Policy, no. 320. Glasgow: Centre for the Study of Public Policy, University of Strathclyde.

Rubenstein, Joshua. 1985. *Soviet Dissidents: Their Struggle for Human Rights*. 2nd ed. Boston: Beacon Press.

Ruble, Blair A. 1987. The Social Dimensions of Perestroyka. *Soviet Economy* 3(2): 171–83.

Ruffin, M. Holt, Joan McCarter, and Richard Upjohn. 1996. *The Post-Soviet Hand-book: A Guide to Grassroots Organizations and Internet Resources in the Newly Independent States*. Seattle: Center for Civil Society International and University of Washington Press.

Russia Journal. 2001. Poll: Russia Needs Professional Army. *The Russia Journal* (22 February). Retrieved 21 May 2001 from http://www.russiajournal.com/news/index.shtml?nd=5517#n5517.

Rutherford, Kenneth R. 2000. The Evolving Arms Control Agenda: Implications of the Role of NGOs in Banning Antipersonnel Landmines. *World Politics* 53 (October): 74–114.

Sakwa, Richard. 2000. Democracy Assistance: Russia's Experience as a Recipient. In *Democracy Assistance: International Co-operation for Democratization*. Edited by Peter Burnell. Portland, Ore.: Frank Cass.

Santiso, Carlos. 2002. Promoting Democracy by Conditioning Aid? Towards a More Effective EU Development Assistance. *Internationale Politik und Gesellschaft* 3: 107–34.

Save the Children, Inc. 1998. Civic Initiatives Program for Democratic and Economic Reform in Russia: Final Program Report. Copy obtained from the World Learning NGOSS Program office, Moscow.

Schmitter, Philippe C. 1977. Modes of Interest Intermediation and Models of Societal Change in Western Europe. *Comparative Political Studies* 10(1) (April): 7–38.

Semyonov, Oleg. 2000. Generals Demand Cannon Fodder. www.gazeta.ru news website (6 April). Reprinted 7 April 2000 in *Johnson's Russia List* #4233. Available at http://www.cdi.org/russia/johnson/.

Sergievskii, Sergei. 2001. Sergei Chikurov: Munitsipalitety dolzhny stanovit'sia konkurentosposobnymi [Sergei Chikurov: Municipalities must become competitive]. *Nezavisimaia gazeta* 163(2473) (4 September).

Sevortian, Anna. 2000. Territoriia NKO: Granitsy otkryty [NGO Territory: Open Borders]. Retrieved 5 October 2001 from the Agency for Social Information (ASI) website http://www.asi.org.ru/asinfo/70565.

Sinelnikov, Andrei. 1998. Russia: Inside the Broken Cell. Retrieved 30 May 2001 from the Family Violence Prevention Fund website: http://www.fvpf.org/global/gf_russia.html.

Skocpol, Theda. 1999. Advocates Without Members: The Recent Transformation of American Civic Life. In *Civic Engagement in American Democracy*. Edited by Theda Skocpol and Morris P. Fiorina. Washington, D.C.: The Brookings Institution/Russell Sage Foundation.

Smith, Jackie G. et al., eds. 1997. *Transnational Social Movements and World Politics: Solidarity Beyond the State*. Syracuse, N.Y.: Syracuse University Press.

SMSP (Soldiers' Mothers of St. Petersburg). 1996. Brochure. Retrieved 15 February 1999 from http://www.openweb.ru/windows/smo/.

Snow, David A., and Robert D. Benford. 1992. Master Frames and Cycles of Protest. In *Frontiers in Social Movement Theory*. Edited by Aldon D. Morris and Carol McClurg Mueller. New Haven, Conn.: Yale University Press.

Sperling, Valerie. 1998. *Foreign Funding of Social Movements in Russia*. Program on New

Approaches to Russian Security, Policy Memo Series no. 26. Cambridge, Mass.: Davis Center for Russian Studies, Harvard University.

———.1999. *Organizing Women in Contemporary Russia: Engendering Transition*. Cambridge, UK: Cambridge University Press.

Starr, S. Frederick. 1988. Soviet Union: A Civil Society. *Foreign Policy* 70 (Spring): 26–41.

Sundstrom, Lisa McIntosh. 2001. Strength from Without? Transnational Actors and NGO Development in Russia. Ph.D. Dissertation. Department of Political Science, Stanford University, Stanford, Calif.

———.2002. Women's NGOs in Russia: Struggling from the Margins. *Demokratizatsiya* 10(2): 207–29.

Tarrow, Sidney. 1992. Mentalities, Political Cultures, and Collective Action Frames: Constructing Meanings through Action. In *Frontiers in Social Movement Theory*. Edited by Aldon D. Morris and Carol McClurg Mueller. New Haven, Conn.: Yale University Press.

———.1998. *Power in Movement: Social Movements and Contentious Politics*. 2nd ed. New York: Cambridge University Press.

Tinker, Irene, and Jane Jaquette. 1987. UN Decade for Women: Its Impact and Legacy. *World Development* 15(3): 419–27.

de Tocqueville, Alexis. 1969. *Democracy in America*. Edited by J. P. Maier; translated by George Lawrence. Garden City, N.Y.: Anchor Books.

UCSMR (Union of Committees of Soldiers' Mothers). 2003. Annual Report 2002. Retrieved 6 April 2004 from http://www.ucsmr.ru/english/ucsmr/report/report 2002.htm.

UNICEF, MONEE Project. 1999. *Women in Transition*. MONEE Project Regional Monitoring Report 6. Florence: UNICEF ICDC.

———.Bureau for Europe and Eurasia (E&E). Office of Democracy and Governance. 1999a. Lessons in Implementation: The NGO Story. Washington, D.C.: USAID.

———.1999b. *FY 2000 Congressional Presentation*. Washington, D.C.: USAID. Retrieved 20 October 2000 from http://www.usaid.gov/pubs/cp2000/eni/russia.html.

———.2000a. *The 1999 NGO Sustainability Index*. 3rd ed. Washington, D.C.: USAID.

———.2000b. Russia: FY 2001 Program Description and Activity Data Sheets. Washington, D.C.: USAID. Retrieved 7 November 2000 from http://www.usaid.gov/country/ee/ru/ru_ads.html.

U.S. Department of State. 2001, 2002, 2003. U.S. Government Assistance to and Cooperative Activities with Eurasia. Retrieved 25 October 2005 from http://www.state.gov/p/eur/rls/rpt/c10250.htm.

U.S. Helsinki Commission. 2004. Briefing: The War in Chechnya and Russian Civil Society. Washington, D.C. (June 17). Transcript available at http://www.csce.gov/briefings.cfm?briefing_id=281.

Urban, Michael. 1997. *The Rebirth of Politics in Russia*. Cambridge, Mass.: Cambridge University Press.

Validata/Yankelovich Partners International. 1995. *Issledovanie otnosheniia k obshchestvennym organizatsiiam i osvedomlennosti ob ikh deiatel'nosti* [Research into attitudes toward public organizations and knowledge about their activities]. Moscow: Validata Yankelovich.

Vallance, Brenda J. 2000. Russia's Mothers—Voices of Change. *Minerva: Quarterly Report on Women and the Military* (Fall-Winter). Retrieved 7 April 2004 from http://www.findarticles.com/cf_dls/moEXI/2000_Fall-Winter/73063468/printjhtml.

Vandenberg, Martina, Daniel MacGrory, and Elena Kochkina. 1996. Russia: Sexual Harassment in the Workplace. In *Seksual'nye domogatel'stva na rabote* [Sexual harassment in the workplace]. Edited by Zoia Khotkina. Moscow: ABA-CEELI.

Vannoy, Dana, Natalia Rimashevskaya, Lisa Cubbins, Marina Malysheva, Elena Meshterkina, and Marina Pisklakova. 1999. *Marriages in Russia: Couples During the Economic Transition.* Westport, Conn.: Praeger.

Van Rooy, Alison. 1998a. The Art of Strengthening Civil Society. In *Civil Society and the Aid Industry: The Politics and Promise.* Edited by Alison Van Rooy. London: Earthscan Publications.

——. 1998b. Civil Society as an Idea: An Analytical Hatstand? In *Civil Society and the Aid Industry: The Politics and Promise.* Edited by Alison Van Rooy. London: Earthscan Publications.

——. 1998c. Introduction: All Roads Lead to Rome. In *Civil Society and the Aid Industry: The Politics and Promise.* Edited by Alison Van Rooy. London: Earthscan.

Van Rooy, Alison, and Mark Robinson. 1998. Out of the Ivory Tower: Civil Society and the Aid System. In *Civil Society and the Aid Industry: The Politics and Promise.* Edited by Alison Van Rooy. London: Earthscan.

Verdery, Katherine. 1996. *What Was Socialism, and What Comes Next?* Princeton, N.J.: Princeton University Press.

Voronina, Olga. 1993. Zhenshchina i sotsializm: opyt feministkogo analiza [Woman and socialism: The experience of feminist analysis]. In *Feminizm: vostok, zapad, Rossiia* [Feminism: East, West, Russia]. Edited by M. T. Stepaniants.

VTsIOM (Russian Center for the Study of Public Opinion [Vserossiiskii tsentr isucheniia obshchestvennogo mneniia]. 1998. Kratkii otchet po massovomu sotsiologicheskomu oprosu "Informirovannost' naseleniia Rossii o deiatel'nosti obshchestvennykh organizatsii" [Short report on the mass sociological survey "Informedness of the population of Russia on the activities of public organizations"]. Moscow: VTSIOM.

——. 2002. Press-vypusk no. 4 (21 February). Retrieved 25 May 2004 from http://www.wciom.ru/.

Wapner, Paul. 1995. Politics Beyond the State: Environmental Activism and World Civic Politics. *World Politics* 47 (April): 311–40.

——. 2002. Horizontal Politics: Transnational Environmental Activism and Global Cultural Change. *Global Environmental Politics* 2 (May): 37–62.

Waters, Elizabeth. 1989. Restructuring the "Woman Question": Perestroika and Prostitution. *Feminist Review* 33 (Autumn): 3–19.

——. 1993. Finding a Voice: The Emergence of a Women's Movement. In *Gender Politics and Post-Communism.* Edited by Nanette Funk and Magda Mueller. New York: Routledge.

Wedel, Janine R. 1998. *Collision and Collusion: The Strange Case of Western Aid to Eastern Europe 1989–1998.* New York: St. Martin's Press.

WFD (Westminster Foundation for Democracy). 2001a. What We Fund. Retrieved 27 April 2001 from http://www.wfd.org/wfd.asp?sn=who_we_are&pg=what _we_fund.

———.2001b. Who We Are. Retrieved 27 April 2001 from http://www.wfd.org/ wfd.asp?sn=who_we_are&pg=about_wfd.

Womack, Helen. 1993. Why Employ Women When There Are Men Out of Work? *The Independent* (London) (21 March).

Yablokova, Oksana. 2004. Soldiers' Mothers Form a Party. *Moscow Times* (9 November).

Yegorov, Ivan. 2000. Shortage of Draftees. *Vremia Novosti* (12 April).

Yermolin, Vladimir. 1999. Sent by the Motherland: A Conscript Cannot Refuse Being Sent to War. *Izvestiia* (30 October).

Young, Dennis R. 2000. Alternative Models of Government-Nonprofit Sector Relations: Theoretical and International Perspectives. *Nonprofit and Voluntary Sector Quarterly* 29(1) (March): 149–72.

Youngs, Richard. 2001. *The European Union and the Promotion of Democracy.* Oxford, UK: Oxford University Press.

Zabelina, Tatiana, ed. 2002. Rossia: nasilie v sem'e—nasilie v obshchestve [Russia: violence in the family—violence and society]. UNIFEM. Retrieved 17 August 2004 from http://www.owl.ru/win/books/camp/book_camp.pdf.

Zakharova, Natalya, Anastasia Posadskaya, and Natalya Rimashevskaya. 1989. Kak My Reshaem Zhenskii Vopros [How We Solve the Woman Question]. *Kommunist* (March): 56–65.

Zaslavsky, Victor. 1982. *The Neo-Stalinist State: Class, Ethnicity, and Consensus in Soviet Society.* Armonk, N.Y.: M.E. Sharpe.

Zavadskaya, Ludmila. 2000. Urgent Legislative Measures and Gender Issues. In *Making the Transition Work for Women in Europe and Central Asia.* Edited by Marnia Lazreg. World Bank Discussion Paper no. 411. Europe and Central Asia Gender and Development Series. Washington, D.C.: World Bank.

Zdravomyslova, E. E., and A. A. Temkina. 1997. Sotsial'naia konstruktsiia gendera i gendernaia sistema v Rossii [Social construction of gender and the gender system in Russia]. In *Materially Pervious Resistor lentil shakily po Zhen skim i gendarme is ledovaniiam 'Valdai-96'* [Materials of the first Russian summer school on women's and gender research 'Valdai-96]. Moscow: MCGS.

Lightning Source UK Ltd.
Milton Keynes UK
UKHW041835010922
408136UK00003B/34/J